Educating Mainland Chinese Learners in Business Education

Kumaran Rajaram

Educating Mainland Chinese Learners in Business Education

Pedagogical and Cultural Perspectives –
Singapore Experiences

 Springer

Kumaran Rajaram
Nanyang Business School
Nanyang Technological University
Singapore, Singapore

ISBN 978-981-15-3393-8   ISBN 978-981-15-3395-2   (eBook)
https://doi.org/10.1007/978-981-15-3395-2

This Springer imprint is published by the registered company Springer Nature Singapore Pte Ltd.
The registered company address is: 152 Beach Road, #21-01/04 Gateway East, Singapore 189721, Singapore

Testimonials

"Dr Kumaran Rajaram has meticulously provided insights into how the World should deal with mainland Chinese students eager for pursuing foreign degrees in business education. The book is a compelling and practical read, with a case study of Singapore as an educational hub for international students, a significant portion of whom are from China. The theoretically sophisticated approach and empirically rich findings reveal why and how a well-programmed curriculum should be in place to help Chinese students transcend cultural boundaries for real education outcomes."

Assoc Professor Yow Cheun Hoe
Director, Chinese Heritage Centre | Head of Chinese | Director, Centre for Chinese Language and Culture
Nanyang Technological University

"This book is a timely contribution to understanding the cultural contexts and nuances of educating mainland Chinese in business education, and beyond. Indeed, a large number of Chinese students, more than six hundred thousand, go abroad annually for their university education, business education included. Understanding how learners from different cultural contexts learn helps us to respect diversified approaches in higher education to cater for diversified learners. With evidence-based findings and probing discussions, the book will advance the scholarship of internationalization of higher education with new perspectives and viewpoints."

Professor Chee-Kit Looi
Co-Director, Centre for Research and Development in Learning
Nanyang Technological University

"The book delivers an exceptional set of ideas, and practical- and policy-related recommendations for positive transformational changes in higher education with focus on specifics of Chinese learners. It builds upon years of experiences and an exceptional level of expertise of a reflective practitioner who carefully detailed and researched specific of Chinese learners. The book presents not only a set of strong theoretical ideas, but it is further empowered through practical case stories, experiential accounts and empirical evidences. A s such, the book will prove to be a powerful resource for practitioners, policy-maker, experts and researchers in higher education contexts whose success is dependent upon positive transformation designed to meet needs of Chinese learners."

Assoc Professor Daniel Churchill
Faculty of Education, The University of Hong Kong

"Accumulating years of management education experience with learning partners from China, the author provide culturally intelligent pedagogies, effectively and efficiently, to navigate imminent Chinese business executives and public servants. For western educators, this book is valuable for insights to decode Chinese learners' behaviors embedded in various schools of Chinese philosophies, especially in blended learning scenarios interacting with theories and frameworks generated by western scholars. This book also furthers design thinking implications for educators to innovate in the process of knowledge creation and distribution. It is also a good reference which facilitates Chinese talent development professionals' collaboration in programme designing process with western educators."

Dr. Li Yan
Senior Lecturer | Director, Mandarin Executive Education, China Programmes
Nanyang Business School, Nanyang Technological University

"Over the years, and especially after China opened up in 1978, countless number of Chinese students went abroad to study, especially in the Western world. The pursuit of a Western and English-based education was highly treasured in China. During this period, Singapore has also played host to thousands of Chinese students in their quest for education. Today, many of them can still be found in our various education institutions, both public and private, and from the primary to tertiary levels. For the education providers, it is very important to know how to best cater to the needs of these Chinese learners. This book is thus very timely in addressing this issue, and the author must be highly commended for providing a very insightful perspective on the subject. This book, I believe, would be very beneficial to all educators"

Professor (Adjunct) Wee Chow Hou
Nanyang Technological University and Singapore University of Social Sciences
Former Business School Dean of National University of Singapore

"Dr Rajaram's book is a significant contribution to the field of cross-cultural business education. Its treatment of learning culture and culture of learning should be well-studied by business educators who teach across international borders. The evidence-based teaching strategies recommended by Dr Rajaram are theoretically innovative and practically viable."

Assoc Professor Andres Carlos LUCO
School of Humanities, Nanyang Technological University

"This book presents a contemporary picture of educating international students. Much of the literature on international education presents an east to west picture; here, internationals students from the eastern hemisphere have to acculturate in the Western context. The gap in such a literature is that there is no one homogeneous east, and it is a different kind of challenge for both students and educators when Chinese students are being educated in another eastern country such as Singapore. The current book, underpinned by good-quality empirical work and theorizing, plugs this gap very effectively."

Assoc Prof Sarbari Bordia
Deputy Director, Higher Degree by Research
Research School of Management, Australian National University

"This text is an important addition to the international research literature on teaching the Chinese learner in higher education. This work builds on and extends research work carried out at the University of Hong Kong on the Chinese learner, edited by Watkins and Biggs (1996 and 2001) at the University of Hong Kong on the Chinese learner. This present text focuses on important new areas in business education and examines the Chinese learner from pedagogical and cultural perspectives based on

Singapore experiences, whereas Watkins and Biggs focused on cultural factors to approaching the Chinese learner based on teaching experiences in Hong Kong. This scholarly work uses evidence-based findings and innovative teaching strategies to inspire future teachers of mainland Chinese students in higher education."

Prof Bob Fox
Curriculum Academic Lead
Office of the Pro Vice-Chancellor (Education)
University of New South Wales
Teaching Fellow, University of Hong Kong

"In a time of globalization of education and a need for the effective delivery of University pedagogy, *Educating Mainland Chinese Learners in Business Education* provides teachers and scholars with a focused look at best practices in mainland China and Singapore. Evidence-based insights take readers into the complexity of cultural values, student-teacher relationships, as well as assessing learning effectiveness among instructional techniques. By reading this book, you will develop a deeper understanding of how to effectively teach and engage Chinese students through customizable instructional techniques."

Prof Robert Sroufe
Murrin Chair of Global Competitiveness
Top Ranked MBA Sustainable Business Practices Program
Palumbo-Donahue Graduate School of Business
Duquesne University

"The book provides a succinct review of cultural theories in the pedagogical context and presents useful research findings related to Chinese learners. These generated theoretically informed and evidence-based recommendations for optimizing the learning effectiveness of Chinese students. The insightful discussions by the author also stimulate interesting future research questions. Given that China is the world's largest source of international students, this book is a timely and valuable read for both researchers, institutions, and instructors interested in the internationalization of higher education!"

Asst Prof Chong SinHui
Division of Leadership, Management and Organisation
Nanyang Business School
Nanyang Technological University

"As globalization continues, it requires that we increasingly seek to better understand those from other cultures, and how to best support them. It is particularly relevant in Singapore, where there is a growing influx of mainland Chinese students (over 300,000 and climbing). This book is designed to help researchers and teachers improve the cultural integration of Chinese international students in Singapore and beyond. Empirically grounded findings, insights, and validated practical recommendations advocated in this book address learning issues of mainland

Chinese learners in culturally dislocated learning environments, which serve as valuable reflections for varying stakeholders in higher education globally."

Asst Prof Ryan Gottfredson
Mihaylo College of Business and Economics
California State University-Fullerton

"This book contains many exciting beginning points with nuanced strategies that include more than traditional approaches to learning about the discipline of business studies, it suggests an approach that matches the cultural, as well as how the philosophical starting points of the students who are leaning this topic in a cross-cultural context and the particular approaches of Chinese students. It also explores the challenges of the how higher education institutions should modify their learning and delivery strategies to match the link between students what and how they learn."

John Hedberg, PhD
Adjunct Professor of Education
School of Education Studies, Macquarie University

"Dr. Kumaran's book provides a systematic exposition of how strategies can be formulated to effectively engage and teach the mainland Chinese students in a western-styled education setting. Recommendations in the book, based on his first-hand experience, have been tested and successfully implemented in his classes. The valuable insights and in-depth evidence-based analysis will be of tremendous interest to educators and scholars in the field of internationalization of higher education."

Dr. Ho Shen Yong
Principal Lecturer | Associate Dean (Academic)
Division of Physics & Applied Physics | College of Science
Nanyang Technological University

"With increasing internationalization of education, educators have to consider the need for change or adaptation of their course pedagogical design and implementation to ensure effective learning for students of different cultural background. This book highlights the relevant research findings and provides guidance to educators who wish to better engage learners from mainland China in learning. Educational researchers, too, will find the summary of extant research on cultural impacts on these students' learning style and possible interventions to increase their learning effectiveness informative for their research."

Assoc Prof Low Kin Yew
Associate Dean (Undergraduate Academic)
Nanyang Business School, Nanyang Technological University

"Mainland Chinese students form a significant market for degree programs, especially graduate programs in business, entrepreneurship, technology and engineering in most International Education destinations such as Singapore, Australia, the USA and the UK. Dr. Rajaram, a Singaporean Business School academic and researcher on education, learning and pedagogy, has written this book based on his painstaking research of learning styles and pedagogy and his innovative teaching methods that he has developed and tested on business students. By developing a theoretical and conceptual framework based on traditional Chinese culture and value systems, Dr. Rajaram is able to effectively discuss the merits of alternative learning styles and pedagogical techniques that are suited to mainland Chinese students. This book is very relevant for researchers in education and pedagogy for understanding effective learning methods and the impact of culture on learning effectiveness especially for mainland Chinese students. The book is also a vital reference source for Educators and Program Directors at the Graduate and Executive programs for design and delivery of programs targeted for main Chinese students and executives".

Professor S. Viswanathan
Nanyang Business School, Nanyang Technological University

Preface

Thirteen years have passed since I started the insightful journey back then in 2006 during my stint as the Head, and Director of Academic Affairs and Business Development managing international students where a large majority were mainland Chinese students. I was intrigued to solve the complex challenges for students in pursuit of their studies at the university setting from a culturally dislocated environment, having to understand the learning styles and culture of learning. I also served concurrently as a research scholar in the area of internationalization of higher education. The inspiration to dive deeper was gathered from the varying complex questions that emerged through the real-life challenges that I had to deal with and have experienced. Back then, the immediate goal is to resolve the issues by addressing the contributing factors, but I did not have the bandwidth to examine them deeper from an evidence-based context to explicitly address the root causes of the problem. Hence, this served as the fundamental motivation in the pursuit of my PhD where I examined on the topic 'Culture Clash: Teaching Mainland Chinese Students Western-Based Education in Singapore'. This study investigated a vital and topical contemporary issue in relation to business education. Educating international students has been a lucrative endeavour for business schools around the world. At the same time, the key notion of ensuring the quality and effective delivery of the course programmes should be reiterated to maintain a high standard and rigor. This requires evidence-based inputs to understand the influence of learning design based on the learning culture, learning characteristics derived from the culture of learning and social and geographical issues that are deeply rooted and complex. However, cross-cultural pedagogical and perceived learning effectiveness issues in business education have been a relatively underresearched topic. Much of the academic success for students is dependent on the educational and cultural congruence between themselves and the institution they study in. The book makes a vital contribution in comprehending the instructional preferences and perceived learning effectiveness in adopting the correct mix of instructional techniques for educating mainland Chinese students undertaking business education in Singapore. As international Chinese students from mainland China are one of the largest cohorts of entrants into both

Eastern and Western business schools, this study makes both theoretical and practical contributions to the field of business education.

The work presented should be of common interest to educators in both the East and West. The focus here are on mainland Chinese learners pursuing their studies in Singapore, but the aspects of perceived learning effectiveness, mix of instructional techniques adopted, learning process and teaching in a culturally dislocated context and effectiveness in knowledge transfer in a rapid changing global environment are a universal concern. Educators globally may be too oblivious and unworrying to ignore this work as irrelevant to them. This is especially true in the current context where international students entail a large percentage of students in the universities from an overall recruitment perspective. This could be evident where my own experiences resonate in undergoing the vast differences in delivering effective knowledge and skills through the correct, customized mix of instructional techniques to local versus international students. The disparity and challenges in embedding general learning effectiveness and instructional techniques theory, without a deep understanding on the cultural and social issues, should not be perceived as quality teaching and learning. When this is viewed and analysed from the lenses of a cross-border context, it seems even more overwhelming, a paradox indeed. When examined, the differences between educational systems intertwined with cultural aspects; in this case, mainland Chinese pursuing their studies in Western curriculum opens a whole framework of complexity in a culturally dislocated environment. In this context, the focus shifts explicitly on the deep values, practices, norms, beliefs and ethical practices, those that are culture- and society (social values and norms)-specific. In many instances, effective learning occurs only when the learning design is customized to the context as deemed requires. K. Rajaram (2013) advocates that much of the academic success for students is dependent on the learning and cultural congruence between themselves and the institution they study in. This work is crucial for educators globally to understand how these mainland Chinese students learn only effectively through the correct mix and customized engagement through the commonly used instructional techniques in a culturally dislocated learning environment. To attain high-quality and effective learning outcomes, the instructional guidelines require evidence-based inputs to have it crafted and calibrated in terms of effective learning and knowledge transfer to these Chinese learners.

This book serves as an essential and timely resource for educators who teach mainland Chinese in Singapore and beyond to enhance the quality of lesson delivery with much higher learning effectiveness. The book serves as an advocate for educators to comprehend, be educated on the surplus theories and deficit theories of Chinese learners and the complexities involved in their pursuit of studies in a culturally dislocated environment. The intricacy of varying interventions to these mainland Chinese students' pursuit of studies in Singapore, i.e. in a culturally dislocated learning context, could be clustered as (1) Western-based curriculum adopted in Singapore; (2) subjected to local accreditation review, adjustments and customization of contents delivery; and (3) being taught by local instructors or Western instructors who may not have an adequate and deep understanding of the learning characteristics, learning style, learning culture and social values of these Chinese students.

The goal of this book is to offer contemporary insights and newest findings with the rapid changes in the field of Internationalization. The new insights involve the analysis, discussion of the evolving and current changes in the literature and evidence-based findings with recommendations tested for its effectiveness measured against the learning outcomes. The contents of this book are written by expanding my previous scholarly works, with some of the article sources reproduced in part in this book with appropriate permissions obtained. The scholarly articles include: (a) Rajaram, K. & Collins, J. (2013). "Qualitative identification of learning effectiveness measures among mainland Chinese Students in culturally dislocated study environments", *Journal of International Education in Business, 6*(2), 179–199; (b) Rajaram, K. & Bordia, S. (2011). "Culture Clash: Teaching western-based management education to mainland Chinese students in Singapore", *Journal of International Education in Business, 4*(1), 63–83; (c) Rajaram, K. (2013). "Followers of Confucianism or a New Generation? Learning Culture of mainland Chinese in pursuit of western based business education away from mainland China", *International Journal of Teaching & Learning in Higher Education, 25*(3), 369–377; (d) Rajaram, K. & Bordia, S. (2013). "East versus West: Effectiveness of knowledge acquisition and impact of cultural dislocation issues for mainland Chinese students across ten commonly used instructional techniques", *International Journal for the Scholarship of Teaching and Learning, 7*(1), 1–21; (e) Rajaram, K. (2013). "Learning in foreign cultures: Self-reports Learning effectiveness across different instructional techniques", *World Journal of Education, 3*(4), 71–95; (f) Rajaram, K. (2014). "East versus West: The descendants of Confucianism vs. evidence-based learning. Mainland Chinese learners in pursuit of western-based education in Singapore", *Journal of Education and Human Development, 3*(1), 239–281.

I trust to dedicate this scholarly work as an avenue of contribution to academics, practitioners and other stakeholders in this field to help them attain their institutional and individualized learning goals.

Singapore, Singapore   Kumaran Rajaram

Contents

Part II Applications to Universities and Higher Education Institutions

Chapter 1
Introduction

The chapter explains the importance and relevance of understanding the pedagogical and cultural nuances and context of mainland Chinese learners and its relevance to internationalization. It commences by discussing the relevance of mainland Chinese learners' pursuit of their studies and rapid internationalization of higher education from a holistic perspective. Then, it discusses the reasons of why international students view Singapore as a viable and one of the more preferred academic locations to pursue their higher studies. Then, a brief discussion on the importance of cultural dislocation facets that needs to be considered as Singaporean and education offshore providers offer higher education through overseas universities is presented. Next, the potential challenges and cultural dislocation aspects in teaching Western-based education to mainland Chinese learners are advocated. Thereafter, the intertwined relationship between cultural dimensions, cultural dislocations and the impact they have on these mainland Chinese students' learning is discussed. The chapter concludes with the significance of cultural integration to learning environment, learning design and teaching and learning.

The aptness of the cultural context in which learning occurs and the way in which learning is facilitated within that context determine the perceived effectiveness and effectiveness of learning outcomes in terms of transfer of knowledge. Culture, learning and communication are intertwined and mutually dependent concepts (Lum 2006). To sustain a global academic reputation, institutions of higher education must endeavour to achieve current and future cultural fit in their offshore operations (Bodycott and Lai 2012). The educational and cultural congruence, between the students and the institution in which they study in, determines the students' academic success (Rajaram and Bordia 2011). The ability to comprehend the subtle yet imperative cultural nuances and embedded complexities on the values, beliefs, cognitive thinking processes and behavioural aspects is key in achieving a conducive learning environment with quality learning outcomes and learning effectiveness.

© Springer Nature Singapore Pte Ltd. 2020
K. Rajaram, *Educating Mainland Chinese Learners in Business Education*,
https://doi.org/10.1007/978-981-15-3395-2_1

1.1 Chinese Learners: Internationalization of Higher Education

The 'Chinese learner' has attracted the spotlight largely due to upsurges in the numbers of mainland Chinese students pursuing their studies in both Anglophone countries such as Australia, Canada, the United States (the 'US') and the United Kingdom (the 'UK') and developed and modernized Asian regions such as Singapore, Hong Kong, Japan, Macau and Korea and developing regions such as Taiwan (Coverdale-Jones and Rastall 2009; Clark and Gieve 2006; Jin and Cortazzi 2006; Ryan and Slethaug 2010; Shi 2006; Turner 2006; Watkins and Biggs 1996, 2001). There are many Asian educational institutions that collaborate with Western universities to offer undergraduate and postgraduate academic and professional development courses or programmes in Asia so that the students need not travel abroad to study. Surprisingly, despite the rapid internationalization of education and workplaces, the perceptions of Chinese learners remain largely based on orthodox and outmoded assumptions.

Ryan and Slethaug (2010) debated:

> Such narrow thinking and lack of attention to the very real challenges and dilemmas that can confront those working on both sides of these systems of cultural practice can cause misunderstandings and inhibit opportunities for the development of innovative, creative and generative ways of teaching and learning. (p. 37)

Rajaram and Collins (2013) further advocated:

> It is essential to understand the composition of these mainland Chinese students in terms of varying demographics like age group, gender, type of business programs, provinces where students pursued their prior education, social background and any prior western exposure, thus enabling instructors to deliver high quality, practical business education to students from a variety of cultures. (p. 195)

Rajaram (2013) also emphasized that:

> There is a shift of Chinese culture of learning due to the changes in China progressively throughout an elongated history by acclimatizing itself to new and ever changing political, social and cultural demands. (p. 369)

In the rapidly evolving new knowledge-based and intellectually advanced economy, the crucial measurement of success for the Asian educational institutions depends largely on how the mainland Chinese students perceive and evaluate the opportunities offered by such foreign institutions. Due to cultural and social dislocation, many mainland Chinese students may experience challenges and stress. Therefore, it is critical for these Asian educational institutions in collaboration with Western universities that offer foreign degrees to appreciate these relevant aspects so as to address them. Much of the academic success of these students is dependent on the cultural and educational congruence between themselves and the overseas university where they pursue their education.

1.2 Singapore as an Academic Location for International Students

The international students view Singapore as an exemplary academic location where they can experience the 'best of both worlds', which is to pursue a Western-based education in an Asian context. Furthermore, it is easier for the mainland Chinese students to culturally adapt to Singapore environment, as there are similarities in language, cultural values, beliefs and social norms between China and Singapore. This led to Singapore as one of their preferred choices in their pursuit of their undergraduate or postgraduate education.

Singapore is a multiracial and multicultural society that functions in a knowledge-based economy. Singapore's known for valuing human resources, and it owes its success to quality human resources. It endeavours to be a global education hub, taking advantage of being a knowledge-based economy where both students and investors can pursue their own specific interests and needs. Investors are well aware that Singapore has a stable government that provides political stability and security, thus enabling good economic conditions. Furthermore, it is easier to conduct business/trade activities in Singapore than in many other countries due to its relatively transparent political system. Of the resources that give Singapore its competitive edge, its strategic location at the crossroads of international shipping is one of the most important. Taking full advantage of its geographical location, Singapore developed into a leading international hub port and maritime centre. It is not only the business/trade activities that benefitted from the location, the education field is also an excellent intermediary between the East and the West. The initial competitive advantage conferred by Singapore's geographical location and natural harbour was buttressed by the free trade policy pursued by the colonial government. Since its political independence, the free trade policy has been sustained through investment in world-class transportation and telecommunications infrastructure, facilities and services.

The emergence of a knowledge-based economy has resulted in four key changes: a rise in the residual component of labour productivity growth; the growth of investment in education; a rise in real stocks of intangible capital (education); and a decline in conventional capital share. In the business/trade aspect, it has the ability to serve as a fine, cheap labour platform base. Extensive air, sea and telecommunications networks link Singapore with major cities and ports in the region and around the world. Singapore is also promoted as a 'smart city', with comprehensive development of information technology infrastructure. From an educational perspective, it serves as an ideal location where students can have close proximity to Western education in an Asian culture. Students are attracted to Singapore as a place for pursuing higher education due to its quality branding and prestigious reputation as a country with well-recognized educational institutions that offer world-class accredited qualifications. This creates the possibility of a new era of Confucianism for the overall economic betterment of Singapore. Moreover, Singapore also serves as an exemplary icon to all the neighbouring countries for its Western-based education offered by foreign universities in partnership with local institutions.

Contemporary business education provides deep knowledge, competencies and skills that compete with rapid changing global expectations and perspectives for future managers and leaders. This prepares students with the relevant industrial exposure and provides them with a global networking platform to enhance their competence. According to the Committee for Private Education 2015–2016 report, 50% of the 135,088 students who commenced their studies in 2015 in private education institutions are foreign students, and 48% of the courses offered by these private education institutions are business and administration courses (Committee of Private Education 2016, Jan 12). This was highlighted in the annual economic review analysis reports for the years 2011–2014, where the total revenue generated was one of the secondary contributing factors to the economic growth of Singapore. Among these international undergraduate students, the biggest cohort was the mainland Chinese students. Local universities and institutions collaborating with overseas universities are taken as the focal platform because these foreign students constitute a growing trend. As of June 2016, the number of foreign students who hold student's pass in Singapore is 66,800 (Population.sg 2016, 25 Aug). International students constitute 30% of the student population in the National University of Singapore and 31% of the Nanyang Technological University in 2015 according to the World University Rankings 2018 (Times Higher Education 2017, 16 Oct). As for the Singapore Management University (2016, 12 Sep), 10% of their undergraduate students and 61% of their postgraduate students in 2016 are international students. The yearly growth in enrolment of international students in business courses is a clear indication of its continuously growing popularity. Such growth presents both opportunities and challenges.

To deal with the intensifying challenges of meeting these international students' educational needs, most educational institutions in Singapore offer a wide range of business courses in comparison to other specialized course programmes. For example, generally the ratio of business courses to other specialized course programmes offered by higher education institutions is approximately 1:3—an apparent sign of the increasing enrolment in business courses among the international students, especially the mainland Chinese students. The high demand may be due to the type and scope of subjects offered in these business course programmes. These subjects are more likely to be within the students' interest, ability to cope and foreseeable future success.

The key challenge in today's international business education is the ability to implement appropriate cross-cultural strategies that facilitate international student education. Offering quality education for international students requires a good understanding of the cultural aspects of education and effective instructional, learning approaches for optimal knowledge transfer. Thus, the key issue is an explicit comprehension of effective use of instructional techniques suitable for these mainland Chinese students to have them learn and gain knowledge most effectively. In this context, this book serves to address the prevailing issues surrounding the influence of cultural values and cultural dislocation on mainland Chinese students' learning effectiveness via the most appropriate instructional techniques that create an optimal educational learning platform.

Singapore is a small city-state with a population of about approximately six million people. It had enjoyed enviable economic growth in the face of the world economic recession in 2008. Despite the recession, due to Singapore's consistent strategic planning, it is one of the few Asian countries least affected by the financial crisis because of its stable governance, sound domestic economic policies, attraction to international talents and so on. These factors encourage investors from various industries to use Singapore as a business base for venture and growth.

> Without any natural resources, the success of Singapore relies entirely on its people. The government's policy is to develop the country into a vibrant international city. One strategy of achieving this objective is to absorb foreign talents. In the area of education, Singapore wants to become the educational hub of Asia. Foreign scholars and students are encouraged to work or study in the country. (Tsang 2001, pp. 347–348)

This is evident in the steady growth in the number of international students in both public and private institutions in recent years. With more international students pursuing their studies in Singapore's educational system, there is an increase in the possibility of them pursuing their careers in Singapore as well, which eventually contributes to the growth of Singapore's national economy. Furthermore, the rising number of international students signifies the high quality of education and recognized qualifications that are offered in Singapore. This enhances credibility of Singapore's education system and facilitates Singapore's goal of becoming a well-recognized educational hub that attracts talents from all around the world.

With China's growing economic and social progression, the mainland Chinese have started to explore opportunities outside their country. Singapore's attraction comes from its superior academic facilities in the region plus cultural similarities to China that allow for easier adaptation. The brain drain problem suffered by China coincides with Singapore's desire to attract foreign talent (Tsang 2001). With China's adoption of an open economy since the late 1970s, more and more mainland Chinese source for opportunities in foreign countries, and for many of them, Singapore is a natural choice (Rajaram 2010; Tsang 2001).

There are many cultural similarities between Singapore and China. Singapore's multiracial culture, which is dominated by the Chinese population, attracts the mainland Chinese, largely due to the cultural and linguistic similarities. Therefore, mainland Chinese tend to blend into Singapore's society much more easily than into Western countries. This has resulted in a vast increase in mainland Chinese students and academics coming to Singapore over the past decade (Bohm et al. 2002). China's economic liberalization in the form of opening up to Western companies comes at a very appropriate time, as Singapore takes on the next phase of its acceleration in attracting foreign talents for the growth of its national economy. It attracts talents through highly recognized and regarded academic pursuits and stable employment. Moreover, Singapore is an excellent place for experiencing and embracing both Asian and Western values. This has been statistically proven in terms of the number of foreign talents, especially mainland Chinese students, coming to Singapore to pursue their higher education.

These mainland Chinese have probably become the largest cluster of foreigners in the institutions collaborating with overseas universities and in overseas universities with Singapore campuses. Their adaptation to the new environment in terms of

culture and learning/teaching styles has a direct impact on their academic performance. These students' main concern is whether they can achieve good academic
results that will then increase their chances for further studies or employment in
their desired career after graduation. As future managers, their performance in
employment depends largely on how well they are trained and equipped with knowledge and skills in their courses of study. Furthermore, those mainland Chinese students who fail to adapt might have to leave the country. Thus, their ability to do well
by learning effectively in their course of study with the correct mix of instructional
techniques has significant personal and organizational performance implications.
There is a high demand for students to learn and acquire knowledge effectively so
as to meet their expectations to do well in their academic pursuits. It is essential to
appreciate that there are distinctive differences in the style of learning in China as
compared to that of a Western-based education in Singapore with partnering overseas universities or that of an education through active and collaborative learning
in local universities in Singapore. The academic success of mainland Chinese students is largely attributed to the effectiveness of a good fit with learning styles
through the identified instructional techniques in the educational institutions.

1.3 Singaporean and Education Offshore Providers Offer Higher Education Through Overseas Universities

The Singaporean higher education sector is extremely competitive, with many
Singaporean and offshore providers from countries such as the United States, the
United Kingdom, France, Australia and others. The Singaporean government,
through the publicly funded universities in Singapore (e.g. National University of
Singapore, Nanyang Technological University and Singapore Management
University, Singapore Institute of Technology, Singapore University of Technology
and Design, Singapore University of Social Sciences), is continuously exploring
possibilities of working with top-ranking universities, especially the universities
from the United States, Europe and Australia, to commit additional educational
resources. Offering quality education for international students requires a good
understanding of the cultural aspects and effective methods of knowledge transfer
which are integrated with optimal learning processes (Rajaram and Bordia 2011).
National culture has long been identified as a major factor influencing organizational direction and performance (Huyton and Ingold 1995). It is also acknowledged
as a key issue impacting on the practices of educational institutions (Bodycott and
Walker 2000; Norris 2000). Giroux (1997) has described 'culture' as the dynamic
interplay between the experiences of people and the social structure at large. It is the
individual perception of one's societal situation. In contrast, Wang (2001) explains
'culture' as one's identification with the shared social construction or sameness that
is shared with others.

As migrants abroad, the mainland Chinese believe that the only way to provide a
better start in life for their children is through education, with many maintaining

high expectations for the quality of education provided by host countries such as Britain, Australia and America. 'The "over-emphasis" on university education and belief that this would confer much status upon the parent within Chinese society' (Pieke 1991, p. 112) means that the number of students who continue in full-time tertiary education is high.

In the knowledge-based economy, how these mainland Chinese students perceive the foreign education is the key determinant of success. There is a collective focus on the critical issues such as cultural factors, family influences, individual personality type, English language competence, motivation for migration and so on (Selvarajah 2006). It is apparent that to successfully maintain their international academic reputation, Singapore's educational institutions must strive to achieve current and future cultural fit. The possibilities for developing an effective emerging framework are endless. Thus, it is critical for educational institutions to appreciate the cultural aspects in terms of their challenges and diversity so that they can better address these relevant issues. Understanding the cultural dislocation facets will then enable the international students—in our case, mainland Chinese students—to acquire knowledge in the most effective manner, which will eventually equip them with competence, experience, exposure, satisfaction and connectedness in terms of quality education.

1.4 Culture Clash: Teaching Western-Based Business Education to Mainland Chinese Learners

Based on research conducted across 50 countries (consisting of a good mix of both Western and Asian countries), Hofstede (1980) developed a typology consisting of four cultural dimensions by which a society may be classified: individualism-collectivism (relates to interpersonal ties), power distance (relates to inequality), uncertainty avoidance (relates to dealing with the unknown and unfamiliar), and masculinity-femininity (relates to the emotional gender roles). Hofstede and Bond (1988) subsequently described another cultural dimension, Confucianism, which is prevalent mainly in Asian countries like Singapore, China, South Korea and Japan. The understanding of Confucian philosophical concepts is important, as Chinese students from mainland China are deeply rooted in Confucian values. Although these students have fairly similar social value systems to those in Singapore, the values of Confucianism, filial piety (respect for one's parents, it is considered the most fundamental of Confucian values, the root of all others); humaneness (the care and concern for other human beings); and ritual consciousness or propriety (the proper way of doing things in the deepest sense), may cause conflicts and challenges to the students in their pursuit of a Western-based education and adopting an active learning approach in a philosophically different curriculum.

However, it has been reported that the measure for some countries, using the Hosfstede's theory, does not appear to reflect the commonly known cultural traits of those countries. For example, Singapore measures as low/weak in uncertainty avoidance, yet the country functions under a governance system that provides high regimentation and stability for its citizens. Examples of strong uncertainty avoidance cultures include France's code law, 'mechanistic system', and examples of weak uncertainty avoidance cultures include the United Kingdom's common law, 'organic system'. However, Hofstede and Bond (1988) found that the uncertainty avoidance dimension is less applicable in Confucian-based cultures, such as the People's Republic of China, South Korea, Japan, Hong Kong, Taiwan and Singapore.

The national culture of a country has an impact on how the people in that country are being nurtured in their personal, social and cultural values. This will translate to the varying aspects in which they operate in. This emphasizes that mainland Chinese students will experience challenges in adapting to the differences in the educational lifestyles inherent in a Western-based education in Singapore. Moreover, this adds to the complexity of cultural values involved in pursuing a Western-based business education that brings in another set of cultural issues to be addressed in delivering the subject modules to mainland Chinese students. Thus, it is expected that mainland Chinese students will adapt to Singapore's culture quite easily in terms of lifestyle but are bound to have effectiveness issues which will surface in terms of the learning and acquiring of knowledge from the course curriculum developed from a Western country (Rajaram 2010; Rajaram and Bordia 2011; Dimmock and Leong 2010).

Confucian philosophy permeated mainstream traditional Chinese values throughout history with its morals and political ideals, playing dominant roles in the past Chinese dynasties. Cultures that are based on the Confucian philosophy develop stability-generating systems that are considerably different from those generated in religion-based cultures, for example, in terms of the values, principles and beliefs in how varying issues are perceived and acted upon. Again, it is anticipated that conflicts between cultures will arise as Western-based education curricula emanated from a religion-based culture. The styles of delivery and methodology utilized will vary, thus having an impact on the effectiveness of knowledge acquirement as well.

1.5   Intertwined Relationship: Cultural Congruence in Students' Learning

The intertwined relationship between cultural dimensions, cultural dislocations and the impact they have on cultural groups from different countries is evident in the literature discussed above. The varying cultural dynamics are expected to have an influence on the students' learning effectiveness, student engagement and the manner in which knowledge is being transferred to the students. It is noticeable that there is a gap, which has not been specifically addressed, that is, the approach by which mainland Chinese students learn effectively. Due to the diversity of scope, only the three most relevant out of the five cultural dimensions from Hofstede's (1980) and Hofstede and Bond's (1988) cultural frameworks will be considered for discussion in this book: the two cultural dimensions of power distance and uncertainty avoidance, together with the third dimension of the philosophy of

Confucianism. The nine cultural dimensions from GLOBE's (Global Leadership and Organisational Behaviour Effectiveness) project have also been duly considered (House et al. 2004). But due to the diversity of its scope, GLOBE's cultural framework has not been adopted. Moreover, when these cultural dimensions are evaluated for their relevance to mainland Chinese students pursuing a business education in Singapore, in comparison with the other cultural dimension frameworks, the rest are evaluated not to have as much impact. Basically, the three carefully identified cultural dimensions—namely, power distance, uncertainty avoidance and the philosophy of Confucianism—are very relevant in measuring the cultural diversity in an internationally based educational and cultural environment. These issues regarding mainland Chinese students' perceived learning effectiveness and learning effectiveness in terms of acquisition of knowledge through Western-based education have not yet been exhaustively researched, and there are many unanswered questions of how to effectively engage these students to acquire knowledge through the correct mix of instructional techniques.

Higher education institutions currently attract students from a variety of cultural backgrounds. A culturally diverse student population has been a common phenomenon in universities in many English-speaking countries, such as the United States, the United Kingdom, Australia and New Zealand, for approximately the past two decades. A relatively new phenomenon is developing where Western-based education is conducted from Asian countries as distance learning operations where the curriculum is either facilitated online or with a campus set-up in Asia with the business operating locally, i.e. the courses or programmes are conducted in the local country itself. As a knowledge-based economy, Singapore is opening up to many Western universities, driving the tertiary educational sector to further expand into a large export market to other Asian countries. The Singaporean higher education sector is made up of several competitive local universities, which have recently been augmented by programmes from several foreign universities from Australia, the United Kingdom, France, the United States, etc. The foreign universities have set up educational programmes in collaboration with local educational providers.

Apart from local Singaporean students, the educational programmes provided by universities or institutions collaborating with overseas universities also attract a substantial number of students from foreign countries, especially mainland China. Much of the academic success for students is dependent on the educational and cultural congruence between themselves and the institution in which they study. Thus, a good understanding of the cultural impact on the adoption of correct mix of instructional techniques and learning styles for students from mainland China is significant in shaping the curricula in these educational institutions. To be successful and maintain an international academic reputation, the collaborative institutions must strive to directly address current and future cultural 'fit' in all their educational operations. The current literature investigating Chinese values in teaching and learning styles proposes that the common challenges mainland Chinese students may face in a Western-style education are lack of abstract thinking, constraints on behaviour caused by embarrassment, over-emphasis on concrete examples, lack of creativity and the need to compromise in group situations.

It is clear that there are educational differences that must be addressed if mainland Chinese students are to reach their fullest potential in distance learning courses and face-to-face courses conducted in Singapore by foreign universities with a Western-based style. There are cultural challenges and adaptability issues involved for mainland Chinese students pursuing a Western-based education in culturally dislocated learning settings. As this is still an evolving field, there is no single, widely recognized and empirically validated framework for evaluating the perceived effectiveness and effectiveness of learning in the pursuit of Western-based education by mainland Chinese students through the adoption of correct mix of customized and effective instructional techniques. Many studies have been conducted theoretically and in isolation, but not integrated within a single framework—for example, Ryan and Slethaug (2010), Coverdale-Jones and Rastall (2009), Shi (2006), Turner (2006), Clark and Gieve (2006), Tsang (2001), Chow (1995), Liu (2006), Nield (2004), Newell (1999), Leung et al. (2008) and Cheng and Wong (1996).

Thus, the strategic purpose of this book is to examine the influence of the perceived learning effectiveness, learning effectiveness and cultural dislocation elements when measured across the commonly used instructional techniques. It focuses on mainland Chinese students pursuing Western-based business undergraduate education in institutions in Singapore collaborating with overseas universities. This book aspires to shed some light on how mainland Chinese students learn effectively, to have them engaged through the commonly used instructional techniques, and, ultimately, identifies the specific and correct mixture of techniques that facilitate optimal learning.

1.6 Significance of Cultural Integration to Learning Environment, Learning Design and Teaching and Learning

Over the years, Singapore has evolved from its traditional British-based educational system to the one that endeavours to meet the needs of individuals and seeks to nurture talents. The strength of Singapore's education system lies in its multilingual policy (English with Malay/Mandarin/Tamil) and a broad-based curriculum where innovation and entrepreneurship command a premium. Individuals acquire the relevant skills and abilities to survive in competitive environments, aspiring for a brighter future. With the nation's rich multicultural heritage, people of the various major ethnic groups (Chinese, Malays, Indians and Eurasians) have gradually acquired a distinct identity as Singaporeans while still maintaining each race's traditional practices, customs and festivals and live together harmoniously. Singapore's high standard of living is also something of which students could be assured of. In the annual survey by the Economist Intelligence Unit, Singapore is ranked 35th in the 2017 global ranking of livable cities (third in Asia) (Today 2017, 16 Aug). It is worth noting that Singapore had an 11-place improvement mainly due to its educational achievements. Singapore was ranked number 1 in Asia in Mercer's 2017 Quality of Living survey, and its infrastructure was ranked the best in the world in the same survey (The Straits Times 2017, 14 Mar). Singapore is also strategically located at the heart of Asia and can be a hub to explore the Southeast Asian region.

As a knowledge-based economy, Singapore is attracting numerous well-established Western universities to collaborate with local universities and higher education institutions. Therefore, the tertiary educational sector in Singapore will further grow into a large export market to other Asian countries. The book discusses and recommends strategies to ensure the quality of education and its compatibility with an Asian client base, both in terms of content of education and services provided to students. Mainland Chinese students are probably the largest cohort of international students who come to Singapore to pursue their education. Within this cohort, the undergraduate students are the largest group (comprising around 68% of the entire student population). Furthermore, there is a pressing need for Singapore, being an education hub aspiring to provide quality education, to acquire an understanding of teaching issues pertaining to this group of international students so as to facilitate and transfer knowledge more effectually. Therefore, it is logical that this research study prioritizes its investigation on this unique and ever growing segment of the international student population.

Higher education institutions and universities were chosen because this has been an emerging group that draws a large volume. The analysis in this book serves as a guide and framework to enhance the teaching delivery by adopting the demonstrably effective instructional techniques for mainland Chinese students. The results and deep discussions can help in the effective development of a curriculum in business education. Although the key research focus is on perceived learning effectiveness and learning effectiveness for mainland Chinese students, the study on each student's outcome in terms of quality and standard (based on perceived learning effectiveness and learning effectiveness) means preparing a competent workforce which will improve productivity for an organization's growth, and that will eventually contribute to the country's economy. This is because of the students' ability to perform and produce tangible results in their future work organizations that largely depends on how well their knowledge has been acquired from their learning outcomes. This book hopes to present research studies that will ultimately enhance Singapore's reputation as a global education hub that provides high-quality education. Consequently, it will help to attract more international students to come to Singapore to pursue their further education despite the global competitive landscape. This would generate more revenue for Singapore and contribute to its economic growth.

A good-quality educational experience is essential for the reputation of an institution that partners with its overseas universities, as well as Singapore as an up-and-coming global educational hub. If students have a good experience in the institutions, they will recommend the institution to other prospective students in the near future. Two good examples are the Singapore University of Social Science (formerly known as SIM University) and Singapore Institute of Management, Global (SIM), institutions that have provided a quality and optimal learning effectiveness platform for its students for the past 10 years. They both have good reputation that strengthens their market position, enabling them to be appealing to prospective students as one of the well-established business-training institutions in Singapore.

Differences exist in the preferred instructional techniques of students in Asian and Western countries. The varying stages of economic development of the countries may influence the modes of instructional approaches to be adopted or used. In contrast to developed countries, Singapore is well-established and rapidly evolving with a consistently growing economy. The instructional approaches used in Singapore will have an impact on what and how mainland Chinese students actually learn, especially those from developing regions with limited modern instructional resources. A Singapore study is timely and contributes to the framework of Western-based education in collaboration with overseas universities. The techniques handled in Singapore's business educational curriculum differ in comparison to other countries. As a multiracial country, Singapore consists of educators who come from varying cultural backgrounds and have differing teaching approaches that impact on the effective delivery of lessons. Thus, adopting an empirically tested framework for standardization will enhance the quality of the higher education institutions, which then contributes to its business growth. Besides, the way the institutions are being regulated in Singapore is unique, which has an impact on the design of the curriculum model in comparison with other countries, where the schools are governed differently. As Wößmann (2001) reported, 'within a country's educational system, the relevant institutions and policies include the ways in which a society finances and manages its schools, how a society assesses student performance, and who is empowered to make basic educational decision, such as which curricula to follow, which teachers to hire, and what textbooks to purchase' (pp. 67–68). Besides, within Singapore, differences prevail in the governance between running full-fledged government-funded institutions versus private institutions collaborating with overseas universities. Therefore, it is imperative to realize, acknowledge and comprehend the explicit cultural dislocation aspects that influence the architecture of effective instructional design and adoption of correct mix of pedagogical approaches for effective knowledge transfer and engagement of students' learning.

The findings and implementation of the studies covered in this book are essential for international trade and investment activities in the educational field, especially for Singapore, which endeavours to be a global education hub now and into the future. As more students are satisfied with the quality of learning outcomes, this will attract an even larger pool of international students, especially mainland Chinese students. Thus, institutions generate more revenue by attracting more potential investors to venture in their growth and boosts international trade operations. Sourcing for investment opportunities is imperative in multinational higher education business today, and assessing the risk profile and reducing the dangers of business deals in foreign environments are unequivocally essential. Thus, Singapore is a stable country with an excellent business and national economic record of accomplishment allowing foreign investors to take advantage of the current business and economic situation by leveraging the growing educational industry.

Cultural factors in the assessment of business opportunities in the Asian region could influence the decisions of potential business ventures. Consequently, application of knowledge about the cultural environment and dislocation aspects can be readily translated into possible advantages by offering higher levels of efficiency and attaining larger profits from the higher education institutions. One of the key responsibilities of the institutions is to comprehend the embedded cultural implications so as to ensure that mainland Chinese students are able to cope and perform to an optimal level of effectiveness. Higher education institutions can perform well by producing quality and highly regarded business graduates through ensuring their students learn effectively. From a business context, the service quality to students is enriched in terms of their academic outcome, thus attracting more students to enroll in the courses offered. The research results that verify the relative cultural influence on perceived learning effectiveness and learning effectiveness via the instructional techniques address the purpose of alleviating business risks due to cultural aspects in general. Moreover, the research affirms the usefulness of applying the results practically in terms of cultural perspectives targeting educational effectiveness in international business education.

There is an ongoing debate in the literature on Chinese learning styles about the instructional techniques that enable the most effective transfer of knowledge. The improvements of Chinese students' perceived learning effectiveness, learning effectiveness and student engagement through the adoption of the instructional techniques have been questioned, and some authors have suggested that the preferred instructional techniques alone present a better indication of effectiveness of learning and attainment of their learning outcomes. Other pioneers in the same field—such as Newell (1999), Richards and Ross (2004) and Chow (1995)—argue that learning effectiveness should be viewed from various aspects of inferences. Pioneers from the cultural field like Hofstede and associates have emphasized cultural values, beliefs, norms and lifestyles as having high influence on perceived learning effectiveness, learning effectiveness and the manner in which these Chinese mainland students may acquire knowledge.

Hofstede (1980) classified those from a background of high power distance as individuals who tend to accept centralized power and rely heavily on superiors for structure and direction. Students from societies having this cultural orientation generally have not been encouraged to make decisions on their own and tend to rely relatively on strong direction. Their learning preference is inclined towards instructional techniques which comprise of higher level of involvement and decision-making from the instructors. Hofstede (1980) reported that individuals from backgrounds of strong uncertainty avoidance would feel uneasy and have a sense of ambiguity, thus preferring to have a structural and systematic approach. Students with a high uncertainty avoidance prefer to be directed and expect a high level of guidance, whereas those with a low uncertainty avoidance prefer to be in situations where there is much less guidance and tend to be more satisfied working independently. It is emphasized that the uncertainty avoidance measure developed by Hofstede is not perfect (Rodrigues 2004). 'Hofstede and Bond (1988) found that the uncertainty avoidance dimension is less applicable in Confucian-based cultures, such as the People's Republic of China, South Korea, Japan, Hong Kong, Taiwan and Singapore' (Rodrigues 2004, p. 612). Cultures that are based on the Confucian philosophy develop stability-generating systems that are considerably different from those generated in religion-based cultures, as how the values and cultural practices advocated in these two cultures differ. Thus, in large power distance and strong uncertainty avoidance societies, individuals in countries whose culture is based on the Confucian philosophy are likely to prefer strong direction and stability (Jarrah 1998).

Anecdotes are abound that learner-centred, active instructional techniques such as flipped classroom approaches, interactive case studies and active and experimental learning activities are more widely used in Western business education, and are not as well-received in many Asian countries (Pun 1989; Boisot and Fiol 1987; Murphy 1987; Rigby 1986; Staw 1982) due to the culture of learning which is shaped by a mixture of cultural values embedded in the learning process. But apparently, there have been many changes in both mainland Chinese students' behaviours and the pedagogies adopted which have happened over the years that need to be understood thoroughly to address the evolving challenges faced in today's context. The research performed supported with the findings will be useful in the design and development of customized and effective instructional methodologies addressing issues pertaining to preferences, cultural dislocation adaptability and effective learning at large.

Having a clear understanding of the cultural dislocation issues embedded in the educational framework and its effect on various instructional methodologies will assist practitioners to design and deliver business curricula effectively. Globally, overseas higher education institutions and universities collaborating with local institutions will benefit from the conceptual framework presented in terms of developing their curricula and educational management strategies. Imperatively, this framework serves as a novel creation where the multileveled, complex and embedded issues are well addressed, hence providing end-users a one-stop guiding conceptual model to work towards quality delivery of lessons.

In addition, there is growing agreement that one of the key drivers of long-term organizational effectiveness is the ability of their employees to learn effectively in an intercultural setting. The mainland Chinese students educated in Singapore are potential future managers and leaders in either Singapore or other global locations. Thus, the ability to equip them with the appropriate knowledge in the most effective manner is vital, as their future performance in organizations depends largely on the understanding of principles, concepts of the content knowledge, skills they have acquired and the opportunity to continuously practice in a learning setting. From that dimensional perspective, this book serves to contribute towards the global knowledge base and economic structure in general. It also contributes to the Singapore setting in particular as it furnishes a guided evidence-based framework and analysis that institution, instructors and other stakeholders can learn from. This is to enhance the quality of the educational service, which optimistically would attract more mainland Chinese students to purse their higher education in Singapore.

References

Bodycott, P., & Lai, A. (2012). The influence and implications of Chinese culture in the decision to undertake cross-border higher education. *Journal of Studies in International Education, 16*(3), 252–270.

Bodycott, P., & Walker, A. (2000). Teaching abroad: Lessons learned about inter-cultural understanding for teachers in higher education. *Teaching in Higher Education, 5*(1), 79–94.

Bohm, A., Davis, D., Meares, D., & Pearce, D. (2002). *Global student mobility 2025: Forecasts of the global demand for international higher education*. Sydney: IDP Education Australia.

Boisot, M., & Fiol, M. (1987). Chinese boxes and learning cubes: Action learning in a cross-cultural context. *Journal of Management Development, 6*(2), 8–18.

Cheng, K. M., & Wong, K. C. (1996). School effectiveness in East Asia: Concepts, origins and implications. *Journal of Educational Administration, 34*(5), 32–49.

Chow, I. H. S. (1995). Management education in Hong Kong: Needs and challenges. *International Journal of Educational Management, 9*, 10–15. https://doi.org/10.1108/09513549510095068

Clark, R., & Gieve, S. N. (2006). On the discursive construction of 'the Chinese learner'. *Language, Culture and Curriculum, 19*(1), 54–73.

Coverdale-Jones, T., & Rastall, P. (2009). *Internationalising the University: the Chinese context*: Springer.

Dimmock, C., & Leong, O. S. J. (2010). Studying overseas: Mainland Chinese students in Singapore. *Compare, 40*(1), 25–42.

Education, C. f. P. (2016, January 12). *Annual report 2015/2016*. Retrieved from https://www.cpe. gov.sg/qql/slot/u754/whats%20new/CPE-AR%202015-16%20(Full)_Low%20Res.pdf

Giroux, H. (1997). Rewriting the discourse of racial identity: Towards a pedagogy and politics of whiteness. *Harvard Educational Review, 67*(2), 285–321.

Hofstede, G. (1980). *Culture's consequence. International differences in work-related values*. Newbury Park: Sage.

Hofstede, G., & Bond, M. H. (1988). The Confucius connection: From cultural roots to economic growth. *Organizational Dynamics, 16*(4), 5–21.

House, R. J., Hanges, P. J., Javidan, M., Dorfman, P. W., & Gupta, V. (Eds.). (2004). *Culture, leadership, and organizations: The GLOBE study of 62 societies*. Thousand Oaks: Sage.

Huyton, J. R., & Ingold, A. (1995). The cultural implications of total quality management – The case of Ritz Carlton Hotel in Hong Kong. In R. Teare & C. Armistead (Eds.), *Services management: New directions, new perspectives*. London/New York: Cassell.

Jarrah, F. (1998). New courses will target transition to university. *China Morning Post, 23*, 28.

Jin, L., & Cortazzi, M. (2006). Changing practices in Chinese cultures of learning. *Language, Culture and Curriculum, 19*(1), 5–20.

Leung, D. Y., Ginns, P., & Kember, D. (2008). Examining the cultural specificity of approaches to learning in universities in Hong Kong and Sydney. *Journal of Cross-Cultural Psychology, 39*(3), 251–266.

Liu, S. (2006). Developing China's future managers: Learning from the west? *Education + Training, 48*(1), 6–14.

Lum, L. (2006). Internationally-educated health professionals: A distance education multiple cultures model. *Education + Training, 48*(2/3), 112–126.

Murphy, D. (1987). Offshore education: A Hong Kong perspective. *Australian Universities' Review, 30*(2), 43–44.

Newell, S. (1999). The transfer of management knowledge to China: Building learning communities rather than translating Western textbooks? *Education + Training, 41*(6/7), 286–294.

Nield, K. (2004). Questioning the myth of the Chinese learner. *International Journal of Contemporary Hospitality Management, 16*(3), 189–196.

Norris, D. M. (2000). *E-business and higher education marketplaces*. Strategic Initiatives, Inc.

Pieke, F. N. (1991). Chinese educational achievement and "folk theories of success". *Anthropology & Education Quarterly, 22*(2), 162–180.

Population.sg. (2016, August 25). *Who's in our population*. Retrieved from https://population.sg/articles/who-is-in-our-population

Pun, A. (1989). *Developing managers internationally: culture free or culture bound?* Paper presented at the symposium presentation at the Conference on International Personnel and Human Resource Management, Hong Kong.

Rajaram, K. (2010). *Culture Clash: teaching western-based business education to mainland Chinese students in Singapore*. Doctoral dissertation. University of South Australia, Adelaide, Australia.

Rajaram, K. (2013). Learning in foreign cultures: Self-reports learning effectiveness across different instructional techniques. *World Journal of Education, 3*(4), 71.

Rajaram, K., & Bordia, S. (2011). Culture clash: Teaching western-based management education to mainland Chinese students in Singapore. *Journal of International Education in Business, 4*(1), 63–83.

Rajaram, K., & Collins, J. B. (2013). Qualitative identification of learning effectiveness indicators among mainland Chinese students in culturally dislocated study environments. *Journal of International Education in Business, 6*(2), 179–199.

Richards, N., & Ross, D. L. (2004). Offshore teaching and learning: An exploratory Singaporean study. *International Journal of Educational Management, 18*(4), 260–265.

Rigby, J. A. (1986). In the schools: California treat: Three days in five ecosystems. *Science and Children, 23*(4), 20–23.

Rodrigues, C. A. (2004). The importance level of ten teaching/learning techniques as rated by university business students and instructors. *Journal of Management Development, 23*(2), 169–182.

Ryan, J., & Slethaug, G. (2010). *International education and the Chinese learner* (Vol. 1). Hong Kong: Hong Kong University Press.

Selvarajah, C. (2006). Cross-cultural study of Asian and European student perception: The need to understand the changing educational environment in New Zealand. *Cross cultural management: An international Journal, 13*(2), 142–155.

Shi, L. (2006). The successors to Confucianism or a new generation? A questionnaire study on Chinese students' culture of learning English. *Language, Culture and Curriculum, 19*(1), 122–147.

Singapore Management University. (2016, September 12). *Statistical Highlights 2016*. Accessed 05 Jun 2018.

Staw, B. M. (1982). Ni Hao: Some reflections on teaching organizational behavior in China. *Exchange: The Organizational Behavior Teaching Journal, 7*(2), 8–11.

The Straits Times. (2017, March 14). *Singapore ranked nicest city to live in Asia for expats, with the best infrastructure in the world: Survey*. Retrieved from http://www.straitstimes.com/business/economy/singapore-ranked-nicest-place-to-live-in-asia-for-expats-survey?login=true

The World University Rankings, 2016–2017, Times Higher Education (2017, October 16). Retrieved from https://www.timeshighereducation.com/world-university-rankings/2017/world-ranking#!/page/0/length/25/sort_by/rank/sort_order/asc/cols/stats

Today. (2017, August 16). *Singapore surpasses Hong Kong on world's most liveable city list for first time*. Retrieved from http://www.todayonline.com/singapore/singapore-surpasses-hong-kong-asias-third-most-liveable-city-economist-report

Tsang, E. W. (2001). Adjustment of mainland Chinese academics and students to Singapore. *International Journal of Intercultural Relations, 25*(4), 347–372.

Turner, Y. (2006). Chinese students in a UK business school: Hearing the student voice in reflective teaching and learning practice. *Higher Education Quarterly, 60*(1), 27–51.

Wang, J. (2001). Contexts of mentoring and opportunities for learning to teach: A comparative study of mentoring practice. *Teaching and Teacher Education, 17*(1), 51–73.

Watkins, D. A., & Biggs, J. B. (Eds.). (1996). *The Chinese learner: Cultural, psychological and contextual influences*. Hong Kong/Melbourne: Comparative Education Research Centre, The University of Hong Kong/Australian Council for Educational Research.

Watkins, D. A., & Biggs, J. B. (2001). The paradox of the Chinese learner and beyond. In *Teaching the Chinese learner: Psychological and pedagogical perspectives* (pp. 3–23). Melbourne: Australian Council for Educational Research.

Wößmann, L. (2001). *New evidence on the missing resource-performance link in education*. Kiel: Kiel Institute for the World Economy.

Part I
Theory and Conceptual Framework

Chapter 2
Characteristics and Complexity of Cultural Values

The chapter begins by furnishing the general characteristics of culture and then with concrete and thorough comprehension of its definitions. This core analysis is further clustered into two subareas to be investigated—namely, general cultural concept and cultural values. Thereafter, a section is explicitly allocated to discuss the theoretical models of culture where the word 'culture' is examined with much deeper intensity to have a clear understanding of the term. This discussion on the theoretical frameworks of culture enables deeper insights and appreciation of the overview of the cultural dimensions. Thereafter, an analysis of Chinese culture follows, thereupon focusing on the concept of Confucianism. This section develops further by categorizing the two traditional Chinese value systems of Yi and Li, followed by the classification of Chinese culture. Next, the chapter examines the distinctive and explicit cultural differences between Singapore and China to address the diversity present in cultural values. The chapter finalizes the discussion on the differences between the different types of educational programmes offered in Singapore and ends with the last section that provides insights on the revolutionization and effects of culture

2.1 Definitions and Characteristics of Culture

The process of how individuals learn and communicate with each other and the cultural values embedded within them makes all these three aspects interdependent and intertwined (Lum 2006). The culture when examined within a learning context comprises varying unique values and beliefs and plays a pivotal role in determining the type of learning design, learning approaches and instructional techniques to be effectively adopted. The learning culture refers to how the learning has been structured and

---

This chapter is improved from K. Rajaram, 2014. East versus West: The Descendants of Confucianism vs. Evidence-Based Learning Mainland Chinese Learners in Pursuit of Western-Based Education in Singapore. Journal of Education & Human Development, 3(1): 239–281

© Springer Nature Singapore Pte Ltd. 2020
K. Rajaram, *Educating Mainland Chinese Learners in Business Education*,
https://doi.org/10.1007/978-981-15-3395-2_2

organized in a contextualized learning space, for example in an institution whereas culture of learning refers to the general approach of how learning takes place among the learners due to the influence of the national culture, learning culture and values, norms that intertwines within the social context and their life. In an institutional context, the learning culture and culture of learning play a vital role in shaping how learning happens and determining the impact towards knowledge transfer. In order for institutions in the higher education to sustain their global academic reputation and image, there is a compelling reason for them to strive to achieve current and future fit in all of their offshore operations (Bodycott and Lai 2012) and perhaps their onshore business activities as well. Students' academic success is attributed to many elements, one of which is the cultural and educational congruence between the institution and its students (Rajaram and Bordia 2011). Rajaram (2014) advocates that the paramount aspects are the quality of education and the collective perception of foreign education by mainland Chinese students which serves as key success factors for both the institutions and their students, in the knowledge-based economy (KBE). Besides these, there are other contributing issues such as English language competence, cultural influences, family influences, individual personality, motivation for migration and so on (Selvarajah 2006). For these relevant issues to be effectively addressed, educational institutions and universities need to be mindful and aware and comprehend the complexities involved in the cultural diversity and the challenges that entail within it. This chapter focuses largely on examining the cultural issues, specifically the cultural dislocation aspects of mainland Chinese students and its influence on the students' learning styles that influence their perceived learning effectiveness and learning effectiveness through the correct mix of instructional techniques adopted.

2.2 The Culture Concept

Culture is viewed to be multidimensional and multifaceted. To have a deeper and holistic understanding, one has to be mindful of the intertwined, closely related issues, embedded principles, values and beliefs and examine the varying levels, dimensions and perspectives involved. The concept is not so straightforward but comprises deeper and embedded complexities. One of the earliest and most widely cited definitions, by Tylor (1881), defined 'culture' as a multifaceted notion that encompasses knowledge, beliefs, morals, customs, laws, art and any other capabilities and habits acquired by man as a member of society. Kim and Mclean (2014) define culture as a collective mindset of shared beliefs, values, behaviours and thinking process, cascaded through multilayers, for example, from a national and/or organizational level. The interpretations of the term culture could be appreciated through the different scholars as follows:

(a) The belief of Hoebel (1960) is inclined towards the sharing of integrated, holistic and learned behavioural characteristics by members of a society. Culture can also be understood as a cluster of unvaryingly approved and shared behaviours within a society or cultural group.

(b) Culture is being disseminated through people in accordance to their expectations and values, so that others could follow. Environment includes man to be part of it (Herskovits 1955).
(c) Culture forms the fundamental basis where essential guidance and directions for desirable behaviour could be relied on. All the historically created designs for living—implicit, explicit, rational, irrational and non-rational—serve as prospective guides for the behaviour of men at any time (Kluckhohn and Kelly 1945).
(d) Culture advocates on how people should relate to each other and respond to erratic situations to deal with human relationships that are to be nurtured in a confirmatory manner. Through providing guidance in our relationships with our surroundings and other people, culture obliges as a mental map to people (Downs 1971).

A compilation of differing yet collective definitions by various authors assists to provide a comprehensive understanding of culture. Culture is characterized as collaborative and collective traits that have an impact through group's response to its environment. External adjustment and integration are attained through a society's culture, achieved through the assistance offered by its members. Rajaram (2010) advocates that relationships are nurtured in an affirmative way through culture which offers a basis on how individuals should relate and respond to each other in varying contexts. In 1984, Hofstede redefined 'culture' as the communal programming of the mind that distinguishes clusters of individuals. The term 'culture' originated from Latin. It is associated with the word *cultus*, which can be interpreted as 'cult' or 'worship'. Members of a cult believe in performing tasks in a particular manner which develop a culture that enshrines those beliefs. Terpstra and David (1985)'s definition assists to delineate the meaning of 'culture' in this context: culture is a learned, shared, persuasive, interconnected set of symbols whose meaning offers a set of directions for members of a society. These directions, taken collectively, provide solutions to challenges that societies must address if they are to remain viable.

With a holistic understanding and integration of varying definitions, 'culture' can be best defined as the collection of beliefs, values, customs and attitudes that differentiate a society from others. Culture can be examined at different levels: (a) international culture (e.g. East versus West); (b) national culture (e.g. Indian, Chinese); (c) regional culture, subculture (e.g. South Asian culture versus East Asian culture, European culture); (d) business culture (e.g. industry or professional culture); and (e) organizational (corporate) culture (e.g. multinational company culture versus state-owned corporation culture). Cultural differences are, more often than not, represented by different backgrounds, languages, perceptions and mentalities. Other cultural differences include beliefs, values, morals, customs, educational background, art and laws.

2.3   Cultural Values

A cultural society or cluster is a more appropriate unit of analysis than an individual person for the assessment of validity of culture-level dimensions (Hofstede 1980, 1991; Schwartz 1992). Theories relating to cultural values, for example, Triandis

(1995), Schwartz (1999) and Trompenaars and Hampden-Turner (2011), concentrate on limited aspects of culture, explicitly on materialism-post-materialism and individualism-collectivism rather than addressing a full range of potentially relevant value dimensions. Empirical work, coupled with these theories, has made use of instruments not validated for cross-cultural equivalence of meaning.

National culture best embodies the values that people embrace. People's attitudes and values are shaped through cultural values that guide their behaviour. Cultural values influence and mould ones' behaviour that implants certain accepted behavioural traits and expectations. Values are defined as conceptions of the required that direct the way social actors such as national leaders, organizational and institutional leaders, policy-makers and individual persons decide on actions, evaluate people and events and explicate their actions and evaluations (Kluckhohn 1951; Rokeach 1973; Schwartz 1992; Schwartz 1999). 'Values' have been described as lasting beliefs that infer specific means of conduct or states of existence which are socially preferable to their opposites (Rokeach 1973). Values concern preferences internalized by the members, whereas social 'norms' concern subjective perceptions of the preferences by a majority of the members of the societies (Pan et al. 1994). A 'value system' is viewed as a relatively permanent perceptual framework that impacts upon an individual's behaviour (England 1978). Cultural values establish the norms or standards by which everything in a society is accessed. Similarly, Williams (1970) pointed out that cultural values correspond to the implicitly or explicitly shared abstract ideas about what is good, desirable and right in society. These cultural values, for example, freedom, prosperity and security, are the foundation for the specific norms that inform people what is suitable in different situations (Schwartz 1999). The manner by which the institutions of society, for example, the family, education, economic, political and religious systems, function their goals and models of operation expresses cultural value priorities (Schwartz 1999).

The value priority aggregation of individuals enables the building up of the value system of a society (Hofstede 1980; Morris 1956). Shared cultural values in a society help to shape the institutional environment that people must adapt to. This results in members of each cultural group to share varying value-relevant experiences, and they are socialized to accept shared social values. People within a particular cultural group may not inevitably hold the exact same values (Hofstede 1984). Due to the varying personalities of individuals and their unique experiences, individual variation in value priorities within cultural groups will exist. The average priorities attributed to societal members' varying values reflect the central thrust of their shared enculturation. The average priorities point to the fundamental shared cultural values. The expectations and hopes to be nurtured in a society can be perceived to be represented by a value system. The values that are embedded within the cultural dimensions reflect the basic issues or challenges that societies have to deal with to regulate human activities (Kluckhohn and Strodtbeck 1961; Rokeach 1973; Hofstede 1980; Schwartz 1999). Hence, this enables us to appreciate and understand the reasons relating to the relational effect between cultural values and the manner in which students learn to acquire knowledge effectively through the different instructional approaches.

2.4   Theoretical Models of Culture

The concept of culture and its underlying dimensions are addressed through various theoretical models. Trompenaars and Hampden-Turner (2011)'s seven dimensions of culture will be one of them. Five of the model's dimensions comprise ways people relate to each other: (1) universalism versus particularism; (2) individualism versus communitarianism; (3) specific versus diffuse; (4) neutral versus emotional; and (5) achievement versus ascription. The sixth dimension relates to the clustering of societies in accordance to the time phase, i.e. sequential time versus synchronous time. The sixth final dimension covers the society's outlook towards the environment: internal direction versus outer direction. Schwartz (1999) advocates three pairs of cultural values, namely, (1) embeddedness versus autonomy, (2) mastery versus harmony and (3) hierarchy versus egalitarianism. Inglehart (2008)'s categorization includes (1) traditional values versus secular-rational values and (2) survival values versus self-expression values.

Hofstede and Global Leadership and Organizational Behaviour Effectiveness (GLOBE) were reported as the most widely used models in organizational cultural-related literature among the other primary predominate national culture models, although with much criticisms and shortcomings (Nardon and Steers 2011). However, among these two models, the inclination of grounding concepts of the emerging cultural dimensions is inclined towards Hofstede and his team's theoretical cultural framework model. In the past two decades, Hofstede's (1980, 1984) typology of cultural dimensions emerges as one of the foremost frameworks for understanding and measuring culture. Harzing's 'Publish and Perish' citation index reports, as of June 2010, there were over 54,000 citations to Hofstede's work (Tung and Verbeke 2010). Despite the criticisms, limitations and shortcomings that were voiced against his work (McSweeney 2002; Oyserman et al. 2002; Signorini et al. 2009), scholars such as Smith and Bond (1999) and Kirkman et al. (2006) have reviewed the literature and concluded that, in general, most large-scale studies published since Hofstede's (1980) work (e.g. Chinese Culture Connection 1987; Schwartz 1992, 1994; Trompenaars 1993) 'have sustained and amplified Hofstede's conclusions rather than contradicted them' (Smith and Bond 1999, p. 56). Nevertheless, readers are to be mindful and aware of that research is not without shortcomings and gaps (Kirkman et al. 2006). Kirkman et al. proposed various recommendations, including distinguishing the effects between country and culture, that have made impact in the research community of international business and management, hence assisted to influence the direction of research since (Beugelsdijk et al. 2017).

The comparative study of work-related values by Hofstede (1980, 1983) covers an exceptionally large number of national cultures, where over the years, the number of studies performed has increased from 40 to 53. The study overlays at least partly with most other cross-national studies as far as the countries covered are concerned (Hofstede and Bond 1984). The extensive analysis consists of 88,000 responses to a questionnaire survey of IBM employees in 66 countries. The study uses a population size that is narrow but comprises of well-matched set of samples (Hofstede and Bond 1984). Hofstede identifies three cultural dimensions through a factor diagnostic treatment of country averages for his value measures. One of these dimensions is further split into two sub-elements, resulting in four dimensions in total, where each of the country involved is given a score. The four dimensions resonate with the central anthropological and societal concerns. They are classified as (a) individualism-collectivism, (b) high-low power distance, (c) high-low uncertainty avoidance and (d) high-low masculinity-femininity. These four dimensions of culture are described and illustrated in detail as follows:

- 'Power distance' is labeled as the first dimension. Power distance is the extent, for example, an organization or society accepts power that is not evenly distributed. Low power distance organizations operate in a highly transparent and open style of working climate, whereas high power distance organizations operate in least transparent and closed working climate. Hofstede and Bond (1984) define culture as the extent to which employees who are less powerful accept that power is distributed unequally. Power distance also refers to the social inequality and the level of authority over others in terms of anthropological and societal issues. In a similar context, it could also be defined as the extent to which relationships between superior and subordinate are distant and formal versus close and informal.
- 'Uncertainty avoidance' is labeled as the second dimension. Hofstede and Bond (1984) define uncertainty as the extent to which others feel threatened by abstruse situations and have created beliefs and institutions that attempt to circumvent these. In contrast, uncertainty avoidance also refers as the extent to which others pursue to curtail uncertainty versus the extent to which they are tolerant of ambiguity. The manner a society deals with conflicts and aggression is linked to the fundamental anthropological and societal issue it is associated with (Hofstede and Bond 1984).
- 'Individualism versus collectivism' is labeled as the third dimension. Individualism refers the extent to which people are oriented towards self-interest, whereas collectivism inclines to an orientation towards the interests of a wider group of which they are a part of. It resembles its standing of the culture on a bipolar continuum. One of the poles, 'individualism', is defined as a situational context where individuals focus only on themselves and their immediate family. The contrary pole, 'collectivism', is defined as a state where individuals belong to in-groups or collectivities who are supposed to look after each other in exchange for loyalty. The basic anthropological and societal element is to associate an individual's level of dependence on the group: i.e. the individual's self-concept as 'I' or 'we' (Hofstede and Bond 1984).
- 'Masculinity versus femininity' is labeled as the fourth dimension. Masculinity relates to the extent to which success is defined in terms of assertiveness, challenge and ambition, rather than in terms of caring and nurturing, which is related to femininity. Hofstede and Bond (1984) define masculinity as a situation where the dominant values in society are success, money and things, whereas its oppo-

site pole, femininity, is a state where the central values in society are caring for others and the quality of life. The basic anthropological and societal concern refers to the choice of social sex roles and their effects on individuals' self-concepts.

Hofstede (2011) at a later phase added two more dimensions to his studies, namely, (a) *long-term orientation versus short-term normative orientation* and *indulgence versus restraint*. Long-term versus short-term orientation dimension relates to the choice of focus on people's efforts: the future, present and/or past. Indulgence versus restraint dimension relates to the gratification in comparison to the control of fundamental human desires in relation to enjoyment of life.

Based on research evidence, Hofstede demonstrated that countries differ drastically in their score on the above discussed. His work has been acknowledged for its research design, systematic data collection and consistent theory to elucidate national variations (Søndergaard 1994). However, as years passed by, three vital limitations and concerns to Hofstede's work were identified by a series of reviewers. First, several authors pointed out the limitations in collating data from employees of a single organization where inferences are made from, and second, others have pointed out that the dimensions that were developed from Hofstede's analysis may be artefacts of the period at which the surveys are carried out (Warner 1981; Lowe 1981; Baumgartel and Hill 1982). Third, questions were raised regarding the validity of inferring values from the attitude surveys alone (Smucker 1982). Despite these limitations, Hofstede's work is widely accepted, receiving no less than 1100 direct references in journals between 1980 and December 2002, and it has provided the basis for 67 replicated studies. As for within the journal citations, Hofstede's dimensions are adopted as a conceptual framework outside its original setting in 293 studies. To account for the latest record by taking reference to the year 2019, his work has a total of 159,336 citations.

The excitedly awaited brief volume on the GLOBE (Global Leadership and Organizational Behaviour Effectiveness) research programme was made available in spring 2004 (House et al. 2004). GLOBE study (2004) introduces the paradigm of 'dimensions', presenting the differences between the cultures of modern nations that could be meaningfully measured and organized along a distinct array of dimensions, representing varying answers to common challenges of human societies (Hofstede 2006). This helps in the derivation of four distinct dimensions, namely, (a) power distance (relates to the issues of inequality), (b) uncertainty avoidance (relates to the issues of dealing with ambiguity and unfamiliarity), (c) individualism-collectivism (relates to the issues of interpersonal ties) and (d) masculinity-femininity (relates to the gender emotional roles). In Hofstede's (1991) research work, a fifth dimension, long- versus short-term orientation (relates to deferment of gratification) was included. GLOBE adopted the dimensions paradigm as well as the five dimensions (Hofstede 2006). The framework was expanded to nine dimensions for conceptual reasons maintaining the labels 'power distance' and 'uncertainty avoidance', however not necessarily their meanings. The framework splits 'collectivism' into two subcategories as 'institutional collectivism' and 'in-group collectivism' and 'masculinity-femininity' into 'assertiveness' and 'gender egali-tarianism'. Long-term orientation was re-named as 'future orientation'. Two more dimensions were added: 'humane orientation' and 'performance orientation'. Further to this, GLOBE distinguishes organizational cultures (practices and values related to the work organization) from societal cultures (practices and values related to the wider society).

Despite Hofstede's seminal work that offers frameworks and set of assumptions for comparing and interpreting national cultural values, criticisms on the research having a Western bias still exist. To have this issue addressed, the study conducted by Bond and his colleagues on the Chinese Culture Connection, 1987, is of a much smaller scope, surveying 100 respondents (50% women) in each of 22 countries across 5 continents. Ward (2002, p. 207) described the study as follows:

> A pivotal element of their study design was a new questionnaire that was developed with input from a number of Chinese social scientists, with the aim of creating an instrument that tapped concerns fundamental to the Chinese worldview. This instrument was termed the Chinese value survey. Both this study and Hofstede's findings identified four primary dimensions with three of them closely aligned, but Bond and colleagues found a unique dimension that appeared to suggest an addition to the then currently accepted cultural varia-tions, yet balancing out western egocentrism.

This dimension is termed the 'philosophy of Confucianism'.

Strong evidence shows that the uniqueness of traditions, ancient beliefs and nuances are preserved in workplace values. The influential work of Hofstede (1980) has extensively popularized the notion that values are somewhat stable over time and that nations are consistently grouped together (Dowling and Nagel 1986; Ronen 1986) according to four key constructs that he labeled 'collectivism' (individual-ism), 'femininity-masculinity', 'uncertainty avoidance' and 'power distance'. Moreover, these four dimensions provide a basis for explaining organizational structures and arrangements, as well as workplace behaviours and pertinent work attitudes (Hofstede 1991). Subsequently, 'Bond and colleagues (The Chinese Culture Connection 1987) identified an additional value indigenous to the Chinese people, which they termed "Confucian work dynamism". This is largely because the principle attributes reflect the teachings of Confucius and the social continuity of an extant civilization of over 2500 years' (Ward et al. 2002, p. 208). Perhaps, it is use-ful and essential to note that Hofstede applied a conventional quantitative design, whereas Bond and colleagues used an idiographic design which is acknowledged as more suitable in cross-cultural research. Nonetheless, there is a dominant perspec-tive that each society has a distinctive set of unwavering cultural values which guide managerial belief and actions which are exemplified in workplace relationships and practices (Adler et al. 1989). Similarly, this can also be applied within the classroom context, where there is a specific cultural group of students who exhibit a particular trend of learning behaviours and styles. The learning culture and culture of learning could be distinctively differentiated across varying cultural groups based on varying aspects, for example, behavioural, cognitive, communication style, norms, beliefs and many others.

Slethaug (2010) acknowledges that the cultural framework of Hofstede (1980) charts the general characteristics of societies; hence one should not generalize and stereotype the findings. But it can be argued that the five cultural dimensions of Hofstede and associates are applicable if the context is used aptly with explicit measurement variables and not generalizing it. The progressively evolving changes in China do influence and shift the traditional cultural values, norms that ultimately influence the learning culture, learning behaviours and preferences. On the other hand, it should be the range of shift in dimensions that needs to be appreciated rather than asserting that the whole complex cultural influences in totality are totally irrelevant now. Likewise, it should not be taken that the traditional cultural values that form this framework have been totally erased.

Many scholars (Rajaram and Bordia 2011; Ryan and Slethaug 2010; Rajaram 2010; Clark and Gieve 2006; Gumingyuan 2001; Nisbet 2003) advocate that students should not be labeled and confined into boundaries, which causes the generation of myths about the groups of students and creates false 'reputations'. To address this, explicit cultural, behavioural values and norms that influences students' learning should be thoroughly and rigorously examined for a deeper understanding. Due to the diversity of the scope, only the three most relevant out of five cultural dimensions (power distance, uncertainty avoidance and philosophy of Confucianism) from Hofstede's (1991) and Hofstede and Bond's (1984) cultural frameworks were considered in the research study reported in this book. When these cultural dimensions are evaluated in relevance to mainland Chinese students' pursuing business education, the dimensions that were not considered have much less impact on cultural dislocation aspects of this study. In conclusion, the three carefully identified cultural dimensions—namely, power distance, uncertainty avoidance and philosophy of Confucianism—are very relevant and apt in measuring the cultural diversity in an international-based educational and cultural environment.

2.4.1 Uncertainty Avoidance

Hofstede's (1980) work clusters the culture of many nations as having a strong uncertainty avoidance nature. Individuals from such cultures prefer more structure as they feel uneasiness in situations of ambiguity and uncertainty. Further to this, the quality of employees in these societies improves by providing security through a higher level of task structure on the job. People from a weak uncertainty culture tend to be relatively tolerant of ambiguity. This enables them to embrace significant autonomy and low structure. Hence, in a cultural context of high uncertainty and power distance, students tend to be inclined towards a much stronger direction, whereas in an environment of low power distance and low uncertainty avoidance, minimal direction is preferred.

The content and the process by which such training is delivered must fit well with participants' cultural backgrounds. Instructional methodologies vary from instructor-centred and directed, didactic such as seminars, lectures and tutorials, to learner centred, experiential such as experiential and simulation exercises. Video presentations, film sharing, displays, handouts, lectures and demonstrations are classified as passive teaching methods, whereas case studies, experiential activities, simulations and active learning with skills acquisition fall under the participative or active teaching methods.

A general perceived expectation of a teacher's role in the Asian context is to teach as being supposedly to be an expert in the subject matter, set the rules and devise detailed and complex examples. This profile of students expects their teachers to deliver highly structured, inflexible and content-driven lectures. Asian students stereotypically tend to rely largely on the teacher and look for instructions that are more definite. They expect their teachers to take the initiative, to lead and to lay clear directions and paths for them to follow.

Rote and repetitive learning is more predominant in Asia's education system, although the context is rapidly shifting with varying early interventions, exposures and influences. Asian cultures place high emphasis on orderliness, systematic approach and conformity. There is a mixed view on the instructional preferences of the Chinese students. One perspective of the literature claims that due to the orientation and learning style of the Chinese students, lecture as more of a one-way content delivery and traditional approach is probably more effective compared to the more dynamic and active style learning approaches, such as action learning, competitive teamwork and role-play exercises. Participative, interactive and competitive activities may not be compatible with Chinese social values (Kumaravadivelu 2003; Chan 1991; Nelson 1995; Carson and Nelson 1996). In a contrary, Shi's (2006) study of 400 middle school students in Shanghai reported that students prefer a more interactive relationship with teachers. However, it is noted that this finding may not be generalized due to the varying variables involved as Shi (2006)'s study argues we need to be mindful of 'their national, regional, economic class and cultural background, as well as age, religion and gender' (pp. 139).

Previous research highlights that mainland Chinese students prefer structured lectures, supplemented with detailed lecture notes. We could also gather that these students' participation in exercises, small group problem-solving, in-basket activities and so on would assist them to emphasize what they have learned from passive note-taking and provide confidence in active involvement. However, we need to realize that the conditioning of how these active learning activities have been designed, organized and executed has to be thought through carefully and contextualized to resonate effectively to the needs of the learning cultural context of these students. On one side, scholars (Chow 1995; Newell 1999) mentioned ritualized behaviour, withdrawal and resentment on the part of these students are often the outcomes of providing and receiving feedback. But again, this could be challenged from the context on whether an appropriate approach was taken to engage these Chinese students, where the cultural aspects are understood well and taken into due consideration. Confrontational decision-making creates a tension quite destructive to the learning process (Chan 1996); hence any form of positive learning is precluded as a high level of discomfort experienced (Chow 1995). In contrary, recent studies by scholars (Ryan and Slethaug 2010; Yang 2009; Chan and Rao 2009;

Rajaram 2010; Shi 2006) report that Chinese learners are active; monitor their own studies; learning from their mistakes or linking past experiences to their studies; prefer a less teacher-directed learning approach; and willing to participate in interactive learning activities. Again, we need to be questioning the background, the level of Western exposure of these Chinese students and which parts of China or Confucian heritage culture (CHC) were they from to have a more accurate characterization. To address these insights at a much deeper level and context, Rajaram and Bordia (2011) advocate that 'Chinese students' learning effectiveness is not directly affected by the active or passive style of teaching approaches rather it is the process of knowledge transfer involved in these instructional techniques at large...' (p.79).

2.4.2   Power Distance

'Power distance' refers to how people view and deal with the integral part of inequities that emerge in the distribution of power, that is, how the culture institutionalizes inequity. Societies in the Western countries, where there is small power distance, inequities are seen as not desirable and preferably reduced, whereas societies elsewhere that are categorized to be high power distance, such inequities are accepted as normal and legitimized in customary and institutional policies (Walker et al. 1996). Thus, people in high power distance cultures incline towards accepting the unequal distribution of power.

Individuals from countries having a culture of large power distance, according to Hofstede (1980)'s study, accept centralized power and rely heavily on superiors for structure and direction. In these cultures, it is accepted that rules and laws differ for superiors and subordinates. Students from these cultures, therefore, require strong directions in decision-making. Frustration and resistance would be the outcomes when independent decisions are required of them. This could be illustrated, for example,

Rodrigues (2004) further illustrated that:

> For example, an assignment which requires them to be independent and resourceful, for example, to go to the library, scan through periodicals, select and read a training-program-relevant article, and link, apply the thrust of it to a theory or concept in the textbook might frustrate or make them uncomfortable. They probably prefer that the instructor assign an appropriate article, give them a clear instruction of what they might look for in the article, and give them some indication as to which particular theory (or theories) or concept(s) in the textbook the thrust of the article applies.

In countries categorized to have a culture of small power distance, the people resist highly centralized power and expect to be at least consulted when making decisions. Students from these cultures of countries may show different levels of resentment towards an instructor who dictates specifically what should be done. Hence, these students would probably prefer assignments that enable them to source or do autonomous research and look for learning materials by themselves, thereafter deciding by themselves on what theories or concepts they have learnt best applies appropriately. They probably require less guidance and direction from instructors as compared to students from large power distance cultures. This could be tied to the culture of learning which has been shaped through how they were expected to behave in their learning process through many years of educational climate that then becomes their preferred and accepted learning culture.

In countries with large power distance cultural orientation, an instructor's reliability, expertise and status would be significant to the students. In the power distance categorization, China is classified to be high in the scale of the power distance measurement. The Chinese students respect the expertise, knowledge and wisdom of the teachers as this is a vital part of their upbringing (Wen and Clément 2003). The teacher is perceived as the guru and provider of knowledge who facilitates a scaffolded structure and detailed information. The students are not willing and uncomfortable to challenge the status quo and the authority figures. As such, it is highly unlikely that students will pose challenging questions to their teachers, especially in open discussions where it could be perceived as a disrespect or making the figure in authority to lose face, if they do so. In comparison with their Western counterparts, Chinese students seldom ask questions, particularly those that challenge or contradict the teacher's viewpoint or critical questions that seen as publicly criticizing the teachers (Chan 1999; Shi 2006). Students are hesitant to ask questions because they assume it is rude to do so during class which may disrupt the lesson (Kumaravadivelu 2003; Ryan and Louie 2005; Chow 1995). However, Chinese students prefer to ask questions or share comments individually with the teachers during class breaks or after the end of class (Shi 2006; Wen and Clément 2003), where it is largely due to the sense of security and comfort Chinese students feel when consulting the teachers privately and face to face (Liu 2006). In contrary, Rajaram and Bordia (2011) reported that 'the cultural dislocation variable of comfort does not affect the learning effectiveness of mainland Chinese students' (pp. 80). The evidence also shows that preference of the instructional techniques may not necessarily correlate to the effectiveness of the students' learning.

2.4.3 Philosophy of Confucianism

Rodrigues (2004) contended that the uncertainty avoidance measure in Hofstede's system is not perfect. The uncertainty avoidance part of the culture is how the people within this culture react to and manage uncertainty in social situations (Walker et al. 1996). Some societies teach their people to accept uncertainty without excessive stress (Walker et al. 1996). In weak uncertainty avoidance cultures, people tend to be tolerant of difference in opinions and are not unduly threatened by unpredictability. On the contrary, in cultures that are high in uncertainty avoidance, uncertainty is viewed as psychologically uncomfortable and disruptive. Hence, uncertainty is dealt through limiting risk by imposing order and structure through rules and dogmas that breed coherence (Walker et al. 1996). Interestingly, the measure for some countries does not resemble the primary cultural traits of those countries. For example, Singapore measures low uncertainty avoidance, yet the country functions under a governance system that provides high regimentation and stability for its citizens, a system which tends to be more predominant in high uncertainty avoidance cultures (e.g. France's code of law, mechanistic system) than in weak uncertainty avoidance cultures (e.g. the United Kingdom's common law, organic system).

Hofstede and Bond (1984) acknowledged that the uncertainty avoidance dimension is less applicable in Confucian-based cultures. Regions with Confucian culture include the People's Republic of China, South Korea, Japan, Hong Kong, Taiwan and Singapore. Cultures that are based on the Confucian philosophy develop stability-generating systems that are significantly different from those generated in religion-based cultures.

Individuals in regions with Confucian culture are likely to prefer strong direction and stability just like societies with high power distance and high uncertainty avoidance (Jarrah 1998). There were numerous studies performed that support this proposition. For example, 'the impression is [that] they [Asian students], one of them are Mainland Chinese students, learn by reproducing and are less able to apply their knowledge to practical situations [compared with Western students]' (Watkins et al. 1991, p. 22). In a study conducted by Pun (1989) on the effectiveness of projects, Chinese learners chose project topics by the accessibility of reference books rather than by the practical importance of the project question. Literature points out that Chinese students prefer learning through concrete facts, precedents and procedures. Furthermore, it is widely believed by the academics in the West that Chinese learners tend to rely more on rote learning than their Western counterparts (Watkins et al. 1991; Ryan and Louie 2005; Kumaravadivelu 2003). Anecdotes abound that learner-centred, active learning methods, used extensively in Western business education (such as case studies and group projects), are not widely accepted as preferred approaches in many Asian countries, one of which is mainland China (Pun 1989; Murphy 1987; Rigby 1986; Staw 1982). This claim could be validated and is consistent with the findings by more recent studies conducted by other scholars (Ho 2010; Leung and Lu 2008; Neild 2004) on Chinese students, where it was also found that Chinese students prefer the teacher-centred teaching methodology. Although Chinese students are exposed to student-centred teaching styles, their adaption to these styles is slow; hence further research is required to investigate which teaching technique will benefit Chinese students (Ho 2010).

We perceive Westerners to pride themselves on their ability to hold individual views and express them candidly, while mainland Chinese to be reserved (Shi 2006), as openness and expressing views outspokenly is generally not encouraged (Chan 1999; Newell 1999; Fox 1994). Generally, the evidence tends to be biased towards Chinese students to be not as to vocally express their thoughts and feelings openly, perhaps largely due to the learning culture that they have been shaped with. However, this is evolving due to the exposure and varying interventions. Inhibition in the expression of feelings is somewhat fading as the newer Chinese generations are more outspoken and expressive on their thoughts due to many varying reasons, i.e. the geographical locations (more advanced provinces in terms of Western and external exposure) where they are from and family backgrounds (more affluent, parents are highly educated, higher class of social backgrounds). Recent studies (such as Littlewood 2009; Ninnes et al. 1999) have argued that these perceptions of Chinese students being less outspoken are often been based on partial knowledge or misunderstandings of Chinese students. These misperceptions have led to negative stereotypes of Chinese students in the Western academia. Rajaram (2010) states:

> The mainland Chinese students generally reported that they learned more effectively via active instructional techniques, with the exception of lectures as the passive instructional technique. This may be due to the increasing trend and exposure to Western values and lifestyles in the learning and teaching actions of courses back in China. As China progresses to become internationally recognized by opening its doors to other countries, there is bound to be an increase of Western exposure influencing the country's educational approach and, importantly, influencing how mainland Chinese students are being taught and their learning styles, as well. (p. 298)

2.5 Chinese Culture

It is vital to examine the cultural values of the mainland Chinese and how these values impact the perceived learning effectiveness and learning effectiveness of the mainland Chinese students, when measured across the commonly used instructional techniques. We adopt the Hofstede's framework to examine and comprehend the effects on the learning process and how they learn effectively based on the dramatic demographic, institutional and economic changes to the Chinese culture over time.

Applying Hofstede's (2010) cultural dimension measurement to the context, the measurement of China's culture is detailed as follows: China has a high power distance. This means Chinese society accepts inequality among people. This means to say certain groups of people would have more power than others, but this inequality of power by varying clusters is generally accepted by the people within this culture. In such a culture, emphasis is placed on hierarchy, seniority, social status and other evolving factors which meant to distribute power distance from high to low. China is low in individualism. The society is highly collectivist where the focus is group interest above the individual interest. Personal relationships prevail over task and company. That is to say that the individuals in this society value social bonding, friendships and relationships. China is a masculine society. It is driven by competition and achievement. The need for success is higher than family or leisure time. This reiterates that the individuals in this society place lesser emphasis on activities that do not necessarily relate to success from their perspective, where they tend to be more task-oriented. China scored low on uncertainty avoidance. The people in this cluster are not comfortable in working with ambiguity and non-familiar environment and context. China scores high in long-term orientation, which could be related to having a very pragmatic culture where peoples' beliefs on truth depend very much on situation, context and time. The Chinese could be reported as persistent and determined in wanting to achieve their long-term goals. The mainland

Table 2.1 Comparison of cultural values (Fan 2000 versus Hofstede 1984)

Hofstede (1984)	Individualism/ collectivism	Uncertainty avoidance	Power distance	Masculinity/ femininity
Fan (2000)	29 conformity	41 prudence	28 hierarchy	71 unity of yin and yang
	35 collectivism	49 conservative	27 deference to authority	8 moderation

Adapted from Fan (2000)

Chinese group is distinctively different as compared to the Chinese diaspora (Chan 2006), where there could come with a mixed values and cultural inclination from other Chinese-speaking countries. China is an emblematic example of a long-term oriented and collective culture (Wu 2002).

We could mention two widely used cultural models, namely, Kluckhohn and Strodtbeck's (1961) five dimensions and Hofstede's (1984) value survey model (VSM). However, these two models are not used in our study due to its narrow scope. Hofstede's VSM is primarily concerned with business culture rather than national culture, and it is overly simplistic as there are only four or five variables to be considered. Fan (2000) reviewed the 40 cultural values from the study by the Chinese Cultural Collection (1987) and revised to provide a new list of 31 Chinese Culture Values (CCVs). The revision was essential, with the total number of values increased by 78 per cent from 40 to 71, with 31 values newly added (44%). These core values are then grouped under categories: national traits, interpersonal relations, family (social) orientation, work attitude, business philosophy, personal traits, time orientation and relationship with nature. Table 2.1 shows a comparison of Fan's (2000) revised cultural values with Hofstede's VSM.

In comparing Hofstede versus Fan's conceptualization, the matching CCVs direct that the Chinese culture is more collective rather than individualistic, being identified to be high uncertainty avoidance and high power distance. In contrary, recent studies (Rajaram 2010; Ryan and Slethaug 2010; Yang 2009; Clark and Gieve 2006; Chan and Rao 2009; Littlewood 2009) have reported a lowered level of uncertainty avoidance and power distance as China which comprises of many states has been progressively exposed to globalization and influenced by the intervention of Western cultures. Another shift was reported on the masculine/feminine dimension, where Chinese culture could not be clearly clustered as masculine nor feminine but, rather, emphasizes the unity of both (Fan 2000).

We could have a deeper appreciation of the cultural dimensions by understanding and comparing the Chinese culture with the American culture. Pan et al. (1994) made a comparison on six main American cultural dimensions with traditional Chinese cultural dimensions and concluded the following, with Chan (2006) reiterating them:

1. The Chinese culture inclines towards the passive acceptance of fate through seeking harmony with nature, whereas the US culture accentuates active involvement and/or mastery in the person-nature relationship. We could interpret that

the Chinese show a more accommodating social tendency working towards harmony and the contentment of the majority.

2. Chinese culture stresses on inner experiences of feeling and meaning, whereas US culture seeks external and holistic experiences. Decisions made by the Chinese are usually based on past experiences and their emotional reactions to these experiences.
3. Chinese culture is characterized by closed world view, treasuring stability and harmony; US culture is characterized by an open view of the world, emphasizing change and movement. The Chinese normally choose to act in a manner that has minimal changes. Perhaps, this could be related to their discomfort towards uncertainty and ambiguity in dealing with issues.
4. Chinese culture counts heavily on affiliation ties and rituals with a historical orientation, whereas US culture places primary faith in rationalism and is oriented towards the future. The Chinese tend not to question the status quo and norms. They prefer to rely on past reported facts and information.
5. Chinese culture accentuates vertical interpersonal relationships, whereas US culture stresses horizontal dimensions of interpersonal relationships. Chinese culture emphasizes the relationship aspects and its resultant happiness, undertaking decision-making based on its expected outcome to be more objective.
6. Chinese culture stresses heavily an individual's responsibilities, duties to family, clan and state, whereas US culture values the individual personality (Chan 2006). In Chinese culture, family, collective focus and team cohesiveness are few of the primary elements in their behavioural philosophy.

Culture is not a stagnant and non-evolving system, although traditional Chinese culture has its own distinct dimensions. Modernization and communistic education are both shaping the contemporary Chinese cultural values. The incessant interaction, dialogues and exchanges with other cultural systems make tremendous and unceasing changes in the nature of Chinese cultural values. Modern China is characterized by tension that is caused by a constant struggle between traditional and modern values, idealistic and pragmatic values and the authoritarian state and market economy. Despite the traditional values that have been deeply ingrained in the Chinese culture, at the same time China is undergoing major rapid changes due to the influences from globalization and economic market development.

A shared characteristic of ethnic Chinese at mainland and overseas is in having the Chinese culture a moderately coherent system of values and norms (Allinson 1989; Bond 1991; Bond and Hwang 1986; Lew 1979; Redding 1990). There are distinguishable core values held commonly by the Chinese notwithstanding their place of residences (Fan 2000), despite differences between the political, social and economic environment between mainland and overseas Chinese experiences. One set of core values are rooted in Chinese culture (Bond 1991), despite the variations that emerge due to the differences among the Chinese of where they reside and the societies they are from. The rudimentary aspect of their identity is embraced through their Chinese culture. The Chinese culture with a tradition of 4000 years of history shapes distinctive core values that are exclusive and consistent. This cultural value system is distinctively Chinese and distinguishes itself not only from Western cultures but also from other Eastern cultures, for example, Japanese culture. The outmoded Chinese culture encompasses diverse and, from time to time, competing schools of thought, including Confucianism, Taoism, Buddhism and so on, and a host of regional cultures. The contemporary Chinese culture in mainland China consists of three major elements: traditional culture, communist ideology and, more lately, Western values.

China entails a long history of mythologies and philosophical writings that guide its people, for example, the Mountain Sea Scripture being one of the oldest writings in China where it contemplates that the combined forces of yin and yang created the world. The universe harmonizes through accomplishing an equilibrium of the positive and negative sides of things (good and evil) that happened. The impact of this ideology was on the two main religions in China, namely, Taoism and Buddhism.

Taoism originated from the teachings of Lao Tze, a philosopher who lived around 300 BC. Its philosophy is closely associated with superstition. It speaks about the duality of yin and yang just like the Mountain Sea Scripture and indicates that individuals need to live in tune with nature. 'Wu wei' (or non-action) is the proper guide to people's behaviours and that the 'tao' (god or creator) would be accountable for their actions and outcomes. However, Taoism philosophy has often been blamed for the decline of the Chinese society in the last 2000 years as *wu wei* has been misinterpreted as doing nothing at all. Buddhism is the other vital influence over Chinese thinking, which became popular in 645 AD after it was founded by a Chinese monk in China (Chun 1991). Buddhism is based upon the individual's place in nature; thus, it is not too far removed from Taoist principles. It is distinguished from Taoism by its emphasis on its believers becoming faultless and god-like beings. Its adapted form, Zen Buddhism, still contained elements of Taoist philosophy, with 'zen' or 'the way' providing people with the means to reach their spiritual state via meditation and disciplined living. Despite great influences from the Taoism and Buddhism philosophies, the main influence on Chinese values, especially learning values, actually came from Confucius. Next, we will discuss the philosophy of Confucianism and its closely knitted and intertwined relationship with Chinese culture.

2.5.1   Confucianism

K'ung-fu-tzu or Master Kung, later named Confucius by Jesuit missionaries, was born in 551 BC. He was a high-office civil servant in China at his time. In contrast to Taoism and Buddhism, Confucius teachings did not commence as a religion as such, but the lessons in practical ethics or set of pragmatic rules for daily life are extracted from the learning of Chinese history (Hofstede and Bond 1984). In fact, Confucian philosophy had such a great influence over the basic values of Chinese civilization that it is frequently perceived as the new religion of China, particularly during the thirteenth century when the social philosophy of Confucianism became intertwined with Taoism and Buddhism, creating Neo-Confucianism. Confucius developed an ethical element in governance by insisting that all rulers must govern with benevolence and justice and that people obey and respect their leaders in return. He trusted that the best possible way forward in a hierarchical Chinese society was to develop a morally motivated bureaucracy. Following his teachings, during the Han dynasty which lasted from 206 BC to 220 AD, imperial rulers introduced the world's first national examinations, so as to no longer limit the accessibility by the elites and give commoners opportunities. The basic Chinese value system today is permeated by the resultant association with ancestor worship and a godly state.

Confucianism is undisputedly the most influential thought structure in Chinese history which shapes the foundation of the Chinese cultural and still provides the basis for the norms of Chinese interpersonal behaviour today (Pye 1972). It has gone through five stages of development in accordance to Yao's (2000) historical perspectives, which are 'Confucianism in formation', 'Confucianism in adaption', 'Confucianism in transformation', 'Confucianism in variation' and 'Confucianism in renovation'. Hence, Yao (2000) reported that Confucianism is 'more a tradition generally rooted in Chinese culture and nurtured by Confucius and Confucians' (p. 17). Shi (2006) argued that Confucianism 'changed throughout a long history by adapting itself to new political and social demands and it is a multi-dimensional concept' (p. 124).

Confucianism is basically the behavioural or moral doctrine that relies on the teaching of Confucius regarding human relationships, virtuous behaviour, social structures and work ethics. In Confucianism, rules are spelled out like a code of conduct for an individual's social behaviour, governing the entire range of human interactions in society. According to Oh (1991), Confucianism, at present, is all about the correct observation of human relationships within a hierarchically oriented society. In particular, the key emphasis on the family is manifested in the five constant virtues and corresponding cardinal relationships (Oh 1991) as:

Constant virtues:

1. Filial piety
2. Faithfulness
3. Brotherhood
4. Loyalty
5. Sincerity

Cardinal relationships:

1. Father and son
2. Husband and wife
3. Elder and younger brother
4. Monarch and subject
5. Between friends

Chen (1986) asserted that the basic teaching of Confucius is distilled in the five constant virtues: humanity, righteousness, propriety, wisdom and faithfulness. Confucius characterized the five basic human relations and principles for each

Table 2.2 Basic human relations versus principles

Basic human relations	Principles
Sovereign and subject (or master and follower)	Loyalty and duty
Father and son	Love and obedience
Husband and wife	Obligation and submission
Elder and younger brothers	Seniority and modeling subject
Friend and friend	Trust

Adapted from Fan (2000)

relation, called 'Wu Lun' (Fan 2000). Table 2.2 summarizes the key aspects as follows.

Of those five basic human relations, three are family relations, which clearly show the importance of family in Chinese society and account for its paternalism. Filial piety and loyalty are generally deemed the most important. When the basic human relations are applied to management, the first and last relations led to the birth of a paternalistic management style in both China and Japan (Hsiao et al. 1990). Confucius used only the male versions of language to define family relations where Confucianism emphasizes the value of harmony, urging individuals to adapt to the collectivity, to control their emotions, to avoid conflict and to maintain inner harmony (Kirkbride and Tang 1992). From Confucianism, two specific Chinese value systems emerged, namely, 'Yi' and 'Li'.

2.5.2   Two Traditional Chinese Value Systems: Yi and Li

Yi can be translated to values such as benevolence, righteousness, morality and faithfulness. Li can be translated to benefit, utilitarianism and profit. The individualism and collectivism (I/C) concepts in Chinese terms can be appreciated by connecting the traditional Chinese collectivistic orientation of Yi and individualistic orientation of Li. The research study by Lu (1998) states there is an interaction between elements of Yi and Li in Chinese cultural value orientations, with a strong tendency towards utilitarian individualism in social relations. The study proposes that the individualism and collectivism (I/C) construct becomes culturally specific and meaningful when connected to a culture's philosophical, rhetorical tradition and framed in conceptual terms that are familiar to the people and cultures under study.

Conventional research regards Confucianism as the upholder of a lineage whose standard recommendations and inspiration have been well-disseminated to the Chinese people, influencing patterns of thought, communication, behaviour and daily life in a holistic manner (Cheng 1987; Jensen 1992; Wright 1975; Yang 1986). Confucianism is believed to glorify and promote collectivism, with its emphasis on the collective good and social harmony as the eventual goal (Bond and Hwang 1986; Yu and Yang 1994):

> Confucian ethics of devotion to family, loyalty to superiors, and self-sacrifice for the benefit
> of the community and state share some similar value orientations of a collectivistic culture
> described by Western scholars … In general, the communication style exhibited by East
> Asian culture is thought to be infused with Confucian humanistic concerns and moral prin-
> ciples. (Lu 1998, p. 94)

Face-saving behaviours, reciprocity and indirectness are considered cultural
norms as well as communicative strategies in social relations (Chang and Holt 1991;
Ma 1992; Scollon and Scollon 1995; Ting-Toomey 1998; Yu 1998).

Indeed, Confucianism was institutionalized as a state philosophy and cultural
ideology in 140 BCE by the ruler of the Han dynasty; and its influence on Chinese
culture and communication cannot be overstated (Lu 1998). However, it cannot be
overlooked that Confucianism is not the only cultural tradition in China. Chinese
culture, the thought process and communication styles have been greatly influenced
and shaped by diverse and varied philosophical traditions such as Taoism, Mohism,
and Legalism, etc.

2.6   Classification of Chinese Culture

The presence of numerous definitions of 'culture' makes it essential to use the most
appropriate definition of the concept to develop a framework. A variety of empirically tested models will be helpful in analysing something complex as cultural values. Different dimensions of cultural values can be examined and compared through
these models. These models are not mutually exclusive nor are they all-encompassing;
rather they offer a variety of approaches in examining cultural similarities and differences. It was clear from Fan (2000)'s study that the matching values from CCVs
indicate that Chinese culture is more collective rather than individualistic, with high
uncertainty avoidance and large power distance.

The construct of individualism and collectivism (I/C) explains and predicts cultural orientations, communication and cultural psychology. Despite this framework's origins from the West, it has been serving as a universal mode of analysis to
distinguish cultures in their value orientations, often cast in dichotomised and polar-
izing terms (Hofstede 1980; Hui and Triandis 1986; Tonnies 1957; Triandis 1995).
In general, collectivism has a tendency to prioritize group goals above individual
goals, whereas individualism has a tendency to place individual goals more importance than group goals. Chinese culture is characterized as collectivistic, whereas
Western culture—for example, the American culture—is considered to be individualistic in its cultural orientation and communication styles (Bond et al. 1985;
Gudykunst and Kim 1984). There remains a need to determine how people living in
collectivistic cultures, over two-thirds of the world population, define and interpret
their collectivistic and individualistic orientations in their own social and cultural
contexts.

In terms of the centrality of culture, we could reiterate that the concern with
existing research on intercultural communication tends to incline more towards

literature validating Western communication theories than exploring other communication frameworks in non-Western cultural contexts. To validate this, we could
site, for example, when investigating on Chinese personality and behaviour, Yang
(1986) located a few methodological defects of which one is the investigator who
has administered an instrument developed and standardized in a Western culture to
a sample of Chinese. The concern of the researcher, including Chinese scholars,
according to Yang, lies in the mechanical application of an instrument without considering its cultural appropriateness. We could clearly see the alarming concern
when the results are being disseminated to scholars globally. Indeed, as Chang and
Holt (1991) pointed out, 'in labeling Chinese society as "collective", few have asked
what the term "collective" means to the Chinese' (p. 252). In fact, the mainland
Chinese translation of 'collectivism' is *jiti zhuyi*, which is a moral aspect that characterizes communist and socialist ideology, requiring total devotion and sacrifice of
self to the communes and the state.

2.7 Cultural Differences and Similarities Between Singapore and China

Then Senior Minister of State, Ministry of Foreign Affairs, Mrs Josephine Teo
informed the House in a Committee of Supply debate in 2016: 'Chinese Singaporeans
feel a cultural affinity with mainland Chinese, with both groups speaking the same
language and celebrating common festivals'; however, the primary difference
between the two countries is 'Singaporeans are diverse yet have an inclusive cultural make-up' (Yong 2016).

Apart from obvious differences between the two countries such as the history,
size and geographical locations, Singapore is distinct from China, as Selmer and de
Leon (1993) point out, in its historical and geographical influences from non-
Chinese population. Singapore experiences strong influences from the non-Chinese
minorities, neighbouring countries and immigrants although the majority of
Singapore population is made up of ethnically Chinese. Singaporeans' everyday life
is a mixture of different cultures. Majority of Singaporeans are bilingual largely due
to its education system. Singapore's colloquial language, Singlish, is distinctive in
its mixture of different languages its people speak and write in, such as English,
Mandarin, Chinese dialects (e.g. Hokkien and Cantonese), Tamil, Malay, etc. We
are able to find food from varying cultures or at times even fusion food in most of
the food centres in Singapore. People are able to access media from varying sources.
In contrast, Chinese culture is more homogeneous where the majority of the population is made up of Han ethnicity. Citizens of one city in China usually shares similar
culture, while Singapore, as a city, is more cosmopolitan.

Singapore has a more Westernized culture than China largely due to its historical
background as a British colony and its geographical location in the middle of trade
path between the East and the West. Moreover, a large majority of Singaporeans,

especially the younger generation, are able to speak and write well in English and have fairly easy accessibility to Western media. The increasing level of Western influence and exposure in Singapore's national culture as a city nation is another primary factor that distinguishes Singapore culture from Chinese culture, where China has varying developments on its numerous provinces across China as a large country.

Confucianism is the cornerstone of traditional Chinese culture. Despite the differences, Singapore leaders, since back from the 1980s, had incessantly and consistently emphasized the necessity to preserve Confucian ethics as a shared Singapore value. This is an effort by the government for nation-building; 'it is also an attempt to reduce the influence of Western values which emphasize individualism and materialism' (Tan 1989, p. 15). Although Singapore has contemporary Westernized images, these do not necessarily reflect the lifestyle of common people. The majority of the working and mature population was born before the major transformation of society in the last 25 years. The ancestral values and mindset that are preserved through the socialization processes of kinship groups are still an essential part of the cultural heritage of the Chinese Singaporeans (Selmer 1987). While Western management values have been embraced to a certain extent in Singapore, 'it is highly doubtful that the adaption is more than superficial and would result in questionnaire responses that are socially desirable' (Selmer and de Leon 1993, p. 72).

> About three quarters of Singapore's population are ethnic Chinese. The other two major races are the Malays and Indians. Singapore has a predominantly Chinese culture. Yet the multi-racial composition of its population suggests that the cultures of Singapore and China should be different, at least to a certain extent. It is unfortunate that China has not been included in Hofstede's (1980) landmark cross-cultural study. The three Chinese-majority societies, namely Hong Kong, Singapore and Taiwan were used as proxies for assessing Chinese cultural values. (Tsang 2001, p. 350)

In a study by Shenkar and Ronen (1987), a survey of work goals on a sample of 163 local managers in China was conducted. The results were then compared with those of Hong Kong, Singapore and Taiwan, where it shows that the three Chinese-dominated regions were more similar to each other in their rankings of the work goals than they were individually to China. The three work goals that differed greatly between mainland China and the other three regions were autonomy, cooperation between co-workers and promotion. Survey participants from mainland China valued the first two work goals more than the last one less than their counterparts in the other three societies (Tsang 2001). Shenkar and Ronen (1987) elucidated these differences using Maoist ideology. Despite these differences, the clustering of work goals among managers from China seemed to be, by and large, in line with the groupings instituted from the other Chinese-dominated societies, signifying the presence of common cultural heritage (Tsang 2001).

Comparing Singapore and China using the Hofstede's (2010) cultural dimensions indexes:

2.7.1   Power Distance

Singapore and China both scored high on the dimension: China at 80 and Singapore at 74. This is likely due to both countries having some basis of their culture on Confucianism. One of the key philosophies in Confucianism is that unequal relationships among people help to maintain stability of the society. Nonetheless, we could also see that Singapore has scored slightly lower in relative, which could be attributed largely due to the impact of its rapid modernization, evolution and the effect of globalization on the education system and workplace climate. China being a large country, despite its fast growth and coming out of its communist approach, the score is slightly higher which could be possibly due to its spillover effect from the lesser advanced provinces within the large country.

2.7.2   Individualism

Both Singapore and China scored low in individualism, where both of them scored 20. This score interprets that both countries are collectivist in their cultures. This comes as not surprising as the majority population in Singapore comprises of Chinese although it is a multiracial society where there are other two primary races including Indians and Malays. In fact, regions with predominant Chinese population scored low on this index, for example, Hong Kong at 25 and Taiwan at 17.

2.7.3   Masculinity

China scored higher at 66 in masculinity than Singapore which scored 48. Singapore's score is more balanced in terms of masculinity/femininity. Singapore's emphasis on the values that arise from the meritocracy system cultivates excellence and higher quality in whatever is being done. So, generally, this encourages leadership that drives others achieve their goals which is rather inclined towards masculinity, whereas China is still more inclined towards relationship to drive the outputs.

2.7.4   Uncertainty Avoidance

Singapore scored very low in this aspect with a rating of 8 as compared to China with a rating of 35. This is an interesting outcome where we could see that Singapore is able to adapt much easily in terms of ambiguity and unsureness compared to China where much closer guidance is generally required to get the tasks done. The difference between the two countries for this uncertainty avoidance measure is relatively large. This could be attributed to the rooted learning culture and values in China that tend to be more conservative and inclined towards a highly structured one, whereas Singapore despite its highly structured persona, its learning practices tend to be more Western-like where students tend to operate in a more autonomous manner in general.

2.7.5 Long-Term Orientation

Both China and Singapore scored high in long-term orientation, with a rating of 87 and 72, respectively. The two countries are both willing to sacrifice for long-term success, for example, being perseverant and thrifty.

Singapore and China have a mutual characteristic in terms of *mianzi* or 'saving face'—for example, correcting mistakes openly in public or in the presence of others; conflict of opinions which results in a disagreement with a senior person or superior; and causing embarrassment to another that may result in losing face for those involved and can be unfavourable in maintaining a cordial relationship that affects business dealings and negotiations. Although further research is required to understand the ways and extent to which cultures between Singapore and China coincide or differ, we could predict these two cultures have more similarities to each other than if each of this culture is compared with many other countries. It is more sensible to expect convergence, instead of divergence, of the two countries. On the one hand, the Singapore government has been energetically promoting Confucianism as its core social value. On the other hand, with the evolving and continuous opening up of China, Western influences are potentially to rise in Chinese society (Tsang, p. 351).

Singapore and China are largely similar culturally; however, we need to acknowledge that they do not share similarity in political and economic system. Although the national culture that is shaped from the style of governance of China may have some effect on Chinese students in terms of their behaviours and the approach in their cognitive thinking, it is likely that mainland Chinese students undergo a considerable amount of adjustment and adaptation in terms of their learning styles, learning techniques and preference in their instructional techniques, when pursuing their studies in Singapore.

2.8 Differences Between Different Types of Educational Programmes Offered in Singapore

In this section, we will examine three large strategies adopted in the offering of the higher educational programmes in Singapore: (1) programmes offered by Singapore local publicly funded autonomous universities; (2) programmes offered by

Singapore local universities partnered with leading international institutions and universities; and (3) programmes offered by Western universities with local private higher education institutions and universities. The primary questions that we will be examining are the following: (1) What are the distinctive variations among these three types of programmes? (2) How do these identified differences affect delivery of contents and students' learning effectiveness?

Singapore is comprise of a wide variety of quality universities ranging from local to international. Primarily, there are six publicly funded universities—the National University of Singapore (NUS), Nanyang Technological University (NTU), Singapore Management University (SMU), Singapore University of Technology and Design (SUTD), Singapore Institute of Technology (SIT) and Singapore University of Social Sciences (SUSS). There are 285 Private Education Institutions registered with Committee for Private Education as of June 2017 (Committee for Private Education 2017). Singapore universities have partnered to offer joint programmes with around 69 high-calibre international universities such as Brown University, King's College London, Waseda University, etc. As for local private institutions that collaborate with overseas university partners to offer educational programmes, examples of the institutions are Yale-NUS College (a partnership between NUS and Yale University) and Singapore-Stanford Partnership (between NTU and Stanford University). Singapore Institute of Management (SIM Global) and Kaplan Higher Education Institute also collaborate with well-established and reputable universities to offer full-fledged and blended distance learning programmes.

Local universities offer programmes that are accredited and fully managed by the in-house experts. When partnered with overseas universities, a large inclination of blended approach in general is adopted, where faculties from the partnered universities will facilitate face-to-face teaching locally. These programmes have adequate control from the parent local university in terms of endorsement and decision-making in offering the academic certification and managing the accreditation process, whereas the programmes offered by institutions in collaboration with their overseas university partners have the control and decision-making power with their overseas partners. The locally situated institution serves more as an administrative bridge between the overseas partner and locally enrolled students. The programmes can be taught by local faculties, or there could be instances where some of the courses of the programme are conducted by faculties of the parent university partners.

2.9   Revolutionization and Effects of Culture

Evolving changes have been making an impact on China for the past two decades. These continuous changes were brought about by the Chinese students who pursue their studies abroad in Western countries and other Asian countries. The rapid economic, social and technological changes have an impact on student's behaviour, communication, leadership and management styles. The opening up to the Western cultures has transformed the economy of China while influencing the value system of the mainland Chinese. The awareness is well embraced by the modern Chinese which is evident in their personal growth and development. Although the Chinese learners are inclined towards more of an authentic repetitive learning approaches due to the influence of learning culture characteristics, such learning context is evolving due to the high level of influences from foreign cultures through varying types of interventions.

The evolution of culture influences the people of the society that leads to the changes in management behaviour, organization system and the learning settings and environment. Culture could be taken as one of the primary determinants and has a high influence on teaching, learning preferences, experiences and its effects on perceived learning effectiveness and learning effectiveness. But there are many other conditions and variables that contribute to it as well. Hence, we need to be mindful that culture is not the only factor (Gu and Schweisfurth 2006). The phrase 'Chinese learner' (Watkins and Biggs 1996, 2001) requests us to view this group as homogeneous; however being aware of their requirements and retorts is determined by their cultural background. Besides culture, there are other influencing aspects, for example, political and economic structure of the provinces the Chinese students are from; family backgrounds (from affluent or poor rural families); learning goals, motivation and mindset of students in pursuing their education; learning climate set for the interaction; the type of professional relationship; and communication styles between instructors and learners. It is vital for educationalists teaching in cross-cultural contexts to reflexive, investigative, empathetic and open attitude. By adopting such an approach, it helps educationalists not to make quick judgement or avoiding making ethnocentric discretions about their learners, largely based on their own stereotyped perceptions, values, belief and norms.

Hence, the next chapter discusses the educational nuances of the instructional techniques that influence effective knowledge acquisition. This chapter also explores questions such as 'how' these mainland Chinese students effectively learn and 'why' in a specific manner, particularly examining their preferred instructional styles. It will be intriguing to explore and understand in context the justifications and rationale of why their preferred teaching styles might not necessarily be the most effective ways in which they learn and acquire knowledge. Hence, this chapter aims to investigate and provide a fundamental understanding, advocating the essential need to espouse the most apposite instructional techniques tailored to the cultural dislocation contexts, examining from the social-cultural lenses. Learning in a well-suited cultural dislocation learning climate enables students to achieve high-quality and effective learning outcomes. Finally, all these issues will be addressed generally in examining on how students are able to learn and achieve their utmost potential, thus achieving optimal academic performance.

References

(The) Chinese Culture Connection. (1987). Chinese values and the search for culture – Free dimensions of culture. *Journal of Cross-Cultural Psychology, 18*(2), 143–164.

Adler, N. J., Campbell, N., & Laurent, A. (1989). In search of appropriate methodology: From outside the People's Republic of China looking in. *Journal of International Business Studies*, 61–74.

Allinson, R. E. (Ed.). (1989). *Understanding the Chinese mind: The philosophical roots.* Hong Kong: Oxford University Press.

Baumgartel, H., & Hill, T. (1982). Geert Hofstede: Culture's consequences: International differences in work-related values. *Personnel Psychology, 35*(1), 192–196.

Beugelsdijk, S., Kostova, T., & Roth, K. (2017). An overview of Hofstede-inspired country-level culture research in international business since 2006. *Journal of International Business Studies, 48*(1), 30–47.

Bodycott, P., & Lai, A. (2012). The influence and implications of Chinese culture in the decision to undertake cross-border higher education. *Journal of Studies in International Education, 16*(3), 252–270.

Bond, M. H. (1991). *Behind the Chinese face: Insights from psychology.* Hong Kong: Oxford University Press.

Bond, M. H., & Hwang, K. K. (1986). *The social psychology of Chinese people.* Oxford: Oxford University Press.

Bond, M. H., Wan, K.-C., Leung, K., & Giacalone, R. A. (1985). How are responses to verbal insult related to cultural collectivism and power distance? *Journal of Cross-Cultural Psychology, 16*(1), 111–127.

Carson, J. G., & Nelson, G. L. (1996). Chinese students' perceptions of ESL peer response group interaction. *Journal of Second Language Writing, 5*(1), 1–19.

Chan, S. (1991). *Asian Americans: An interpretive history.* Boston: Twayne Publishers.

Chan, C. S. (1996). Combating heterosexism in educational institutions: Structural changes and strategies. *Primary Prevention of Psychopathology, 17*, 20–35.

Chan, S. (1999). The Chinese learner–a question of style. *Education+ Training, 41*(6/7), 294–305.

Chan, K. (2006). Consumer socialization of Chinese children in schools: Analysis of consumption values in textbooks. *Journal of Consumer Marketing, 23*(3), 125–132.

Chan, C. K., & Rao, N. (2009). *Revisiting the Chinese learner: Changing education, changing context.* Dordrecht, Springer and the Comparative Education Research Centre, University of Hong Kong.

Chang, H. C., & Holt, G. R. (1991). More than relationship: Chinese interaction and the principle of kuan-hsi. *Communication Quarterly, 39*(3), 251–271.

Chen, C. (1986). *Neo-Confucian terms explained.* New York: Columbia University Press.

Cheng, C. Y. (1987). Chinese philosophy and contemporary human communication theory. In D. L. Kincaid (Ed.), *Communication theory: Eastern and Western perspectives* (pp. 23–43). San Diego: Academic Press.

Chow, I. H. S. (1995). Management education in Hong Kong: Needs and challenges. *International Journal of Educational Management, 9*, 10–15. https://doi.org/10.1108/09513549510095068

Chun, C. N. (1991). *The Asian mind game.* Basingstoke: Maxwell Macmillan International.

Clark, R., & Gieve, S. N. (2006). On the discursive construction of 'the Chinese learner'. *Language, Culture and Curriculum, 19*(1), 54–73.

Community of Private Education. Retrieved September 24 2017., from https://www.cpe.gov.sg/for-students/registration-status-of-private-education-institutions-peis-in-singapore#

Dowling, P. J., & Nagel, T. W. (1986). Nationality and work attitudes: A study of Australian and American business majors. *Journal of Management, 12*(1), 121–128.

Downs, J. F. (1971). *Cultures in crisis.* Beverly Hills: Glencoe Press.

England, G. W. (1978). Managers and their value systems: A five country comparative study. *Columbia Journal of World Business, 13*(2), 35–44.

Fan, Y. (2000). A classification of Chinese culture. *Cross cultural management: An international Journal, 7*(2), 3–10.

Fox, H. (1994). *Listening to the World: Cultural issues in Academic Writing*. ERIC.

Gu, Q., & Schweisfurth, M. 2006. Who adapts? Beyond cultural models of "the" Chinese learner, Language, Culture and Curriculum, 19(1), 74-89

Gudykunst, W. B., & Kim, Y. Y. (1984). *Communicating with strangers: An approach to intercultural communication*. Addison Wesley Publishing Company.

Herskovits, M. J. (1955). *Cultural Anthropology*. New York: Alfred A. Knopf.

Ho, R. (2010). Assessment of Chinese students' experience with foreign faculty: A case study from a Chinese University. *Journal of Teaching in International Business, 21*, 156–177.

Hoebel, A. (1960). *Man, culture and society*. New York: Oxford University Press.

Hofstede, G. (1980). *Culture's consequence*. Newbury Park: International Differences in Work-Related Values.

Hofstede, G. (1983). National cultures in four dimensions: A research-based theory of cultural differences among nations. *International Studies of Management & Organization, 13*(1–2), 46–74.

Hofstede, G. (1984). The cultural relativity of the quality of life concept. *Academy of Management Review, 9*(3), 389–398.

Hofstede, G. (1991). *Cultures and organizations: Software of the mind*. London: McGraw-Hill.

Hofstede, G. (2006). What did GLOBE really measure? Researchers' minds versus respondents' minds. *Journal of International Business Studies, 37*(6), 882–896.

Hofstede, G. (2010). The GLOBE debate: Back to relevance. *Journal of International Business Studies, 41*, 1339–1346.

Hofstede, G. (2011). Dimensionalizing cultures: The Hofstede model in context. *Online Readings in Psychology and Culture, 2*(1), 8.

Hofstede, G., & Bond, M. H. (1984). Hofstede's culture dimensions: An independent validation using Rokeach's value survey. *Journal of Cross-Cultural Psychology, 15*(4), 417–433.

House, R. J., Hanges, P. J., Javidan, M., Dorfman, P. W., & Gupta, V. (Eds.). (2004). *Culture, leadership, and organizations: The GLOBE study of 62 societies*. Thousand Oaks: Sage publications.

Hsiao, F. S. T., Jen, F. C., & Lee, C. F. (1990). Impacts of culture and communist orthodoxy on Chinese management. In *Advances in Chinese industrial studies*, vol. 1, Part A, pp. 301–314.

Hui, C. H., & Triandis, H. C. (1986). Individualism-collectivism: A study of cross-cultural researchers. *Journal of Cross-Cultural Psychology, 17*(2), 225–248.

Inglehart, R. F. (2008). Changing values among western publics from 1970 to 2006. *West European Politics, 31*(1–2), 130–146.

Jarrah, F. (1998). New courses will target transition to university. *China Morning Post, 23*, 28.

Jensen, V. J. (1992). Values and practices in Asian argumentation. *Argumentation and Advocacy, 28*, 155–166.

Kim, S., & McLean, G. N. (2014). The impact of National Culture on informal learning in the workplace. *Adult Education Quarterly, 64*(1), 39–59.

Kirkbride, P. A., & Tang, S. F. Y. (1992). Management development in the Nanyang Chinese societies of Southeast Asia. *Journal of Management Development, 11*(2), 55–66.

Kirkman, B. L., Lowe, K. B., & Gibson, C. B. (2006). A quarter century of culture's consequences: A review of empirical research incorporating Hofstede's cultural values framework. *Journal of International Business Studies, 37*(3), 285–320.

Kluckhohn, C. (1951). Values and value-orientations in the theory of action: An exploration in definition and classification. In T. Parsons & E. Shils (Eds.), *Toward a general theory of action* (pp. 388–433). Cambridge: Harvard University Press. https://doi.org/10.4159/harvard.9780674863507.c8

Kluckhohn, C., & Kelly, W. H. (1945). The concept of culture. In R. Linton (Ed.), *The science of man in the world crisis* (pp. 78–106). New York: Columbia University Press.

Kluckhohn, F. R., & Strodtbeck, F. L. (1961). *Variations in value orientations*. Evanston: Row, Peterson and Co.

Kumaravadivelu, B. (2003). Problematizing cultural stereotypes in TESOL. *TESOL Quarterly, 37*(4), 709–719.

Leung, M. Y., & Lu, X. H. (2008). Impacts of teaching approaches on learning approaches of construction engineering students: A comparative study between Hong Kong and mainland China. *Journal of Engineering Education, 97*(2), 135–145.

Lew, W. J. F. (1979). A Chinese woman intellectual: Family, education, and personality. *Education Journal, 7,* 166–197.

Littlewood, W. T., & 李德桓. (2009). *Participation-based pedagogy: How congruent is it with Chinese cultures of learning?*

Liu, S. (2006). Developing China's future managers: learning from the West? *Education+ Training, 48*(1), 6–14.

Lowe, E. A. (1981). Culture's consequences: international differences in work-related values. *Journal of Enterprise Management, 3*(3), 312.

Lu. (1998). An Interface between individualistic and collective orientations in Chinese cultural values and social relations. *Howard Journal of Communications, 9*(2), 91–107.

Lum, L. (2006). Internationally-educated health professionals: A distance education multiple cultures model. *Education+ Training, 48*(2/3), 112–126.

Ma, R. (1992). The role of unofficial intermediaries in interpersonal conflicts in the Chinese culture. *Communication Quarterly, 40,* 269–278.

McSweeney, B. (2002). Hofstede's model of national cultural differences and their consequences: A triumph of faith-a failure of analysis. *Human Relations, 55*(1), 89–118.

Morris, V. C. (1956). Physical education and the philosophy of education. *Journal of Health, Physical Education, Recreation, 27*(3), 21–32.

Murphy, D. (1987). Offshore education: A Hong Kong perspective. *Australian Universities' Review, 30*(2), 43–44.

Nardon, L., & Steers, R. M. (2011). The culture theory jungle: Divergence and convergence in models of national culture. In *Cambridge Handbook of Culture, Organizations, and Work* (pp. 3–22). Cambridge, UK: Cambridge University Press.

Neild, K. (2004). Questioning the myth of the Chinese learner. *International Journal of Contemporary Hospitality Management, 16*(3), 189–196.

Nelson, G. (1995). Cultural differences in learning styles. In J. Reid (Ed.), *Learning styles in the ESL/EFL classroom* (pp. 3–18). Boston: Heinle & Heinle.

Newell, S. (1999). The transfer of management knowledge to China: building learning communities rather than translating Western textbooks? *Education+ Training, 41*(6/7), 286–294.

Ninnes, P., Aitchison, C., & Kalos, S. (1999). Challenges to stereotypes of international students' prior educational experience: Undergraduate education in India. *Higher Education Research & Development, 18*(3), 323–342.

Nisbet, R. E. (2003). *The geography of thought.* London: N. Brealey Publishing.

Oh, T. K. (1991). Understanding managerial values and behaviour among the gang of four: South Korea, Taiwan, Singapore and Hong Kong. *Journal of Management Development, 10*(2), 46–56.

Oyserman, D., Coon, H. M., & Kemmelmeier, M. (2002). Rethinking individualism and collectivism: Evaluation of theoretical assumptions and meta-analyses: American Psychological Association.

Pan, Z., Chaffee, S., Chu, G., & Ju, Y. (1994). *To see ourselves: Comparing traditional Chinese and American cultural values.* Boulder: Westview.

Pun, A. (1989). *Developing managers internationally: Culture free or culture bound?* Paper presented at the symposium presentation at the Conference on International Personnel and Human Resource Management, Hong Kong.

Pye, L. W. (1972). *China: An introduction.* Boston: Little Brown.

Rajaram, K. (2010). *Culture clash: Teaching western-based business education to mainland Chinese students in Singapore.* Unpublished doctoral dissertation). University of South Australia, Adelaide, Australia.

Rajaram, K. (2014). Business endeavours in savoury snack industry: Old Chang Kee. *International Journal of Business and Social Science, 5*(6).

Rajaram, K., & Bordia, S. (2011). Culture clash: Teaching Western-based management education to mainland Chinese students in Singapore. *Journal of International Education in Business, 4*(1), 63–83.

Redding, G. (1990). *The spirit of Chinese capitalism* (Vol. 22). Berlin/Boston: Walter de Gruyter.

Rigby, J. A. (1986). In the schools: California treat: Three days in five ecosystems. *Science and Children, 23*(4), 20–23.

Rodrigues, C. A. (2004). The importance level of ten teaching/learning techniques as rated by university business students and instructors. *Journal of Management Development, 23*(2), 169–182.

Rokeach, M. (1973). *The nature of human values*. New York: Free Press.

Ronen, S. (1986). *Comparative and multinational management*. New York: Wiley.

Ryan, J., & Louie, K. (2005). Dichotomy or complexity: Problematising concepts of scholarship and learning. In M. Mason (Ed.), *Proceedings of the critical thinking and learning: Values, concepts and issues, 34th annual conference of the philosophy of education society of Australia* (pp. 401–411). Hong Kong: Philosophy of Education Society of Australia.

Ryan, J., & Slethaug, G. (2010). *International education and the Chinese learner* (Vol. 1). Hong Kong: Hong Kong University Press.

Schwartz, S. H. (1992). Universals in the content and structure of values: Theoretical advances and empirical tests in 20 countries. *Advances in Experimental Social Psychology, 25,* 1–65.

Schwartz, S. H. (1994). Are there universal aspects in the structure and contents of human values? *Journal of Social Issues, 50*(4), 19–45.

Schwartz, S. H. (1999). A theory of cultural values and some implications for work. *Applied Psychology, 48*(1), 23–47.

Scollon, R., & Scollon, S. W. (1995). *Intercultural communication: A discourse approach*. Oxford: Blackwell.

Selmer, J. (1987). Swedish managers' perceptions of Singaporean work related values. *Asia Pacific Journal of Management, 15*(1), 80–88.

Selmer, J., & de Leon, C. (1993). Organizational acculturation in foreign subsidiaries. *Thunderbird International Business Review, 35*(4), 321–338.

Selvarajah, C. (2006). Cross-cultural study of Asian and European student perception: The need to understand the changing educational environment in New Zealand. *Cross cultural management: An international Journal, 13*(2), 142–155.

Shenkar, O., & Ronen, S. (1987). Structure and importance of work goals among managers in the People's Republic of China. *Academy of Management Journal, 30,* 564–576.

Shi, L. (2006). The successors to Confucianism or a new generation? A questionnaire study on Chinese students' culture of learning English. *Language, Culture and Curriculum, 19*(1), 122–147.

Signorini, P., Wiesemes, R., & Murphy, R. (2009). Developing alternative frameworks for exploring intercultural learning: A critique of Hofstede's cultural difference model. *Teaching in Higher Education, 14*(3), 253–264.

Slethaug, G. (2010). Something happened while nobody was looking: The growth of international education and the Chinese learner. *International education and the Chinese learner,* 15–36.

Smith, P. B., & Bond, M. H. (1999). *Social psychology across cultures* (2nd ed.). Boston: Allyn and Bacon.

Smucker, J. (1982). Greet Hofstede: "Culture's consequences". *Sociology Reviews of New Books, 9*(2), 55–56.

Søndergaard, M. (1994). Research note: Hofstede's consequences: A study of reviews, citations and replications. *Organization Studies, 15*(3), 447–456.

Staw, B. M. (1982). Ni Hao: Some reflections on teaching organizational behaviour. *Exchange: The Organizational Behaviour Teaching Journal, 7*(2), 8–11.

Tan, C. H. (1989). Confucianism and nation building in Singapore. *International Journal of Social Economics, 16*(8), 5–16.

Terpstra, V., & David, K. H. (1985). *The cultural environment of international business* (2nd ed.). Cincinnati: South-Western Pub. Co..

Ting-Toomey, S. (1998). Intercultural conflict styles: A face-negotiation theory. In Y. Y. Kim & W. B. Gudykunst (Eds.), *Theories in intercultural communication* (pp. 213–235). Newbury Park: Sage.

Tonnies, F. (1957). *Community and society*. New York: The Michigan State University/Harper & Row.

Triandis, H. C. (1995). *Individualism & collectivism*. Boulder: Westview Press.

Trompenaars, F. 1993. Riding the Waves of Culture, Nicholas Brealey, London.

Trompenaars, F., & Hampden-Turner, C. (2011). *Riding the waves of culture: Understanding diversity in global business*. London/Boston: Nicholas Brealey Publishing.

Tsang, E. W. (2001). Adjustment of mainland Chinese academics and students to Singapore. *International Journal of Intercultural Relations, 25*(4), 347–372.

Tung, R. L., & Verbeke, A. (2010). *Beyond Hofstede and GLOBE: Improving the quality of cross-cultural research*. Dordrecht: Springer.

Tylor, E. (1881). On the origin of the plough, and wheel-carriage. *The Journal of the Anthropological Institute of Great Britain and Ireland, 10*, 74–84.

Walker, A., Bridges, E., & Chan, B. (1996). Wisdom gained, wisdom given: Instituting PBL in a Chinese culture. *Journal of Educational Administration, 34*(5), 12–31.

Ward, S., Pearson, C., & Entrekin, L. (2002). Chinese cultural values and the Asian meltdown. *International Journal of Social Economics, 29*(3), 205–217.

Warner, M. (1981). Culture's consequences. *Journal of General Management, 7*(1), 75–78.

Watkins, D.A. and Biggs, J.B. 1996. (Eds), "The Chinese Learner: cultural, psychological and contextual influences", University of Hong Kong, Hong Kong: Comparative Education Research Centre

Watkins, D.A. and Biggs, J.B. 2001. The Paradox of the Chinese Learner and Beyond. In: D.A., Watkins and J.B. Biggs, (Eds) (2001) Teaching the Chinese Learner: Psychological and Pedagogical Perspectives: Hong Kong, CERC and Melbourne, ACER. 3-26

Watkins, D., Reghi, M., & Astilla, E. (1991). The-Asian-learner-as-a-rote-learner stereotype: Myth or reality? *Educational Psychology, 11*, 21–33.

Wen, W.-P., & Clément, R. (2003). A Chinese conceptualisation of willingness to communicate in ESL. *Language Culture and Curriculum, 16*(1), 18–38.

Williams, R. M. (1970). *American society: A sociological interpretation*. New York: Knopf.

Wright, A. F. (1975). *Confucianism and Chinese civilization* (Vol. 138). Stanford: Stanford University Press.

Wu, P. C. (2002). Cultural dimensions at the individual level of analysis. *International Journal of Cross Cultural Management, 2*(3), 275–295.

Yang, K.-S. (1986). Chinese personality and its change. In M. H. Bond (Ed.), *The psychology of the Chinese people* (pp. 106–170). Hong Kong: Oxford University Press.

Yang, Z. (2009). The effect of mother tongue transfer on English writing. *Teaching and Management, 11*(3), 16–20.

Yao, X. (2000). *An introduction to Confucianism*. Cambridge: Cambridge University Press.

Yong, C. (2016, April 8). *Singapore's value lies in its 'unique culture'*. The Straits Times. Retrieved from http://www.straitstimes.com/singapore/singapores-value-lies-in-its-unique-culture?login=true

Yu, N. (1998). *The contemporary theory of metaphor: A perspective from Chinese*. Amsterdam: John Benjamins Publishing.

Yu, A. B., & Yang, K. S. (1994). The nature of achievement motivation in collectivist societies. *Cross Cultural Research and Methodology Series-Sage, 18*, 239–250.

Chapter 3
Educational Context: Students' Perceived Learning Effectiveness and Learning Experiences

The chapter commences with a discussion on Singapore as an educational hub for international students. A brief explanation is covered on active versus passive learning that relates to the context of the usage of the terms 'active techniques' and 'passive techniques'. The selection of the correct fit of instructional techniques in teaching through various contexts, especially in cultural dislocation and social aspects, is discussed. The concept of learning effectiveness for of students' learning is presented. Next, the academic literature on the perceived learning effectiveness among different instructional techniques and teaching mainland Chinese students is presented. The methodology, analysis and findings on the qualitative research to comprehend the mainland Chinese students' 'perceived learning effectiveness' are described and explained. The findings on the perceived learning indicators across multiple instructional techniques and individual instructional strategies are presented and discussed. The chapter wraps up by offering the recommendations to understand the cross-cultural learning and teaching issues for these mainland Chinese students pursuing their studies in culturally dislocated context

The consistency of providing quality education to students determines the long-term success and sustainability of educational institutions. To achieve this goal, a good comprehension of the learning culture, identifying the right fit, correct type of instructional techniques that need to be adopted with a constant alignment to the evolving rapid changes, is required. For the purpose of this book, the varying types of instructional techniques, with the more relevant and appropriate ones for the mainland Chinese learners, are thoroughly discussed with varying cultural dislocation aspects; hence, the correct mix is recommended. By adopting the appropriate mix of instructional techniques with a thorough understanding of the learning culture and culture of learning, we could achieve quality learning process that leads to higher level of perceived and actual learning effectiveness. The key long-term driver

This chapter is improved from Rajaram, K., & Collins, J. B. (2013). Qualitative identification of learning effectiveness indicators among mainland Chinese students in culturally dislocated study environments. *Journal of International Education in Business, 6*(2), 179–199.

of success in terms of delivering consistent quality and rigorous learning deliverables for educational institutions will be the ability to create an ecosystem that facilitates effective learning, which translates into the capability to speedily produce, recognize and amalgamate knowledge delivery.

3.1 Educational Hub for International Students

Singapore, with its strategic geographical location, bridges the Western and Eastern economies. In terms of education field, therefore, its advantageous location enables it to aim to be a global educational hub. In fact, Singapore is ranked 6th in the world and 1st in Asia in 2017 in the 'U21 Ranking of National Higher Education Systems' for its provision of quality higher education (Universitas 21 2017). For this ranking, 50 countries are ranked on the basis of 25 attributes in each of four areas: resources, environment, connectivity and output. As tertiary education can prepare an individual to contribute to one's future workspace creatively and effectively, it is the key to an individual's successful career. A quality system of higher education should be congruent with national aims and personal desires and aptitudes. For Singapore, which relies mainly on its human resources for economic development, it is imperative to continue to value and prioritize high-quality and rigorous education. This was well evident by the report released by Universities 21 called 'U21 Ranking of National Higher Education Systems' where Singapore emerges as the top 11th country worldwide and 1st in Asia for its provision of quality higher education. The goal of this report analysis is to offer insights into aspects on (a) how quality education systems contribute to authentic ideas, business processes, activities and operations as well as bilateral trade relations and (b) provide insights into areas for improving living standards. In this report, Mr. Satish Bakhda, Rikvin's Head of Operations, mentioned 'As Singapore is strategically placed in the heart of Asia, it has become an esteemed business epicenter that serves as a gateway between Western and Eastern economics. As education contributes to new business ideas and activity, it would then make sense to offer the best tertiary education options that are directly relevant to businesses here'. Rikvin, Singapore Company Incorporation Specialists, has identified four contributing aspects to Singapore's rise as an education hub for students from all over the world. The four factors are, namely, (a) wide variety of quality educational institutions; (b) edu trust quality assurance; (c) cost of education; and (d) environment and living climate.

(a) Wide Variety of Quality Educational Institutions
   Singapore offers a diverse and wide range of courses from a variety of quality universities ranging from local to international. Besides the six local universities, many foreign universities also have Singapore campus, such as the University of Chicago Booth School of Business. In the private education sector, there are 6880 establishments in Singapore as of 2015.

(b) Edu Trust Quality Assurance
   In accordance with the Singapore Private Education Act, all private education institutions (PEIs) are required to be registered with the Singapore Committee

for Private Education (CPE). The validity of PEIs registration varies based on how it performs in line with the CPE's registration criteria to be offered a longer validity period of registration.

(c) Cost of Education

According to the report by Business Standard, management education in the United States and United Kingdom is more expensive than in Singapore (approximately 20–25% cheaper). For example, the total fees for a full-time MBA programme in Oxford (University of Oxford, SAID Business School 2017) and Cambridge (University of Cambridge, Judge Business School 2017) can cost up to £55,000, top MBA programmes in top US schools (Wharton, University of Pennsylvania 2017) can cost around USD $70,000, while a full-time MBA programme in Singapore (National University of Singapore, Nanyang Technological University, Singapore Management University 2017) costs around S$62,000 per year. Hence, Asian students do not need to go far to experience and enjoy high-quality education, and students around the world can also benefit from this.

(d) Environment and Living Climate

Singapore offers a relatively safe, low-crime environment that facilitates business-related and social activities. Backed by sound corporate governance and political stability, Singapore is also a model for efficiency. This in turn supports education and business activities as well.

As China is fast growing economically and socially, many Chinese begin to explore opportunities outside their country. Many Chinese choose to come to Singapore as it offers quality education, conducive academic environment and cultural and linguistic similarities with China that allows Chinese students to settle in easily. Indeed, mainland Chinese tend to blend in Singapore's society more readily than into other Western countries (Tsang 2001). These are probably some of many reasons for an increase in mainland Chinese students and academics coming to Singapore over the past decade (Bohm et al. 2002). Other potentially possible factors attracting mainland Chinese students include Singapore as an excellent place for experiencing both Asian and Western cultures, the well-recognized academic systems and the stable environment for employment.

All the reasons stated above led to the Mainland Chinese students becoming the largest cluster of foreigners in the public and private international institutes in Singapore. Their ease of adaptation to new cultural and learning/teaching environments has a direct impact on their academic performance. These students' main concern is whether they can achieve good academic results to increase their chances for further studies or employment in their desired careers after graduation (Bodycott 2009; Bohm et al. 2002). As potential future managers and leaders, their performance in employment depends largely on how well they are trained to be equipped with necessary knowledge and skills in their courses of study. Chinese students who fail may be required to leave the country. Thus, doing well academically by acquiring knowledge and learning most effectively has both personal and organizational performance implications (Tsang 2001).

3.2   Active Versus Passive Learning

Let us first examine the words 'active' and 'passive' to have a clearer comprehension in context to the learning context. The term 'active' learning is used in context where more collaboration and participation are required through, for example, exchanges and communication between the instructor and students and among students themselves. In contrast, the term 'passive' learning is used on instances where the action is inclined towards a one-way delivery by the instructors or a transfer of information without much contribution, inputs and/or sharing by the learners.

Similarly, in our context we will use the terms 'active techniques' and 'passive techniques'. Rodrigues (2004) has classified ten commonly used techniques into these two categories based largely on frequency of interactivity, exchanges of perspectives participation among instructors-students or among students and the level of collaboration among students during their learning process. Rajaram (2010) leverages on Rodrigues (2004)'s work but further categorized and fine-tuned the classification in subcategories with much more specific qualifying criteria and detailing the clarity of how many more other authentic and varying instructional techniques could be easily clustered into one of the categories that fits or overarches the qualifying requirements.

3.3   Instructional Techniques

The selection of the correct fit of instructional techniques in teaching through various contexts requires one to reflect on varying questions, such as: (1) Why are these instructional techniques the best fit based on the context? (2) How does these instructional techniques appropriately engage the students? (3) How to use these instructional techniques to have the knowledge transfer facilitated more effectively?

The choice of instructional techniques in teaching requires a consideration of how best to engage the students and transfer knowledge effectively. The effectiveness of instructional techniques has to be investigated from various perspectives, for example, the cultural context, institutional context, social context and its values, the contextualized learning culture and culture of learning from the national and/or institutional levels, etc.

Students from different social and cultural backgrounds respond to the use of different instructional techniques differently. It is the varying emphasis on learning processes that are adopted in a culture that nurtures that cluster of learners to be inclined towards the different learning styles and preferences (Kemp 2010; Holland 1989; Kolb and Fry 1975; Watkins et al. 1977). In Singapore, Western-based business education is facilitated by faculty of different racial profiles or cultural background. Hence, generally the instructional approaches adopted are more catered towards the local learners' preference. However, the instructional techniques to be adopted for mainland Chinese students cannot be identical to the type of instructional techniques adopted for the local students in Singapore. This could be attributed to the learning culture that these students have been exposed to all their years in the education system. Rodrigues (2004) categorized ten commonly used instructional techniques into (1) four active techniques, 'case studies', 'individual research projects', 'classroom discussions' and 'group projects', and (2) six passive techniques, 'lectures by instructors', 'reading textbooks', 'guest speakers', 'videos shown in the classroom, 'classroom presentation by students' and 'computerized learning assignments'. Using inappropriate instructional techniques leads to undesirable and negative learning outcomes, such as students' frustrations, disengaged from lessons, ineffective knowledge transfer and unable to transfer intended skills and competencies to students. When the content knowledge is disseminated ineffectively, that causes students not able to acquire the essentials adequately affecting their learning outputs. Rajaram (2010) advocates one to be mindful and aware of the values, norms, beliefs and preferences when teaching in cross-cultural context. Instructors need to use the correct mix of instructional techniques so as to attain an optimal learning experience for students by being mindful of the varying social and cultural factors.

Inappropriate and poor usage of instructional techniques are situations without a deep awareness, causing a high sense of unfamiliarity and discomfort for students. Alternatively, it could be without any mindful and progressive adaptive interventions or when the instructional techniques used are not what the students' value in terms of their perceived learning effectiveness that causes negative repressions to occur. If inappropriate instructional techniques are adopted, then student frustration may be one of the outcomes. Teaching effectiveness in a cross-cultural context could be achieved by adopting a correct mix of appropriate instructional techniques by which the students learn best and gain optimal knowledge. The selection of the techniques depends on (1) the subject matter; (2) location where the instruction occurs; and (3) the country or countries which the foreign students come from.

Mainland Chinese students bring distinctive values from their cultural backgrounds. There are obvious differences in the instructional techniques used between China and Singapore. Hence, maximizing student learning requires selection of instructional techniques that best help them leverages on the learning characteristics of Confucian heritage that could be carefully calibrated and contextualized to meet the requirements of a Western-based educational curricula and business practices. This enables both matching of instructors' delivery approach with students' preferences and shifting of students' preferences to fit the types of assessment being carried out.

3.4 Learning Effectiveness

Learning is shaped by cultural, social, psychological, personal and contextual influences (Gu and Schweisfurth 2006), and it happens in countless varying forms. Students learn through varying approaches by seeing and hearing, reflecting and acting, reasoning rationally and instinctively, memorizing and envisaging and illustrating analogies and creating mathematical models (Felder and Silverman 1998). To shift or transform learners' mindset beyond their preferred learning style, a developmental growth process should be adopted (Frontczak 1990, 1999; Kolb 1984). Felder and Silverman (1998) advocate three primary variables that affect students' learning, namely, (a) innate ability, (b) prior preparation and (c) the fit between the instructor's teaching approach and students' learning style. We could extend this debate further by stating that this process is further complicated by the fact that different instructors prefer to adopt different teaching styles based on what they perceive to be effective as per their experiences. For example, some instructors use traditional lectures and/or interactive style lectures; others use hands-on experiential and active learning approaches. Some focus on grounded principles while others more on applications. Some emphasize on memorizing and others on the ability to comprehend deeply and apply. The instructional methodology adopted largely depends on the intended learning outcomes and what the teachers want to equip these students with, skills, applied knowledge, contents, facts and so on.

Learners who prefer intuitive over sensory perception respond much better when concepts are emphasized (abstract contents) over facts (concrete content) (Felder and Silverman 1998). The usage of films, pictures and charts is more comfortable to learners whose preference is more inclined towards visual perception. Students are able to learn through multiple learning modalities, namely, concrete experience, conceptualization, reflective observation and experimentation proposed by McCarthy (1980) to facilitate effective learning and augment the learning ability of students.

Having an adequate fit of learning activities with students' learning styles enhances learning outcomes that are validated by two theoretical frameworks, namely, Felder and Spurlin (2005) learning style index and Kolb's (1984) two-dimensional model (Frontczak 1990; Tom and Calvert 1983; Merrison et al. 2003). The effectiveness of learning is affected by the learning circumstances, for example, the learning climate and environment (Dunlosky et al. 2013), the means of how effectively the instructional techniques are adopted and used and profile characteristics of the learners. Rajaram and Collins (2013) advocate that for effective learning to occur, a balanced approach and compatibility are required between the learning styles of students and the correct mix of instructional techniques, learning activities adopted. The fit of the learning activities to Karns's four learning style types is presented in Table 3.1.

Saravanamuthu and Yap (2014) describe that this Western Chinese learning disengagement is attributed to learning shock (Gu 2005), role shock (Minkler and Biller 1979) and language shock (Agar 1996) that beset learners transiting between cultures. Learning shock refers to challenging experiences and not comfortable

Table 3.1 Karns' four learning styles types

Type of learners	Learning activities
1. Accommodators	Respond to field trips, simulations, group projects and case
	Studies, in class participation and guest speakers
2. Convergers	Respond to experiential learning but want to focus on the
	Principles behind what is experienced
3. Divergers	Respond to brainstorming, group activities and lectures
4. Assimilators	Respond to term papers, readings and individual work

Source: Karns (2006), extracted from Rajaram and Collins (2013)

feelings in unfamiliar learning circumstances, which is compounded by unfamiliarity with the practices of teaching and learning and inadequate language ability (Gu and Maley 2008). Adaption to these unfamiliar learning environments becomes a hindrance due to the cognitive, affective and psychological influences that contributes to emotional and psychological anxiety (Saravanamuthu and Yap 2014). However, scholars (Gu and Schweisfurth 2006; Zhou et al. 2008) claim that the Chinese students intentionally and consciously strive to regulate their learning impetus strategies to the foreign learning environment.

Mismatches exist between the learning styles of mainland Chinese students and the traditional teaching styles adopted by professors delivering Western-based curricula. This leads to students' distraction and monotony that cause them to perform poorly on tests, get them discouraged and, in some cases, have them changed to other courses and even drop out of the institutions. Hence, we should be clear that the perceived effectiveness in learning is influenced by the adoption of the correct mix of instructional techniques that fit the cultural context and learning styles of students, which may not be easily standardized.

3.5   Perceived Learning Effectiveness Among Different Instructional Techniques

An extensive body of literature addresses the issues on teaching and learning approaches for mainland Chinese students (Bu and Mitchell 1992; Biggs 1994; Chan 1999; Coverdale-Jones 2006; Clark and Gieve 2006; Jin and Cortazzi 2006; Louie 2005; Liu 2006; Littlewood 2009; Martinsons and Martinsons 1996; Ryan and Hellmundt 2005; Ryan and Louie 2007; Ryan and Slethaug 2010; Rajaram and Bordia 2011; Shi 2006; Turner 2006). Yet, the literature lacks an all-inclusive approach assimilating specific aspects of cultural dislocation and learning principles that influence effective learning strategies for Western-based education. Some scholars, Chan and Rao (2009), Coverdale-Jones and Rastall (2009), Yang (2009) and Ryan and Slethaug (2010), have called out for such studies, but only students' learning styles and preferences for lesson delivery have been examined so far. There are no studies so far that measures perceived learning effectiveness or learning effectiveness indicators for preferences of instructional techniques in pursuit of a Western-based education in a culturally dislocated context of a cosmopolitan country, such as Singapore. We note, however, student's preference of instructional techniques may not necessarily equate to most effective perceived learning and learning effectiveness.

There is evidence to support that sociocultural background of students is associated to their preference of their learning styles and choice of instructional techniques preferred over others. Cultural norms and values of the students' country of origin influence their choice of learning and instructional approaches, before they are fully adapted and assimilated to the unfamiliarity and newness of the culture, which requires a prolonged exposure. Effectiveness in the usage of the same instructional techniques may vary from one culture to another. Some scholars (Holland 1989;

Kolb and Fry 1975; Watkins et al. 1977) reported that it is the learning culture where the student is from that develops one's learning style and it is the learning style that leads to the varying pedagogical preferences. Asian and Western learners embrace differing pedagogical preferences (Lindsay and Dempsey 1983). Choo (2007) claims that Chinese students' learning styles and experiences in China are not compatible with the Western teaching styles in business schools. In fact, the Western teaching styles create 'negative emotions, anxiety, fear and confusion among Chinese students' (p.156). He reiterates that there are distinctive differences in Chinese students' learning styles compared to their Western counterparts. Scholars (Pun 1989a, b; Jarrah 1998; Ladd and Ruby 1999) reported that Western learners learn through more towards the exploration and collaborative approaches, while Chinese learners expect the teacher to lead, guide in the learning process and provide the information readily. Hammond and Gao (2002) asserted that contemporary Chinese education is characterized by rote learning, repetition and memorization, where this approach a conservative attitude to learning and Biggs (1996) described it as superficial learning. On the contrary, scholars (Ryan and Slethaug 2010; Rajaram and Bordia 2011; Littlewood 2009; Ryan and Louie 2007; Rajaram 2010) disagree and argued that students' learning and teaching preferences and choice in their style/approach of learning approaches are influenced by the learning design and assessments that support that, not traditionally stereotyped and perceived cultural aspects. This could be further validated where Zhang (2006) found that Chinese students prefer teaching styles that allow collaborative work and creativity-generating.

'Western' and 'Asian' values are not fixed perspectives that remain discrete, homogenous and unchanging. We should not label and encourage stereotyping of students without examining deeper into the contextual issues (Ryan and Slethaug 2010; Rajaram 2013; Ninnes et al. 1999). These contextual issues include the influence of instructional approaches, learning tasks or types of assessment on students' learning behaviours and attitudes or whether participative and interactive learning is facilitated or hindered.

Confucius philosophy largely influences the Chinese learning principles that emphasize on willpower, effort or concentration of the mind. For mainland Chinese students, education focuses on testing of storage of knowledge through rote memorization (Kumaravadivelu 2003; Ryan and Louie 2005) but at the expense of creativity (Chan 1999) and prone to plagiarism (Phan 2006; Kirkpatrick 2004). The Chinese learners still embrace the same set of learning attitudes such as focus, diligence, concentration and endurance of hardship (Li 2001) and the rationale behind the attitudes, i.e. egalitarianism, 'you can achieve it if you want to' (Lee 1996, p. 39).

Interestingly, the learning beliefs and behaviours of these mainland Chinese students are frequently viewed as the opposites of Western academic values. Chinese learners often prefer not to express their views (Chan 1999) so as to portray themselves as humble and not to unnecessarily affront others. Some scholars also label Chinese students in general as being rote, passive and superficial learners lacking critical thinking skills (Ninnes et al. 1999; Ryan and Louie 2005; Kumaravadivelu 2003). However, the myths of Chinese learners being submissive, rote learners have been refuted by Rajaram, K. (2010), Rajaram K. (2013) and many other scholars (Chalmers and Volet 1997; Chan and Drover 1997; Coverdale-Jones and Paul Rastall

2009; Greake and Maingard 1999; Hellmundt 2001; Jones 1999; Littlewood 2001; Ninnes et al. 1999; Watkins and Biggs 1996, 2001). It was argued that it was partial knowledge or indeed a misunderstanding that created the negative stereotypes (Littlewood 2009; Ninnes et al. 1999). Memorization is in fact related to understanding and can be used to deepen one's comprehension of information, i.e. it should not be stereotyped as mechanical rote learning as perceived by some researchers from the Western culture. But the stereotypes of Confucian heritage culture (CHC) and Chinese students continue to exist (Ryan and Slethaug 2010). For example, Wen and Clement (2003) claim that Chinese students are passive because they are unwilling to participate in classroom. The students are being labeled of this characteristic as they are submissive to authority. However, there has been a profound and rapid shift on the social and cultural aspects on Chinese learners away from the rooted values of Confucius' teachings. Hence, it is essential to re-examine the instructional approaches adopted for more effective facilitation of learning.

3.6 Teaching Mainland Chinese Students

There has been extensive literature addressing the preferred teaching techniques of mainland Chinese students. However, a holistic framework that encompasses aspects such as culture, social values, behavioural norms, cultural dislocation challenges and learning styles is still lacking. These aspects contribute as diverse yet collective touch points for the development of high-quality and effective instructional and learning strategies for the mainland Chinese students in pursuit of a Western-based education overseas.

Chinese learning principles are grounded in Confucian philosophy. A primary emphasis of Confucian tradition is education that is vital both for individuals and for the society. In fact, the Confucius's *Analects* had reference to 'learning' in the whole literature (Lee 1996). Confucianism has evolved through five principal stages, namely, 'Confucianism information', 'Confucianism in adaption', 'Confucianism in transformation', 'Confucianism in variation' and 'Confucianism in renovation'. Yao (2000) conveyed that Confucianism is more of a tradition largely rooted in Chinese culture and nurtured by Confucius and Confucians. However, Shi (2006) is of the view that Confucianism vicissitudes throughout an elongated history by acclimatising itself to evolving social and political demands through a multidimensional concept.

Studies from scholars (Ryan and Slethaug 2010; Rajaram and Bordia 2011, 2013; McNaught 2012; Yang 2009; Littlewood 2009; Chan and Rao 2009; Shi 2006) discoursed the changing learning approaches of mainland Chinese students. They urged instructors to shift their mindset from the fixed perceptions of 'Western' and 'Asian' values. There is a pressing need to re-examine the adoption and customization of the instructional approaches for the mainland Chinese students to respond to the rapid shift in Chinese learners' learning requirements. Teachers adopting a mindful leadership when working in a cross-cultural classroom need to be sensitive to the role of culture, social aspects and its effects to teaching and learning as well.

Mainland Chinese students' preferred teaching techniques and their learning styles have been explored by Nakamura (1964), Redding (1990), Martinsons and Martinsons (1996) and Biggs (1994). Aside from these, more recent studies include Cheng and Wan (2016) and Chi et al. (2017). It appears that no study has looked exclusively at perceived learning effectiveness of preferred instructional techniques and the optimization of knowledge acquired for Chinese students pursuing Western-based education away from their home country. No studies have explicitly examined this aspect yet; studies have only examined the students' learning styles and preference in the delivery of lessons. There has been no clear indication or evidence on the measure of perceived effectiveness of students' learning via their preferred instructional techniques. We noted that students' preference for a certain instructional technique may not necessarily equate to their most effective approach of learning. The primary concern is to identify the correct mix and types of effective instructional techniques most suitable to be adopted to facilitate these mainland Chinese students. To address the 'gaps' on this context, a study was performed by Rajaram and Collins (2013), to understand issues surrounding the influence of students' own views of learning effectiveness via their perceptions on the most appropriate instructional techniques.

3.7 Method

3.7.1 Profile of Mainland Chinese Students

For both the qualitative and quantitative studies presented in this book, the profile of mainland Chinese students is identified from the provinces, i.e. Shanghai, Zhejiang, Anhui, Shandong, Beijing, Guangdong, Henan and Jiangsu, that are more affluent, westernized, educated, politically advanced and possessed a stronger business sense. This classification will enable the analysis to be concrete and grounded as students are coming from by and large the same previous educational backgrounds, learning culture and social and economic backgrounds.

3.7.2 Participants

We conducted interview preliminarily to comprehend participants' ideas of 'perceived learning effectiveness'. A total of 20 participants represent Eastern and South Eastern regions where mainland Chinese were identified. The following criteria were imposed to ensure the student sample provided consists of a reasonable representation: (1) Chinese students from mainland China; (2) pursuing undergraduate business studies offered by overseas universities affiliated with local higher education institutions; (3) studying in institutions (i.e. if it is classified as private-based) that have earned 4-year Singapore Edu Trust licences; (4) students' International English Language Testing System (IELTS) scores no lower than 6.0 (competent language user in written and verbal forms); and (5) preinterviewed to ensure that students could articulate their thoughts reasonably well with fluent, logical flow and clarity.

3.7.3 Procedure

The interview was conducted for approximately 2 h per student over the 20 student participants. Interview sessions were facilitated by an external consultant who is fluent in both English and Chinese and has worked in various parts of China and with extensive understanding of the culture, language and the dialects spoken there. All interviews were audio-taped and then independently transcribed over a period of approximately 6 months. To ensure the accuracy and consistency of interview transcriptions, all were revetted by the principal researcher and a research assistant.

The major research question was:

RQ1. How do mainland Chinese undergraduate students conceptualize 'learning effectiveness' in their pursuit of Western-based business education?

The following sub-questions also helped in forming exploratory interviews:

RQ1a. How do these students perceive learning effectiveness in terms of quality of learning and scope of knowledge covered?

RQ1b. What are the relative differences in quality of students' learning across the instructional techniques?

RQ1c. Which qualitative indicators emerged readily from students themselves vs which others required prompting?

RQ1d. Which instructional techniques fit the way the students like to learn?

RQ1e. Which of the instructional techniques provided the most attractive learning environment?

RQ1f. How are the instructional techniques increasing the awareness of the subjects?

These primary questions were addressed through the conduct of interviews. Some other major issues on the influencing attributes of students' learning effectiveness also surfaced. Semi-structured approach was adopted for the interviews where the interview questions were asked in a sequential order. This allowed students to share their experiences with the interviewer and to identify aspects of instructional techniques that facilitated their learning in different ways.

3.7.4 Analysis

The key themes from all interviews with regard to each instructional technique are analyzed by the principal researcher. Main themes were compiled in accordance with the broad clusters they are classified under. From these data sheets, responses to every interview question were scrutinized to determine what participants reported, how they justified their thinking and what key themes emerged from specific questions asked. The themes and findings for each of the interview questions were summarized using the template (Table 3.2) in understanding how the questions were commonly and individually comprehended by the interviewed Chinese students.

Table 3.2 Thirty Qualitative indicators of learning effectiveness (both emergent and prompted) for 10 instructional techniques reported during interviews with 20 Chinese students studying business in Singapore

< Emergent Prompted >	1-CasStd	2-InRsPrj	3-GrpProj	4-ClsDisc	5-Lec	6-RdTxt	7-GstSpkr	8-Vid	9-ClsPrsnt	10-CmpLrn	Totals
Common themes across many instructional techniques											
1. Quality of learning/optimal knowledge acquisition	9	14	7			9	16				55
2. Ability to relate and apply in a practical context	15	9	3	3			7	8	9		54
3. Reiterate, refresh, facilitate to remember information	15	7	5	6			11	3			47
4. Critical and analytical thinking	11						6		6		23
Themes specific to individual instructional techniques											
5. Easier to understand	9										9
6. Learn from current knowledge and others	6										6
7. In-depth and diverse coverage of information	5										5
8. Facilitate, apply from own and others' perspectives	4										4
9. Easier to visualise and picture >	4										4
10. Learn from varying opinions' views	2										2
11. Ability to challenge the norm >	2										2
12. Allows one to express views and opinions		2							7		9
13. Allows one to think in varying modes		8									8
14. Improve spoken language and written skills >		5									5
15. Understanding the flow >		5									5
16. Thinking diversely		4									4
17. Independent learning >		3									3
18. Efficiency in knowledge acquisition >		2									2

19. Clarify and share ideas with group mates			13								13
20. Facilitate learning >			12								12
21. Knowledge transfer >			7		5						12
22. Greater sense of security					7						7
23. Enhancing understanding			5								5
24. Greater control in the learning process			5								5
25. Effectiveness and relevance >								9			9
26. Personal self-improvement >									9		9
27. Vibrant and interesting learning environment >									7		7
28. Improve presentation skills									6		6
29. Sharing information/ability to think thoroughly								4			4
30. Flexibility of learning										4	4
Total for each instructional technique	82	59	40	26	12	9	40	24	44	4	340

Extracted from Rajaram, K. and Collins, J., (2013)

Consensual qualitative research (CQR) technique is used to first analyse the interviews (Hill et al. 2005). To address the cultural sensitivity of the data of varying and diverse perspectives, two primary researchers and one external auditor were involved in this CQR team. Subsequently, the frequencies of similar responses were tallied within each broad cluster to distinguish between frequently mentioned attributes of learning effectiveness and notions which were rarer or idiosyncratic, thus moving the study from 'strictly qualitative' towards mixed-methods research.

3.7.5   Findings

3.7.5.1   Qualitative Indicators of Perceived Learning Effectiveness

Twenty mainland Chinese students reported a total of 340 indicators of learning effectiveness across the 10 instructional techniques. Most indicators received multiple mentions that could be summarized into 30 qualitative categories (Table 3.2). Out of the 30 categories, 19 (flush left) emerged without prompting, while 11 (flush right, italics) required some urging and prompting from the interviewer before students could clearly articulate them. Four categories were common to nearly all techniques: 'critical and analytical thinking'; 'reiterating, refreshing and facilitating in order to remember information'; 'relating and applying knowledge in practical contexts'; and 'learning quality for optimal knowledge acquisition'.

Table 3.2 also highlights how differently the 20 students react to the different instructional techniques. 'Case studies' technique evoked a different cluster of learning effectiveness indicators than did 'individual research projects' or 'group projects' or 'class discussions. Students find values in each instructional technique, but, apart from the four techniques mentioned, the perceptions of the remaining six techniques were quite varied.

Students used themes 'reiterate', 'refresh' and 'facilitate' to describe what they perceive as creating learning effectiveness from the instructional techniques. Majority of students reported that effective knowledge transfer happens when there is reiteration, refreshment and facilitation to remember information. They view their ability to relate and apply knowledge in practical contexts as effective knowledge acquisition and self-improvement. When knowledge acquisition is optimal, quality learning is the result. Students view optimal knowledge acquisition being achieved when detailed information is provided. Sharing of different perspectives and ideas from external experts also contributes to quality learning with optimal knowledge acquisition. Also highlighted in the interviews was the effectiveness of learning through sharing and clarifying of ideas a with group mate. This effect has been reported by Mickaelsen et al. (2002) as the 'developmental exchange' which characterizes team-based learning and other learner-centric pedagogies. Students also rated instructional techniques which provide a greater sense of security as more effective. Students commonly related instructional approaches' learning effectiveness to their flexibility.

Table 3.2 shows 30 qualitative indicator categories summarized from 340 students' explications of learning effectiveness for 10 instructional techniques resulting from interviews with the 20 mainland Chinese undergraduate business students. Table entries are ordered in two ways: first by commonality across multiple instructional techniques and second by whether each indicator emerged spontaneously from students' own thinking or whether indicators required prompting to provoke deeper thinking and intellectual probing of students' conceptualizing.

3.8 Perceived Learning Effectiveness Indicators Common Across Multiple Instructional Techniques for Mainland Chinese Students

3.8.1 Knowledge Acquisition and Quality of Learning

The links between acquiring new learning, application and learning quality were the most frequently mentioned (n = 55). Quality of learning was determined to be providing the students with a way of knowledge acquisition and optimal application for five out of the ten instructional techniques, i.e. 'case study', 'individual research project', 'group project', 'reading textbook' and 'guest speaker': 'You can apply the information that you learned […] useful learning tools in improving my learning and acquisition of knowledge' [s8]. There is a good fit in terms of quality learning with optimal knowledge gain. Their processes highlighted interrelating ideas, developing linkages, consolidating and critical thinking:

I am able to relate and link-up to how it is in the practical context and what I have been taught in the theory lessons. This definitely assists me to learn effectively in the application part of the learning that allows critical thinking [s15].

Effective learning was facilitated when newly acquired cognitive content were analysed, thus enabling knowledge construction in a logical and meaningful manner:

It allows me to apply what has been taught as it makes me understand the contents and allows them to be analyzed thoroughly. So, the process of going through this allows me to apply the knowledge gained [s2].

3.8.2 Relating Knowledge and Applying in Practical Contexts

Relating to and application of new and existing knowledge in a practical manner emerged as a common indicator for seven out of ten instructional techniques: 'case study', 'individual research project', 'group project', 'classroom discussion', 'guest speaker', 'video' and 'classroom presentation'. This indicator emphasizes the practical aspects of knowledge acquirement: 'We are able to learn the practical aspect of the knowledge that is being taught' [s7]. These approaches not only relate to theoretical concepts but also allow in-depth thinking, learning and acquiring of knowledge: 'It does allow me to learn by applying to a practical context. It allows me to think and apply the theoretical knowledge that I have acquired' [s18]. The association of theoretical knowledge with real-life situations enables application of the concepts. There were 54 mentions of associating and making links between factual information via its learning processes by encouraging the students to think thoroughly.

3.8.3 Reiterate and Refresh to Facilitate Remembering the Information

Learning effectiveness was conceptualized as reiterating, refreshing and 'facilitating to remember' as a common indicator 47 times and for 6 out of 10 techniques: case study, individual research project, group project, classroom discussion, guest speaker and video. This indicator reflects students' notions of effectiveness as promoting greater ease in refreshing acquired knowledge and revisiting acquired information: 'I feel it is effective as it makes me understand and refresh the theories by linking up to how it is used in the practical reality' [s20]. The reiteration of information enables them to refresh and relate factual information, thus facilitating links to past experiences and relating them back to the initial situation: 'We do share and link up the past experiences that we have, which allows me to link up to the knowledge and information that is being taught' [s4].

3.8.4 Critical and Analytical Thinking

Critical and analytical thinking emerged 23 times and as a common indicator for 3 out of the 10 techniques: 'case study', 'guest speaker' and 'classroom presentation'. This indicator illustrates learning through thinking and reflection and leads to effective knowledge acquisition. Furthermore, critical and analytical thinking is associated with exploring and analysing issues from different viewpoints, thus amplifying learning:

It allows me to think and analyze the contents much more deeply and also provide opportunities to share and ask questions if in doubt and seek for clarifications as well [s16].

Detailed and in-depth analysis on specific issues using clear reasoning skills demonstrates effective learning: 'It challenges us more and makes us develop what we have learned by reasoning. I can learn by developing from the current knowledge' [s13].

3.9   Indicators Specific to Individual Instructional Strategies

3.9.1   Case Studies

Seven indicators characterized various aspects of learning effectiveness specific to case studies as instructional techniques. 'By using case studies, I am able to think on my own and apply by using whatever knowledge and information that I had been taught and knew previously' [s1]. Through discussions with peers, knowledge acquisition is reinforced: 'It allows different opinions and views – the way others think in a specific manner. Case study requires you to read and apply more. It allows the students to think more and develop more' [s9]. Learning is enhanced by building on the existing and available information. Case studies are easy to access, but it also allows for broadening of one's perspective through exploration of diverse and varying perspectives. When information is fully analysed and then applied, learning can be enhanced through better appreciation of the issues. Application of theories promotes critical thinking as student has to express his own viewpoints and support his argument with factual evidence. The varying opinions and views allow opportunities to test the norms and to challenge the status quo while exploring the limits of the case. Case study contents are easily understood and visualized: 'It allows me to picture the entire issue more easily. It also allows me to think and analyse the learned knowledge with much better understanding' [s20]. The ability to see the picture allows sharing of diverse perspectives between students without losing the case's context.

3.9.2   Individual Research Projects

Seven indicators described learning effectiveness specific to individual research projects. They promote independent and critical thinking and lead to student's acquiring the useful skill of leading research projects independently: 'Research projects provide me an opportunity to think thoroughly with the information obtained and allow me to also express my views on certain specific issues as well' [s11]. Students make their own decisions after exploring various possibilities. This promotes student's thinking and problem-solving skills through allowing students to think thoroughly and to learn by applying the acquired information. There is also an improvement in the quality of spoken and written language skills:

It improves my English very well. When I start to research for the individual research project questions, it forces me to read and write things down, so it improves my English proficiency [s5].

Learning independently through uncomfortable and challenging situations without much external help enables better learning:

This mode literally puts me on a platform to learn independently without much guidance or assistance from my teachers and peers. This helps me to learn much better as it teaches me to be independent, helping me to learn in an uncomfortable and challenging situation [s10].

Research projects also create avenues for students to express their views, to learn through feedback from peers and lecturers, others' experiences and to acquire knowledge from wider perspectives and frameworks of understanding:

By involving the research projects, it makes me refresh and link up to the facts and information that I have been taught. This allows me to share and reiterate the information that I have acquired [s19].

3.9.3   Group Projects

Two indicators described learning effectiveness specific to group projects. Such projects provided students chances to share their ideas and refresh their learning: 'The process of sharing with others makes us learn more by refreshing the learned knowledge' [s2]. This process allows students to learn from others' varied perspectives and provide opportunities to challenge and appreciate others' opinions that surface from these discussions:

It does allow me to share my ideas with group mates and also learn from them as well. At times, I do also disagree with the views proposed by the group mates [s17].

Learning from other people's views and ways of solving problems broadens student's own perspective and is a more effective way of knowledge acquisition than acquiring information from a single channel:

The different views and sharing from different people in the group allows me to learn much more and makes me look at things from different angles of thoughts. This then enhances my effectiveness in my learning [s8].

Furthermore, when students teach each other, it not only allows the weaker student to benefit from the learnings of his peers but also encourages and motivates students to do better:

During the group discussions, I am able to share my views as well as listen to others' views, which allows me to learn more effectively. Sometimes, I do disagree with what my group mates suggest and support my argument with the facts that I have collected [s3].

3.9.4 Classroom Discussions

Five indicators highlighted learning effectiveness of classroom discussions. Knowledge is more easily accessible and relatable when it is linked to past experiences: 'We do share and link up the past experiences that we have, which allows me to link up to the knowledge and information that is being taught' [s20]. Also, understanding and learning are enhanced as information becomes clearer:

Classroom discussions allow me to discuss my viewpoints at the very instant on the topics that are being taught, at the very day, and as such, it increases my awareness of the subject matter concerned [s6].

With the new information acquired, students are able to think broader and deeper, enhancing their understanding and learning. Students experience greater control in the learning process as the discussions allow flexibility in managing the amount of guidance required:

If I need more assistance in a particular aspect of the topic, I can spend more time in clarifying that with the instructor. Alternatively, I can also share and exchange thoughts more, if that is required for diversity in addressing a particular aspect of a topic [s4].

3.9.5 Lectures

Surprisingly, only two indicators surfaced describing learning effectiveness in relation to lectures. When experts directly deliver the instructional content to the students, it allows easy understanding and absorption of information by students:

If the teacher is very experienced, then we can learn a lot. But the teacher must be able to put across the information in a much simpler manner so that the students are able to cope well by relating the contents [s4].

Students are able to feel more certainty and ease when knowing that the information comes from experienced individuals. This allows better concentration and absorption of the student and more content transfer per unit time:

I feel comfortable from the learning pointers shared by the teachers as I could be assured that the information is accurate and reliable. It allows me to have a sense of security and feel at ease [s7].

3.9.6 Reading Textbooks

Nine indicators characterized the quality of learning and knowledge acquisition of reading textbooks which was linked to their ability to learn and acquire more information. It allows specific details to be accessible to students, hence, promoting better understanding of material. Furthermore, reading textbooks assist the students to enhance their language proficiency and vocabulary:

Can improve a lot as by reading, I learn new words and my vocabulary improves, as well. New information can be learned, so I think it improves my learning quality [s2].

Reading textbooks only provides minimal guidance students needed to specifically seek others for the necessary clarifications:

I agree as most of the time there is not much opportunity to share with others what we have read unless we are being specifically asked to do so, which is on very rare occasions [s19].

3.9.7 Videos

Four indicators emerged for the specific learning effectiveness for videos approaches. Knowledge is acquired in a different yet interesting manner, by visualizing and listening:

By seeing the videos, I am able to better understand the concepts that have been taught to me [s15]. When I see the video, I am able to see and appreciate the real operations which happen in the industry.

Most of the video content is useful and relevant. Students are able to discuss the acquired information and challenge differing opinions after viewing the videos, which facilitates deep thinking: 'It does allow us to share our views and thus, allows us to think about certain issues more deeply before coming to a decision' [s19].

3.9.8 Class Presentations

Three indicators were identified in relation to class presentations. Students develop self-confidence with exposure to frequent mandatory presentations:

I am much more comfortable and confident now compared to a year ago as it literally forces me to understand the contents well and thereupon express my points by putting forth my thoughts and ideas [s6].

Post-presentation feedback from peers and instructor helps students to learn from their mistakes. Students also develop skills through answering or clarifying questions posed during the post-presentation sessions. A vibrant, exciting and interesting learning environment is facilitated as disagreements on assumptions and challenges on status quo are negotiated:

It makes me think and understand the contents, so it helps me in my thinking process and understanding. Then, during my digesting of the information, it also allows me to question and clarifies some key issues that come from the contents [s14].

As there has been a lack of opportunities to present and share one's during high school period in China, it helps that students are exposed to chances to present in order to acquire the necessary presentation skills. Presentation is also a process that requires understanding and thinking critically about the contents covered:

It does provide me the challenge to overcome my fear to present in front of a group. Although initially, I found it so difficult to adjust, now I am looking forward to it as I know it allows me to build up my confidence and it also gives me a platform to engage with my other classmates and also learn from the questions that are being posed by the lecturers during the question and answer sessions [s1].

3.9.9 Computerized Learning Assignments

Flexibility was the only indicator reported in support of computerized learning, although it was surfaced four times. Computerized learning allows for flexibility in managing one's time for learning and allowing the student to be an independent learner:

It does allow me to share my opinions freely, more importantly, in my own free time, but I find that the expressing of ideas and thoughts done via the e-platform, by the written mode – I have my own difficulty, and it has its own limitations as well [s11].

Although it offers flexibility, its learning effectiveness was compromised in these students' views:

Although it provides the flexibility of learning at any time, but I find it is not very user-friendly in terms of my learning and acquiring of more knowledge. So, I would say that the quality of my learning is not improved very much via this mode of delivery [s3].

3.10   Discussion and Recommendations

3.10.1   Discussion

On one side the predominant view in the literature states that mainland Chinese students prefer passive-oriented instructional approaches such as lectures, demonstrations, handouts, displays, films and videos. Experimental exercises, case studies, role-playing and simulations belong to participative teaching methods and are thought to be least preferred. Problem-solving and explorative teaching methods employed in the West would not fit with the Confucian-derived preference for rote learning (Thompson and Gui 2000). These claims were challenged by other scholars (Ryan and Slethaug 2010; Rajaram 2010; Littlewood 2009; Ryan and Louie 2007; Rajaram and Bordia 2011, 2013) who caution not to stereotype Chinese learning approaches and describe them as discrete, homogeneous and unchanging. Conversely, in our study four of the commonly used instructional techniques – case study, individual research project, group project and classroom discussions – through self-reports by students describe to be excellent avenues for effective learning in terms of knowledge acquisition for mainland Chinese students. This claim could be further validated by the study by Rajaram and Bordia (2013), where 402 mainland Chinese students from China reported that the active instructional techniques (case studies and group projects) are among the highest rated techniques in terms of perceived learning effectiveness. Furthermore, when the four active and six passive instructional techniques were measured across the cultural dislocation elements (comfort, familiarity and knowledge transfer) both in a combined and individual context, the active instructional techniques were rated highly.

Despite the literature suggesting that mainland Chinese students are rote learners, our study interview results show that repetitive learning approaches may not be their only preferred choice in terms of knowledge acquisition and perceived learning effectiveness. Participants chose case study as their first priority over the other instructional techniques:

I strongly feel that case study approach helps me to gain the practical application experience and links it to the theory concepts that I have been taught. By doing so, it enhances the quality of my learning process […].

Other active techniques that emerged high in terms of perceived learning effectiveness and knowledge acquisition are individual research projects, group projects and class discussions. The perceived effectiveness for the individual research project approach was justified as it made the students apply the information by digesting and analysing the contents to make logical and meaningful deductions: 'In terms of trying to digest and analyse the information obtained, it helps me to be more effective in terms of my learning'; and: 'I agree. It makes me digest the information and then summarise it, which, in a way, improves my understanding of the subject concerned. It also literally forces me to analyse, read and write down my finding'. Students testified that group projects improved the quality of their learning through the process of rationalizing the problem – 'Group projects allow me to share my views and opinions with my group mates and I also listen to their sharing. Thus, I believe that this definitely improves the quality of my learning' – and also learning from the various viewpoints and others' different ways of thinking: 'I personally feel that it is much better than doing it myself because others might have some new ideas and these could be used to improve the quality of my learning'. Classroom discussions enabled students to acquire, learn more easily and increase their awareness by relating to their past experiences: 'We do share and link up the past experiences that we have, which allows me to link up to the knowledge and information that is being taught'. Classroom discussions created an engaging and interesting environment to acquire knowledge:

Classroom discussions allow me to discuss my viewpoints at the very instant on the topics that are being taught, at the very day, and as such, it increases my awareness of the subject matter concerned.

Classroom discussions enabled students to examine issues from a diverse perspective, resonate with past experiences and relate them back to the situational context, accordingly: 'We do share and link up the past experiences that we have, which allows me to link up to the knowledge and information that is being taught'.

However, students expressed concerns and challenges for two passive instructional approaches – reading textbooks and computerized learning. Much letter guidance and minimal face-to-face contact hindered their learning. Moreover, despite them meeting the basic IELTS requirements, their language proficiency was not adequate enough to always understand and appreciate contents delivered through these instructional techniques. Face-to-face learning contexts were generally preferred compared to a self-directed autonomous style of learning. This could be associated with minimal sharing and exchange of views that are achieved through these approaches. Students needed to specifically seek others for the relevant clarifications:

I agree as most of the time there is not much opportunity to share with others what we have read unless we are being specifically asked to do so, which is on very rare occasions.

Students testified that the knowledge acquiring through the computerized learning technique was not productive: 'No, because via online and computerised learning, it eliminates the face-to-face sessions; thus, the information delivered is not very effective'. The students identified several reasons to justify their point, as highlighted in the interviewees' quotes:

I don't think so as there are quite a number of unfamiliarity issues that I need to handle, which I am not too comfortable with. Firstly, as there is no face-to-face contact, I am not able to clarify my enquiries and doubts with the teachers instantly, so this gets me frustrated because I have to express my clarifications in the written form, which I have loads of difficulty in doing due to my proficiency in the English language.

There is also a lot of possibility of misunderstanding the contents.

Problem-solving capabilities are often deserted as students' accomplishments are mostly evaluated through written examinations that may not necessarily be designed to examine holistic competencies or employability skills, beyond academic abilities. Mainland Chinese students may be concrete and pragmatic when evaluating ideas, but they can also suffer from a lack of creativity and possibilities of exploring unfamiliar tasks to be assigned. Group work can work well with mainland Chinese students but may need to be structured differently from those designed for Western students. Scholars (Chan 1997; Ryan and Slethaug 2010; Shi 2006; Clark and Gieve 2006; Yang 2009) described the observations from their studies of Chinese learners as follows: are active; monitor their studies; learn from their mistakes or link to their past experiences as reflections; prefer a student-centred approach to a teacher-centred approach; and are willing to participate in interactive and cooperative learning activities. However, these findings on the shift in learning approaches are reported largely by Chinese learners from China and Hong Kong based rather than from those who are outside their home countries, especially pursuing a cross-cultural Western-based curriculum study. Tang (1996) specifically pointed out that mainland Chinese students will work collaboratively but prefer to do it informally outside of class as part of their learning process. Chinese students are not comfortable in expressing their opinions in public. Their classroom activities and learning process are usually dominated by lectures with limited questioning or discussions. Chinese students' classroom culture discourages active and critical enquiry as they stereotypically behave in accordance with the social expectations of their roles. Although it is rare for them to express their disagreements explicitly to their teachers, they do not accept the teachers' information blindly as well (Shi 2006). Most Chinese students feel that fruitless teaching takes place if they are repeatedly asked in the class to solve a problem by themselves or to express their opinions. They assume that it is not crucial for a learner to have his or her own opinions and thoughts. It could be logically interpreted based on the sociocultural dimension that Chinese students' unwillingness to participate in class can be related to their willingness to submit to authority which could be attributed to the cultural values and norms embedded in behaviours that influence their learning attitudes and behaviours.

3.10.2 Recommendations

We examined the perceived learning effectiveness through a qualitative approach to have a deeper understanding on the cross-cultural learning and teaching issues for these Chinese mainland students pursuing their studies in culturally dislocated context. Overgeneralizing of the use of different instructional techniques emerges as a caution to be noted from the study findings. We recommend the following to be understood well and apply the right instruction for students' effective learning and knowledge acquisition: first, to optimize students' learning, essential characteristics like exposure, the right mix of techniques, addressing comfort and familiarity aspects should converge to maximize module appeal and effectiveness. Second, students' preference of teaching techniques may not necessarily facilitate them to acquire knowledge optimally and effectively. For example, students may be comfortable being taught with a particular technique, but that does not necessarily mean it facilitates effective learning. Third, instructors must be mindful, comprehend the diverse learners' characteristics and apply correct mix of teaching techniques based on learners' prior knowledge; experience; educational, family and social background; cultural exposure; beliefs; values; maturity level; and type of learners (auditory, visual or kinaesthetic). Fourth, the class size and the style of delivery approach (e.g. seminar style, workshop, lecture style with either large class size or small class size) need to be given due consideration. This influences the level of interactiveness and the manner in which the teaching approaches are operationalized. Fifth, the traditional one-way lecture style should be shifted to be more participative and interactive to encourage participation that allows students to be engaged and learn effectively with critical and reflective thinking. Finally, it is essential to understand the composition of these mainland Chinese students in terms of their varying demographics like age group, gender, type of business programmes, provinces where students pursued their prior education, social background and any prior Western exposure, thus enabling instructors to deliver high-quality, practical business education to students from a variety of cultures. Mainland Chinese students do not appear to be rote-learners when responding to questionnaires about their educational preferences. Literature shows that it is a mistake to assume mainland Chinese students as rote-learners. Memorizing and understanding are not separate parts but are one connected and interlocking procedure. Mainland Chinese students rely on memorization as part of the learning process. The Chinese system of learning is to become well-versed with the text, to comprehend it, to reflect on it and then to question it. There is a cross-difference in the learning of Western and Chinese students. Western students largely view understanding as a rapid insight, while Chinese students view comprehending of concepts as a lengthy process that entails substantial mental effort. All 20 participants reported a change in their preference for teaching approach since their exposure to Western-based education, but, more importantly, all 20 also agreed that they preferred a less guided and structured style of delivery. Case studies are tied with lectures as students' single-most preferred choice for effective knowledge acquisition – a new finding for curriculum developers and classroom instructors.

References

Agar, M. (1996). *Language shock: Understanding the culture conversation*. New York: Harper Paperbacks.

Ballard, B., & Clanchy, J. (1991). *Teaching students from overseas: A brief guide for lecturers and supervisors*. Melbourne: Longman. Cheshire.

Biggs, J. (1994). Asian learners through western eyes: An astigmatic paradox. *Australian and New Zealand Journal of Vocational Educational Research, 2*(2), 40–63.

Biggs, J. (1996). Western misperceptions of the Confucian heritage learning culture. In D. Watkins & J. Biggs (Eds.), *The Chinese learner: Cultural, psychological, and contextual influences* (pp. 45–67). Hong Kong: Comparative Education Research Centre.

Bodycott, P. (2009). Choosing a higher education study abroad destination: What mainland Chinese parents and students rate as important. *Journal of Research in International Education, 8*(3), 349–373.

Bohm, A., Davis, D., Mergers, D., & Pearce, D. (2002). *Global student mobility 2025: Forecasts of the global demand for international higher education.* Sydney: IDP Education Australia.

Bu, N., & Mitchell, V. F. (1992). Developing the PRC's managers: How can Western experts to be more helpful? *Journal of Management Development, 2*(11), 42–53.

Chan, S. (1997). Migration, cultural identity and assimilation effects on entrepreneurship for the overseas Chinese in Britain. *Asia Pacific Business Review, 3*(4), Summer), 211–222.

Chan, S. (1999). The Chinese learner – A question of style. *Education & Training, 41*(6/7), 294–304.

Chan, D. W., & Drover, G. (1997). Teaching and learning for overseas students: The Hong Kong connection. In D. McNamara & R. Harris (Eds.), *Overseas students in higher education* (pp. 46–61). London: Routledge.

Chan, C. K., & Rao, N. (2009). *Revisiting the Chinese learner: Changing education, changing context.* Springer and the Comparative Education Research Centre, University of Hong Kong.

Chalmers, D., & Volet, S. (1997). Common misconceptions about students from South-East Asia studying in Australia. *Higher Education Research and Development, 16*(1), 87–98.

Cheng, M. H. M., & Wan, Z. H. (2016). Unpacking the paradox of Chinese science learners: Insights from research into Asian Chinese school students' attitudes towards learning science, science learning strategies, and scientific epistemological views. *Studies in Science Education, 52*(1), 29–62.

Chi, X., Liu, J., & Bai, Y. (2017). College environment, student involvement, and intellectual development: evidence in China. *Higher Education, 74*(1), 81–99.

Choo, K. L. (2007). The implications of introducing critical management education to Chinese students studying in UK business schools: Some empirical evidence. *Journal of Further & Higher Education, 31*(2), 145–158. https://doi.org/10.1080/03098770701267614

Clark, R., & Gieve, S. N. (2006). On the discursive construction of the Chinese learner. *Language, Culture and Curriculum, 19*(1), 54–73.

Coverdale-Jones, T. (2006). Afterword: The Chinese learner in perspective. *Language, Culture, and Curriculum, 19*(1), 148–153.

Coverdale-Jones, T., & Rastall, P. (Eds.). (2009). *Internationalizing the University: The Chinese context.* Houndmills: Palgrave Macmillian.

Coverdale-Jones, T., & Rastall, P. (2009). *Internationalising the university: The Chinese context.* London: Palgrave Macmillan.

Dunlosky, J., Rawson, K. A., Marsh, E. J., Nathan, M. J., & Willingham, D. T. (2013). Improving students' learning with effective techniques: Promising directions from cognitive and educational psychology. *Associations for Psychological Science, 14*(1), 4058.

Felder, R. M., & Silverman, L. K. (1998). Learning and teaching styles in engineering education. *Engineering Education, 78,* 674–681.

Felder, R. M., & Spurlin, J. (2005). Reliability and validity of the index of learning styles: A meta-analysis. *International Journal of Engineering Education, 21*(1), 103–112.

Frontczak, N. (1990). The role of learning styles in marketing education. In J. Doutt & G. Mckinnon (Eds.), *Proceedings of the Western marketing educators' association* (pp. 57–62). Las Vegas: Western Marketing Educators' Association.

Frontczak, N. (1999). Students evaluation of an experiential learning technique: The marketing plan assignment. In M. Curren & K. Harich (Eds.), *Proceedings of the Western Marketing Educators' Association.* Palm Springs: Western Marketing Educators' Association.

Greake, J., & Maingard, C. (1999). NESB postgraduate students as a new university: Plus ca change, plus c'est la meme chose. In Y. Ryan & O. Zuber-Skerritt (Eds.), *Supervising post-*

graduates from non-English speaking backgrounds (pp. 40–60). Buckingham: The Society for Research into Higher Education and Open University Press.

Gu, Q. (2005). 'Enjoy loneliness' – Understanding Chinese learners' voices. *Humanising Language Teaching, 7*, at www.hltmag.co.uk

Gu, Q., & Maley, A. (2008). Changing places: A study of Chinese students in the UK. *Language and Intercultural Communication, 8*, 224–245.

Gu, Q., & Schweisfurth, M. (2006). Who adapts? Beyond cultural models of 'the' Chinese learner. *Language, Culture and Curriculum, 19*, 74–89.

Hammond, S., & Gao, H. (2002). Pan Gu's paradigm: Chinese education's return to holistic communication in learning. In X. Lu, W. Jia, & R. Heisey (Eds.), *Chinese communication studies: Contexts and comparisons* (pp. 227–244). Westport: Ablex.

Hellmundt, S. (2001, December). *The Internationalisation of the Tertiary curriculum: Strategies to link critical theory and intercultural understandings.* Paper presented at the Australian Association for Research in Education Conference, Fremantle.

Hill, C. E., Hess, S. A., Knox, S., Ladany, N., Thompson, B. J., & Williams, E. N. (2005). Consensual qualitative research: An update. *Journal of Counseling Psychology, 52*(2), 196–205.

Holland, R. P. (1989). Learner characteristics and learner performance: Implications for instructional placement decision. In B. J. R. Shade (Ed.), *Culture, style and the educative process* (pp. 167–183). Springfield: Charles C. Thomas Publisher.

Jarrah, F. (1998). New courses will target transition to university. *China Morning Post, 23*, 28.

Jin, L., & Cortazzi, M. (2006). Changing practices in Chinese cultures of learning, language. *Culture and Curriculum, 1*(1), 5–20.

Jones, J. (1999). From silence to talk: Cross cultural ideas on students' participation in academic group discussion. *English for Specific Purposes, 18*(3), 243–259.

Kemp, L. (2010). Teaching & learning for international students in a learning community: Creating, sharing and building knowledge. *Journal of Scholarly Teaching, 5*, 64–74.

Kirkpatrick, A. (2004). Some thoughts on the Chinese learner and the teaching of writing. *The East Asian Learner: An Academic Journal for Teachers and Researchers, 1*(1), 6–15.

Kolb, D. (1984). *Experiential learning*. Englewood Cliffs: Prentice-Hall.

Kolb, D. A., & Fry, R. (1975). Toward an applied theory of experiential learning. In C. Cooper (Ed.), *Studies of group process* (pp. 33–57). New York: Wiley.

Kumaravadivelu, B. (2003). Problematizing cultural stereotypes in TESOL. *TESOL Quarterly, 37*(4), 709–719.

Ladd, P. D., & Ruby, R. (1999). Learning style and adjustment issues of international students. *Journal of Education for Business, 74*(6), 363–367.

Lee, W. O. (1996). The cultural context for Chinese learners: Conceptions of learning in the Confucian tradition. *The Chinese learner: Cultural, psychological and contextual influences, 34*, 63–67.

Li, J. (2001). Chinese conceptualization of learning. *Ethos, 29*(2), 111–137.

Littlewood, W. (2001). Students' attitudes to classroom English learning: A cross-cultural study. *Language Teaching Research, 5*(1), 3–28.

Littlewood, W. (2009). Participation-based pedagogy: How congruent is it with Chinese cultures of learning? In P. Cheng & J. X. Yan (Eds.), *Cultural identity and language anxiety* (pp. 179–202). Guilin: Guangxi Normal University Press.

Liu, S. (2006). Developing China's future managers: Learning from the west? *Education & Training, 48*(1), 6–14. https://doi.org/10.1108/00400910600645699

Lindsay, C. P., & Dempsey, B. L. (1983). Ten painfully learned lessons about working in China: The insights of two American behavioural scientists. *The Journal of Applied Behavioral Science, 19*(3), 265–276.

Louie, K. (2005). Gathering cultural knowledge: Used or use with care? In J. Carroll & J. Ryan (Eds.), *Teaching international students: Improving learning for all* (pp. 17–25). London: Routledge Falmer.

Martinsons, M. G., & Martinsons, A. B. (1996). Conquering cultural constraints to cultivate Chinese management creativity and innovation. *Journal of Management Development, 15*(9), 18–35.

McCarthy, B. (1980). *The 4MAT system teaching to learning styles with right/left mode techniques.* Barrington: Excel.

McNaught, C. (2012). SOTL at cultural interfaces: Exploring nuance in learning designs at a Chinese university. *International Journal for the Scholarship of Teaching and Learning, 6*(2), 1–7.

Merrison, M., Sweeney, A., & Heffernan, T. (2003). Learning styles of a campus and off-campus marketing students: The challenge for marketing educators. *Journal of Marketing Education, 25*(3), 208–217.

Mickaelsen, L. K., Knight, A. B., & Fink, D. (2002). *Team-based learning: A transformational use of small groups.* Westport: Prager.

Minkler, M., & Biller, R. (1979). Role shock: A tool for conceptualizing stresses accompanying disruptive role transitions. *Human Relations, 32*, 125–140.

Nakamura, H. (1964). *Ways of thinking of eastern people.* Honolulu, HI: University of Hawaii Press.

Nanyang Technological University, Nanyang MBA-Admissions & Fees – Fees & Financial Aid. Retrieved September 25, 2017., from http://www.nbs.ntu.edu.sg/Programmes/Graduate/NanyangMBA/admission/Pages/Fees-and-Financial-Aid.aspx

National University of Singapore, MBA – Tuition Fees & Payment Schedules. Retrieved September 25, 2017., from http://mba.nus.edu/en-SG/fees-finances/tuition-fees/

Ninnes, P., Aitchison, C., & Kalos, S. (1999). Challenges to stereotypes of international students' prior educational experience: Undergraduate education in India. *Higher Education Research & Development, 18*(3), 323–342.

Phan, L. H. (2006). Plagiarism and overseas students: Stereotypes again? *ELT Journal, 60*(1), 76–78.

Pun, A. S. L. (1989a). Developing managers internationally: culture free or culture bound, symposium presentation at the Conference on International Personnel and Human Resource Management, Hong Kong, 13 December.

Pun, A. S. L. (1989b). *Action learning in the Chinese culture: Possibility or pitfall.* In Manchester International Human Resource Development Conference, Manchester.

Rajaram, K. (2010). *Culture Clash. Teaching western-based business education to mainland Chinese students in Singapore,* Thesis (PhD) (assessed and graded distinction by two prominent and well-established research scholars), University of South Australia.

Rajaram, K., & Bordia, S. (2011). Culture clash: Teaching Western-based management education to mainland Chinese students in Singapore. *Journal of International Education in Business, 4*(1), 63–83.

Rajaram, K., & Bordia, S. (2013). East versus West: Effectiveness of knowledge acquisition and impact of cultural dislocation issues for mainland Chinese students across ten commonly used instructional techniques. *International Journal for the Scholarship of Teaching and Learning, 7*(1), 1–21.

Rajaram, K., & Collins, J. B. (2013). Qualitative identification of learning effectiveness indicators among mainland Chinese students in culturally dislocated study environments. *Journal of International Education in Business, 6*(2), 179–199.

Redding, G. (1990). *The spirit of Chinese capitalism* (Vol. 22). Walter de Gruyter.

Rodrigues, C. A. (2004). The importance level of ten teaching/learning techniques as rated by university business students and instructors. *Journal of Management Development, 23*(2), 169–182. https://doi.org/10.1108/02621710410517256

Ryan, J., & Hellmundt, S. (2005). Maximising international students' cultural capital. In J. Carroll & J. Ryan (Eds.), *Teaching international students: Improving learning for all* (pp. 13–16). Abingdon, United Kingdom: Routledge.

Ryan, J., & Louie, K. (2005). Dichotomy or complexity: Problematising concepts of scholarship and learning. In M. Mason (Ed.), *Proceedings of the critical thinking and learning: Values, concepts and issues, 34th annual conference of the philosophy of education society of Australia* (pp. 401–411). Hong Kong: Philosophy of Education Socitey of Australia.

Ryan, J., & Louie, K. (2007). False dichotomy? 'Western' and 'Confucian' concepts of scholarship and learning. *Educational Philosophy and Theory, 39*(4), 404–417.

Ryan, J., & Slethaug, G. (2010). *International Education and the Chinese learner* (pp. 13–89). Hong Kong: Hong Kong University Press.

Saravanamuthu, K., & Yap, C. (2014). Pedagogy to empower Chinese learners to adapt to western learning circumstances: A longitudinal case-study. *Cambridge Journal of Education, 44*(3), 361–384. https://doi.org/10.1080/0305764X.2014.914154

Shi, L. (2006). The successors to Confucianism or a new generation? A questionnaire study on Chinese students' culture of learning English. *Language, Culture and Curriculum, 19*(1), 122–147.

Singapore Management University, Lee Kong Chian School of Business, Master of Business Administration – Admissions – Programme Fees. Retrieved September 25, 2017., from https://business.smu.edu.sg/mba/admissions/programme-fees

Tang, C. (1996). Collaborative learning: The latent dimension in Chinese students' learning. In D. A. Watkins & J. B. Biggs (Eds.), *The Chinese learner: Cultural, psychological, and contextual influences* (pp. 183–204). CERC and ACER: Hong Kong.

Thompson, E. R., & Gui, Q. (2000, September/October). The appropriateness of using Hong Kong to make inferences about business students in mainland China, Journal of Education for Business, 48–56.

Tom, G., & Calvert, S. (1983). Learning style as a predictor of student performance and instructor evaluations. *Journal of Marketing Education, 5*(2), 14–17.

Tsang, E. W. K. (2001). Adjustment of mainland Chinese academics and students to Singapore. *International Journal of International Relations, 25*, 347–372.

Turner, Y. (2006). Chinese students in U.K. business school: Hearing the student voice in reflective teaching and learning. *Higher Education Quarterly, 60*, 27–51.

Universitas 21. The leading global network of research universites for the 21st century. Retrieved September 25, 2017., from http://www.universitas21.com/article/projects/details/153/executive-summary-and-full-2017-report

University of Cambridge, Judge Business School, MBA-Fees & Funding. Retrieved September 25, 2017., from https://www.jbs.cam.ac.uk/programmes/mba/fees-funding/

University of Oxford, SAID Business School, Oxford MBA – Fees & Funding. Retrieved September 25, 2017., from https://www.sbs.ox.ac.uk/programmes/degrees/mba/fees-funding

Watkins, H. A., Moore, C. A., Goodenough, D. R., & Cox, P. W. (1977). Field-dependent and field-independent cognitive styles and their educational implications. *Review of Educational Research, 47*(1), 1–64. https://doi.org/10.3102/00346543047001001

Watkins, D., & Biggs, J. (Eds.). (1996). *The Chinese learner: Cultural, psychological and contextual influences*. Hong Kong/Melbourne: Comparative Education Research Centre, the University of Hong Kong/The Australian Council for Educational Research Ltd..

Watkins, D., & Biggs, J. (Eds.). (2001). *Teaching the Chinese learner: Psychological and pedagogical perspectives*. Hong Kong/Melbourne: Comparative Education Research Centre, the University of Hong Kong/The Australian Council for Educational Research Ltd..

Wen, W.-P., & Clément, R. (2003). A Chinese conceptualisation of willingness to communicate in ESL. *Language Culture and Curriculum, 16*(1), 18–38.

Wharton, University of Pennsylvania, MBA Program – Tuition and Financial Aid Information. Retrieved September 25, 2017., from https://mba.wharton.upenn.edu/tuition-financial-aid/

Yang, Z. (2009). The effect of mother tongue transfer on English writing. *Teaching and Management, 11*(3), 16–20.

Yao, X. (2000). *An introduction to Confucianism*. Cambridge University Press.

Zhang, L. (2006). Preferred teaching styles and modes of thinking among university students in mainland China. *Thinking Skills and Creativity, 1*, 95–107.

Zhou, Y., Jindal-Snape, D., Topping, K., & Todman, J. (2008). Theoretical models of culture shock and adaptation in international students in higher education. *Studies in Higher Education, 33*, 63–75.

Chapter 4
Learning Styles of Mainland Chinese

The chapter presents the academic evidence addressing the educational perspectives in relation to mainland Chinese students. It focuses on five key aspects—namely, (a) evaluating principles of learning styles which contributes to optimal learning effectiveness and perceived learning effectiveness; (b) the stereotypes of the learning styles of mainland Chinese students; (c) changes and shifts in Chinese culture of learning; (d) practical challenges and implications in the pursuit of Western-based education and (e) the deliverables of Western-based education for mainland Chinese students and the different types of instructional approaches.

This chapter first presents the general context of the education system in Singapore, thereafter addressing the learning style theories, followed by explicitly identifying the learning behavioural styles of mainland Chinese students. The individual aspects of the mainland Chinese students' learning styles are further examined: (a) emphasis on the perception of the concrete; (b) practicality as a central focus; (c) rote versus repetition style of learning; (d) classroom behaviour; (e) medium of instruction and (f) analysis and identification of gaps in current knowledge. Next, the evolving changes in the Chinese culture of learning are investigated. Thereupon, the challenges and adaptability issues on the pursuit of a Western-based education versus the Chinese-oriented education are discussed. The discussion is further extended to examine the applicability of Western concepts to China. Vital aspects related to the learning styles of mainland Chinese students, namely, (a) students' participation in classroom activities; (b) use of typical management training techniques and (c) teacher-student relationship and active versus passive teaching

This chapter is improved from Rajaram, K. (2013). Followers of Confucianism or a New Generation? Learning culture of mainland Chinese: In pursuit of western based business education away from mainland China. *International Journal of Teaching & Learning in Higher Education,* 25(3), 369–377 and Rajaram, K., & Bordia, S. (2011). Culture Clash: Teaching Western-based management education to mainland Chinese students in Singapore. *Journal of International Education in Business,* 4(1), 63–83.

approaches, are also explored and debated. In this chapter the two key theoretical frameworks for the context of learning effectiveness and instructional approaches—namely, (a) Morey and Frangioso's (1988) six effective learning principles and (b) four active (A-like) and six passive (P-like) instructional techniques identified by Rodrigues (2004)—are discussed. This primes to the next section on the identification of the gaps in current knowledge. Lastly, the key pointers discussed are reinforced.

4.1   Singapore's Education System

Singapore government's philosophy is to create a high-quality life for all Singaporeans through maximization of economic growth, political stability and being inclusive as a multiracial society (Civil Service College 2017). Singapore government is well aware of evolving challenges of the twenty-first century, having recognized the growing impact of globalization, explicitly, enhancing national economic competiveness in the global marketplace and nurturing social cohesion in the city-state.

Low (2001) describes Singapore government's position in education, suggesting that 'the role of education and human resource development in economic growth and development is unequivocal and, in the Singapore context, public policies and strategies in education, training and manpower development serves as a leading edge that have paid off handsomely in the economic and social-political success it enjoys today' (p. 305).

Education forms a vital part of Singapore's public policy agenda. As the progress of the country is closely linked to its economic development and racial harmony, the local government must consciously and continuously align and transform the education system to the changing needs of the economy. The Singapore government is committed on improving the education and training system to stay competitive and relevant to the changes in global economy. To uphold Singapore's competitiveness in the global economy, the economic committee advocates the design of education is to optimize each of the individual's potential enhancing creativity and flexibility in their thinking skills (Ministry of Trade and Industry, Singapore 1986). A report by the economic planning committee in 1991 emphasizes the importance of creativity and innovation (Ministry of Trade and Industry, Singapore 1991). This translates in action to have schools and universities to be called upon to play a key role in bringing about this change (Lee 1996). The proposed reforms in the education system and the introduction of TSLN's (Thinking Schools, Learning Nation) vision, coupled with the implementation of the SEM (Singapore Educational Model), are part and parcel of the larger social re-engineering project initiated by the government to strengthen its socio-economic position in the regional, global and market context. In 2011, the Ministry of Education of Singapore took on a vision of 'student-centric, value-driven' education for Singapore where everyone in the community should work together to develop every student into an engaged learner. The ministry also introduced a reform: 'many paths, new possibilities'. It is calling for the education policy to be more inclusive that provides better access and wider opportunities for Singapore students, to prepare them for the future (Ministry of Education 2017).

The transformation is not just on the K-12 and tertiary education, it even includes upgrading of the adult workforce. The recent governmental effort includes Workforce Singapore (WSG) and SkillsFuture (SSG) Singapore, where both are statutory board under the Ministry of Education (MOE). WSG was set up to oversee the transformation of the local workforce and industry to meet ongoing economic challenges, and SSG's goal is to drive and coordinate the implementation of the national SkillsFuture movement, promote a culture and holistic system of lifelong learning through the pursuit of skills mastery and strengthen the ecosystem of quality education and training in Singapore (SkillsFuture Singapore and Workforce Singapore 2017).

4.2   Cultural Implications on Learning and the Education System: International Students in Western-Based Education

Some of the challenges faced by international students in pursuing a Western education include language and communication, learning styles and previous experiences (Baron and Strout Dapaz 2001). However, the primary challenge remains in the divergence of second language ability that may possibly place an international student at a disadvantage (Atkins and Ashcroft 2004).

Common patterns of learning are seen on individuals within a culture (Oxford and Anderson 1995). As such, in our case, mainland Chinese students are expected to be displaying largely the common patterns and trend in terms of their learning. Learners from the West (e.g. United States) are largely influenced by the individualist culture which shapes their learning culture. Hence, the students from the West are open to challenges from authority, i.e. knowledge and instructors as subject matter experts. These students are accustomed to verbal communication in their learning process (Cagiltay and Bichelmeyer 2000), and their preference is inclined towards experiential or kinesthetic learning rather than rote memory learning. Chinese learners display distinctive differences from Western learners as they accept knowledge without much questioning and reply on rote memory as they display traits such as being compliant, passive and obedient. These Chinese students tend to lack in critical thinking skills (Biggs 1991; Chen 2009; Reid 1987) and are sturdy visual and auditory learners (Zhang and Evans 2013).

Cultural differences can also affect communication, for instance, the variance in non-verbal signs in different cultures (Wayman 1984; Ball and Mahony 1987; Garcha and Russell 1993; Natowitz 1995). A lack of awareness of local idioms and slangs also leads to cultural misunderstandings (Lacina 2002).

Cultural differences present itself in educational differences that cause learning styles across educational systems to vary (Atkins and Ashcroft 2004). In some countries, students gain knowledge through imitation and observation, while in others, for example in North America and United Kingdom, critical thinking skills and independent research emerge as the main focus of students' development (Wayman 1984; Garcha and Russell 1993; Notowitz 1995; Kamhi-Stein 1998). Group achievement may be considered far more important than individual accomplishment in certain other cultures (Wayman 1984; Garcha and Russell 1993). Cultural conditioning is reflected in the learning style preferences of students (De Vita 2002); international students tend to exhibit a broader range of learning styles than local students, which in turn can put them at a disadvantage when exposed to an educational environment biased towards the home student, i.e. Singapore, Western-based learning styles.

In most societies, education systems are political and function as an instrument to facilitate the younger generation's amalgamation into existing social systems where China qualifies as one of these societies. The first lesson that many mainland Chinese students learn during their early days of school is obedience to authorities through observation of proper codes of conduct, including sitting posture, behaviour and responses towards their teachers. This approach of restrictive education system conforms to the societal norm, demands obedience and urges students to follow norms or instructions. An individual's development is hence interrelated with social involvement. The underlying principle of education must be viewed not so much as an encouragement to promote individuality; rather, it is to make individuals apprehend that they are part of a collectivity; thus, they have to conform to the norms and values of the collective. The teacher-centred education has created a strong dependence on expert knowledge that represses initiative and creativity on the part of learners (Liu 2006). This educational influence shapes the behaviour and work values of an individual and makes an impact on the individual's adult life. It is not surprising that the behaviour of a mainland Chinese is often described as lacking initiative, dependent on higher authorities in decision-making and unwilling to take on responsibilities. Such behaviour will not assist the students in preparing themselves to the rapid changes taking place in Chinese enterprises, let alone competing at an international level in this globalized world.

To influence and shift the mindset, outlook, attitudes and behaviour of Chinese employees, Chinese state-owned enterprises can learn from the experiences of foreign-invested companies. Besides the efforts of individual organizations to train and nurture their employees, teachers who facilitate management modules can also contribute through facilitating effective learning processes to transform these students to become effective leaders. The way forward is to inquire and examine the existing models of management education and explore new possibilities for teaching and learning.

Chinese students are placed in the limelight due to rapid increases in the numbers studying in Anglophone countries such as Australia, the United States, Canada and the United Kingdom (Clarke and Gieve 2006; Coverdale-Jones and Rastall 2009; Rajaram 2010; Ryan and Slethaug 2010; Shi 2006; Turner 2006; Watkins and Biggs 2001). Despite rapid internationalization of education and workplaces, the views of the Western world on Chinese learners remain largely based on stereotypical and outmoded assumptions. Ryan and Slethaug (2010) suggested:

> Such narrow thinking and lack of attention to the very real challenges and dilemmas that can confront those working on both sides of these systems of cultural practice can cause misunderstandings and inhibit opportunities for the development of innovative, creative and generative ways of teaching and learning. (p. 37)

Offering quality education for international students entails a good understanding of the cultural aspects and effective methods of knowledge transfer which are integrated with optimal learning processes (Rajaram and Bordia 2011). The shift of Chinese learning culture due to rapidly changing Chinese political, social and cultural environment to acclimatize itself to the new globalized and highly technology-dependent world remains to be further examined at a much deeper level.

Researchers are still trying to understand the influence of culture on Chinese students' reluctance on participating in class (e.g. Yu 2016; Chris and Arthur 2014). With the increase in popularity of distance learning due to the increase in Internet access, research interests are also shifting towards the influence of culture on Chinese students' online classroom behaviour (Zhang 2013; Tian and Qian 2014). This is illustrated through a study done by Zhang (2013) on online US education environment on how the Confucian heritage culture affects students coming from mainland China, Taiwan and Hong Kong. She finds that the Confucian culture, especially the idea of power distance, affects these students' online learning. Students' respect for authority, in this case the instructors, prevented them from seeking help from the instructors, instead, they turned to their peers for help.

4.3 Learning-Style Theory: Theory of Learning Effectiveness—Morey and Frangioso's (1988) Six Effective Learning Principles

From the literature, we could conclude that the term 'learning styles' is largely used inaccurately and often interchangeably with terms such as 'learning modalities' and 'cognitive' styles. Students do not learn in the same manner as they come with different talents and strengths, where these strengths determine each student's learning style. These individual learning preferences, strengths or talents are termed as learning modalities (a combination of perception and memory). The learning modality theory advocates that learners have a preference in how they receive and store information through one or more of the sensory modalities such as auditory, visual, kinesthetic and tactile. Cognitive styles are resonated to be biologically based, hence relatively stable. There are numerous overlapping and opposing theories. Despite authors using varying terminologies to label them, the two broadly accepted cognitive styles are the wholist-analytic dimension and verbal-imagery dimension (Riding and Read 1996). Imagers incline to think pictorially, whereas verbalizers epitomize information in words form. Each of these two groups of learners best learns from their own ways, i.e. imagers learn best from information represented in the pictorial, while verbalizers learn best from text and words. Next, wholists views information from a global, top-down perspective, whereas analytics cluster information into its smaller parts. Wholists are inclined towards 'breadth-first' structure where a holistic view of a topic is furnished before details are introduced, whereas analytics prefer a depth-first approach where each topic is examined in full before moving on to the next one.

Since the mid-1970s, numerous theories and opinions on learning styles have evolved where there has been a rising growth on its research in terms of its definitions and dimensions (Wintergerst et al. 2003; Oxford and Anderson 1995), but there is little agreement on the exact definition of the learning styles. Some scholars reiterate the concept of multiple intelligence, while others subscribe to the sensory pathways or working memory in deciding how students learn. The lack of academic clarity in this field has resulted in no universally accepted model of learning styles. However, a number of scholars have attempted to identify the most influential models of learning styles (Coffield et al. 2004) and break down the processes and concepts that underlie the term, learning styles. Although acknowledging the possibility of oversimplifying a complex subject, learning styles may be categorized into three interrelated elements (Cassidy 2004): (a) instructional preferences, predispositions towards learning in a particular manner, for example, independently or collaboratively or in a specific setting (time of the day or environment, for instance); (b) learning strategies, adaptive responses to learning specific subject matter in a particular context; and (c) information processing, typical modes of perceiving, storing and organizing information, for example, pictorially or verbally.

Learning styles assist in describing an individual's way of processing information (Naserieh and Sarab 2013) and act as catalyst through which learners deal with their learning challenges (Barmeyer 2004). Teachers' awareness of students' learning styles on their learning process is crucial (Sun and Teng 2017). If the teachers are aware of learners' individual differences, they tend to align their instructional strategies to meet the learners' individual needs (Sadeghi et al. 2012). Individual differences could be largely related to culture and learning aptitude and demographic variables such as age and gender (Ehrman et al. 2003). Extending further, it could be further categorized into three areas, namely, learning strategies, learning styles and affective elements such as interaction between learners and instructors, anxiety, empathy, self-efficacy and motivation (Ehrman et al. 2003). Learning strategy choices is significantly influenced by learning styles that assist to inform their preferences to instructors who are able to manage learners' anxiety (Ehrman and Oxford 1990). The accurate identification of a learner's learning style assists instructors to guide learners by designing and adopting instructional strategies that meet the learners' needs (Huang et al. 2018). Consequently, the lack of awareness of learners' styles will possibly have the instructors adopt inappropriate instructional techniques that affect students' enthusiasm and learning motivations that negatively limit their learning outcomes (Oxford 2003).

Learning style refers to the elements of individual differences that are imperative to knowledge and skills acquirement (Shade 1989a). People sharing a common historical and geographical background generally share a similar distinctive learning style as they are required to adapt to a unique set of environmental expectations together (Shade 1989b). The distinctive learning style of a nation and/or culture is reflected through the institutionalization and reinforcement via its child-rearing practices and education systems.

There are many aspects of individual differences that shape the way in which one acquires knowledge and skills. Although there are various learning-style theories, the differences in the learning-style characteristics among people from different nations have not been sufficiently researched on. In their search for the underlying developmental causes of variations in individual learning styles, Berry (1976), Witkin and Berry (1975) and Witkin et al. (1962) came across one of the most influential explanations for the emergence of cross-national differences in learning style. In accordance to this conceptualization, individuals' learning style differs along a field-dependence and/or field-independence dimension. Communities that rely on individuals' entrepreneurial abilities for survival, such as hunting, tend to adopt the field-independence approach, while those that depend on cooperative means of production, such as agriculture, tend to adopt a field-dependence style.

> Individuals preferring a field-independent style are characterized by easiness in abstracting important information from a distracting background, and a lack of interest in the opinions of external referents ... In contrast, individuals possessing a field-dependent style are characterized by a difficulty to perceptually differentiate a figure from its background and a willingness to be informed by the opinions of external referents. [Rodrigues 2004, pp. 610–11]

Studies have examined the impact of national culture on student learning. However, no research was found to examine the influence of national culture (i.e. at a deeper level, it would be the subcultures of provinces or cluster of provinces) on the students' preferences on the instructional techniques adopted in a Western-based education in terms of achieving optimal perceived learning effectiveness.

There has been no single set of widely recognized and empirically validated criteria to evaluate the perceived effectiveness of instructional methodologies on teaching mainland Chinese students in a Western-based education. Although there are many isolated studies performed, no integrated framework has been developed yet.

Contemporary organizations consist largely of knowledge workers creating knowledge and innovation. It is vital to adopt and train these students using the correct mix of instructional techniques to enable them to acquire knowledge optimally. In fact, if students are able to be taught more effectively, they are able to acquire knowledge more efficiently and do much better in achieving the intended learning outcomes. In today's globally competitive and fast-evolving education field, having the students learn effectively is a strategic advantage. Students learn in varying ways, by visualizing and hearing; reflecting and acting; reasoning rationally and instinctively; memorizing and visualizing and illustrating analogies and constructing mathematical frameworks. The adoption of instructional approaches varies; for example, some instructors use lectures, others use demonstrations or discussions, some focus on principles and others on applications and understanding, and others emphasize on memorizing. Felder and Silverman (1998) advocate that a students' learning depends on (a) native ability, (b) prior preparation and (c) compatibility of the students' learning style inline to the instructor's teaching approach. Mismatches potentially exist between the common learning styles of mainland Chinese students and how contents are preferably delivered to them. As a consequence of mismatch, students may easily become bored and inattentive in class, do poorly on tests, get discouraged by the curriculum and in some cases, change to other courses or drop out of the institute. Majority of the instructional components correlate to one another. A student who favours intuitive over sensory perception, for example, would respond well to an instructor who emphasizes concepts (abstract content) rather than facts (concrete content): a student who favours visual perception would be most comfortable with an instructor who uses charts, pictures and films (Felder and Silverman 1998).

A theoretical framework consisting of six effective learning principles that leads to effective learning was developed by Morey and Frangioso (1998). The framework largely uses two principles of understanding: 'mental models or paradigms' and 'systems thinking—variation'. It also comprises two principles of skills: 'ability to challenge assumptions' and 'listen to understand'. Further are two principles of processes: 'Learning cycle: observe, assess, design, implement (OADI) cycle' and 'teach others'. Learning can still occur in the absence of the six principles, however, if the six principles are practiced and mastered, learning has occurred most effectively. Figure 4.1 shows Morey and Frangioso's (1998) model represented in a diagrammatic form.

4.3.1 Understanding

First, the two principles for understanding involve the aptitude of a learner to acquire information in an effective way within the sphere of comfort and expediency. Effective learning is the ability to understand an immense amount of information in

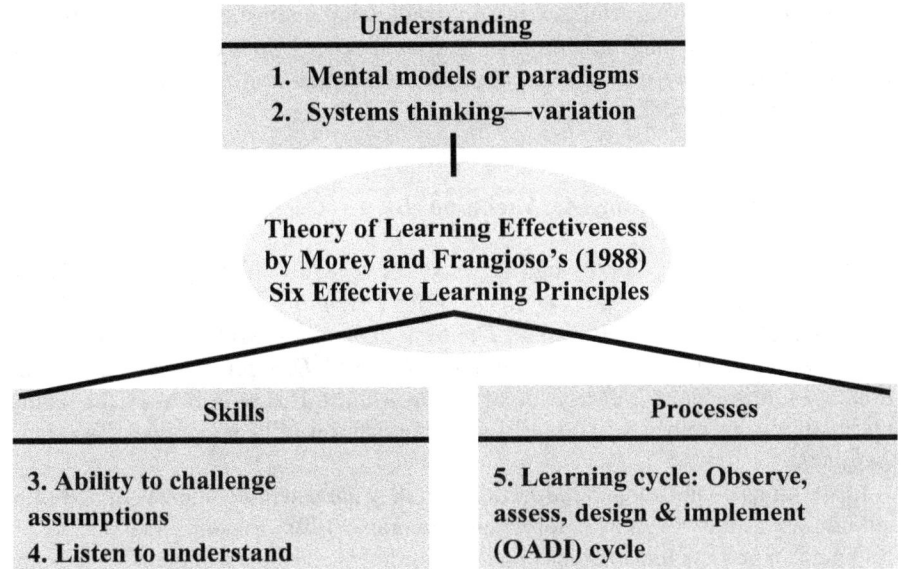

Fig. 4.1 Morey and Frangioso's (1998) six effective learning principles. (Adapted from Morey and Frangioso 1998)

an easy and comfortable means. The two main aspects are (a) mental models or paradigms and understanding and (b) systems thinking—variation.

4.3.1.1   Mental Models or Paradigms

Morey and Frangioso (1998) had adapted the mental models or paradigms from Senge, Peter, *The Fifth Discipline*, Doubleday, New York, 1990, and Covey, Steven R, *Principle-Centered Leadership*, Simon and Schuster, New York, 1992. Let's discuss one of the two principles, 'understanding: mental models or paradigms'.

Individuals view the world through the lens of their experiences and assumptions. That lens deviates as a result of what is perceived and depends on the interpretation of what is being viewed. The same facts and situations can be interpreted differently based on the lens through which they are viewed. Individuals operate from their own postulations and contexts; therefore, a lot of times, there is no strict 'right' or 'wrong' on one issue when people disagree. It is a result of the interpretation they have from the lens they see the facts or situations from.

Morey and Frangioso (1998, p. 309) add to this aspect of the principle:

Usually, we perceive and then analyze information in the manner that we understand. For example, the same situation in a particular context can be analyzed in various angles depending on how we view the situation based on our own past experiences and information gathered.

Learning occurs or accelerates when an individual understands that their beliefs are the outcomes of their assumptions and experiences. In a contrary, if it is not understood, then they may discard any likelihoods that are opposed to their own perceived mental model.

4.3.1.2 Systems Thinking *(A)*: Variation *(B)*

Morey and Frangioso (1998) had adapted the systems thinking (A)—variation (B)—model from (A) Senge, Peter, *The Fifth Discipline*, Doubleday, New York, 1990, and (B) Deming, W Edwards, *The New Economics*, MIT Press, Cambridge, MA, 1994. Peter Senge (1990), the author of *The Fifth Discipline*, said that systems thinking—variation—is a discipline of seeing wholes. It is a framework for seeing interrelationships rather than things, for seeing patterns of change rather than static snapshots.

Most things do not happen independently; they are usually outcomes of complex and non-linear relationships (Morey and Frangioso 1998; Edwards 1982). System thinking is a process that enables one to comprehend systems and describe them in a better and accurate manner, through a systematic and organized approach. It provides the appropriate tools to understand systems and facilitate the description of a new language.

The vital aspect of systems thinking for learning is the comprehension of the events that drives the outcome of complex interactions. Morey and Frangioso (1998) describe that 'if we attempt to learn from the outcome of a life experience without an understanding of the complex system that created that outcome, we will create false assumptions that will negatively impact future learning' (p. 309). In a similar context, a deep understanding of events influences the outcome of systems and randomness that potentially could be linked to the principle of variation. It can be concluded that learning by reflecting on an event with either the false assumption that an event occurred because of the system when it was actually random or to think it was random when it was because of the system is to be avoided. Thus, it is essential for students to understand the relationships and linkages between various issues coupled with the evolving changes, rather than seeing it from only one single and fixed perspective.

4.3.2 Skills

4.3.2.1 Ability to Challenge Assumptions

The following discussions will address the next two principles classified under the 'skills' segment. First is the ability to challenge assumptions—not only is the world viewed through the lens of one's assumptions, but one needs to have the aptitude to dispute those assumptions (Morey and Frangioso 1998). To learn effectively, one's assumptions need to be understood accurately, and they can then be challenged.

Challenging assumptions is not easy for those who recognize their identities with their beliefs. For this group of people, learning will be challenging. When someone questions a basic assumption, an effective learner must sense that there is more to the truth than what they believe in. The experience could be viewed as a thought-provoking opportunity for learning if one is comfortable when challenged on their personal assumptions. This opens up opportunities of seeing the world from fresh with new perspectives through a new lens. In summary, an effective learner is able to challenge assumptions; hence, learning is facilitated through the emergence of new and refreshing views.

4.3.2.2 Listen to Understand

Morey and Frangioso (1998) had adapted the 'listen to understand' concept from Covey, Steven R, *Principle-Centered Leadership*, Simon and Schuster, New York, 1992. The second principle means that there are no opportunities to learn from others if one is always talking and not listening (Morey and Frangioso 1998).

Morey and Frangioso (1998, p. 309) illustrated it as follows:

> This is a basic, yet difficult skill. Typically, our natural tendency is to first tell others about what we know and then ignore their responses as we prepare our response. Learning requires deep listening where we are trying to understand not only another person's viewpoint, but also the assumptions of their viewpoint. This skill builds on the ability to challenge assumptions. When we try to understand the assumptions of others, it opens up the possibility that our assumptions may be misguided.

When an individual does not allow their own assumptions to be challenged, they tend to be withdrawn from the possibility of learning. The individual cannot fully appreciate the person whom they are communicating with. Hence, deep listening skills enable one to challenge the status quo and hear the perceptions of others so that one's own assumptions can be reviewed. This communication process involves listening and acknowledging the viewpoints and assumptions of others, which enables to attain the intended learning outcomes.

4.3.3 Processes

4.3.3.1 Learning Cycle: Observe, Assess, Design and Implement (OADI) Cycle

The last two principles fall under the category of processes. Morey and Frangioso (1998) had adapted the 'Learning Cycle: Observe, Assess, Design and Implement (OADI) Cycle from Kim, Daniel, 'The link between individual and organizational learning', *Sloan Management Review*, Fall 1993, pp. 37–50. The learning cycle

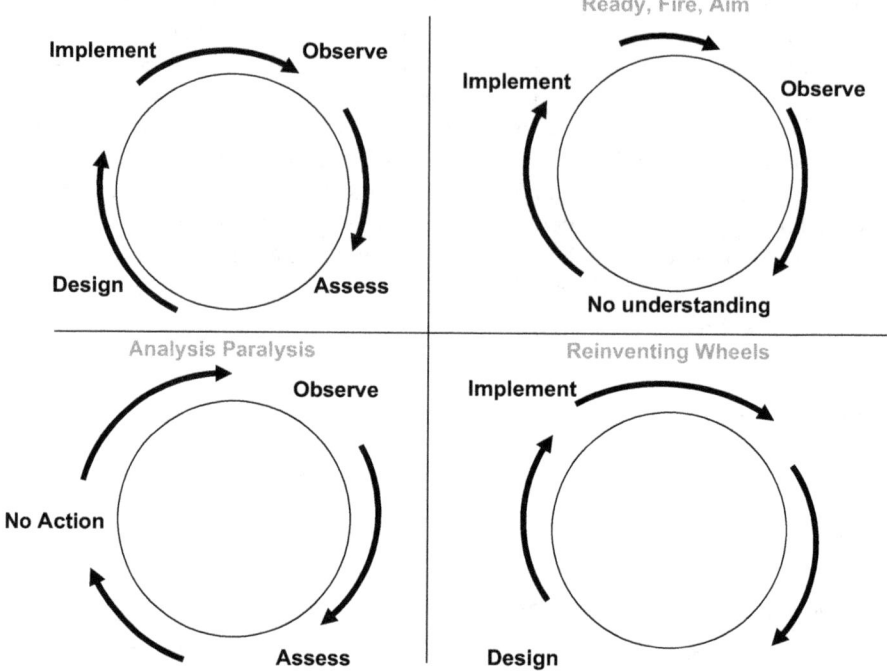

Fig. 4.2 Learning cycle. (Adapted from Daniel 1993)

comprises the following: a complete observe, assess (reflection, gain understanding), design (develop theory, prediction, vision) and implement (test) process cycle (Morey and Frangioso 1998).

In the OADI cycle, people experience concrete events and actively observe what is happening (Daniel 1993). They evaluate (consciously or subconsciously) their experiences with the observations and design and develop an abstract concept that responses to the assessment. The design is put to the test in the concrete world that produces new concrete experiences facilitating another cycle. The design and implementation stage of the cycle may be excluded. A person's learning cycle, before the implementation stage, involves their personal experiences and past encounters that will cause them to decide on how they could handle and approach future issues that might arise.

Figure 4.2, adapted from Bohlin and Brenner (1996), illustrates the general learning mistakes that occur when the cycle is ignored.

Morey and Frangioso (1998, p. 310) state:

> In the OADI cycle, people experience concrete events and actively observe what is happening. They access (consciously or subconsciously) their experience by reflecting on their observations and then design or construct an abstract concept that seems to be an appropriate response to the assessment. They test the design by implementing it in the concrete world, which leads to a new concrete experience, commencing another cycle.

4.3.3.2   Teach Others

The second principle is 'teach others where teaching is the ultimate win-win activity of all the principles, this one has the greatest total impact on the effective learning of a learning environment' (Morey and Frangioso 1998, p. 310). Morey and Frangioso (1998) had adapted this principle from Covey, Steven R, *Principle-Centered Leadership*, Simon and Schuster, New York, 1992. Besides arming the receiver with new knowledge, teaching others reinforces and internalizes learning in the teacher. Transfer of knowledge fails if teachings do not literally force one to understand the information clearly. Teaching is an element intertwined with the learning process that allows enhancement of learning that would eventually contribute to higher order of learning effectiveness.

4.3.4   *Valuing the Principles*

To attain quality deliverables in an institution, it is recommended to adopt the measurements of learning effectiveness from the framework of processes, skills and understanding. An institution committed to effective learning must measure their performance accurately, adopt the correct mix and customize the instructional techniques to achieve optimal maximum knowledge transfer of the students. Having a clear and deep understanding on how students learn most effectively via the correct mix of instructional techniques enables the institutions to tailor-make to fit their learning needs. The correct usage of the effective learning principles through the appropriate instructional techniques would influence a change in students' learning behaviours and the culture of learning. An institution that advocates the value of learning but uses inappropriate instructional techniques not in congruence with it will most probably receive unsatisfactory outcomes. The primary long-term driver of success for educational institutions will be effective learning, which translates into the ability to speedily produce, recognize, amalgamate and implement the correct mix of instructional techniques through a good appreciation of the learning culture and culture of learning.

Morey and Frangioso (1998, p. 314) mentioned that:

> Learning is accelerated if each of the six principles of effective learning are understood and utilized. To create a culture where the six principles thrive, metrics must be available so the educational institution can align itself to value the principles.

A conductive learning environment can be created with a good balance between the underlying principles of effective learning and by-products of learning itself that produces quality students equipped with higher knowledge competence.

4.4 Deficit Theories?: Misconceptions and Stereotypes of the Confucian Heritage Learning Culture

The observations and much written work about the cultural and social aspects on Chinese students learning have been amalgamated (McMahon 2011) to create what has been loosely been called 'the Chinese learner' (Cortazzi and Jin 2001; Lee 1996; Samuelowicz 1987; Turner 2006; Watkins 2000; Watkins and Biggs 1996, 2001). Western views of 'the Chinese learner' have been biased and remain largely based on stereotypical and outmoded assumptions (Ryan 2010) despite the intensified internationalization of education through global cultural flows of students and teachers between schools and universities in Anglophone countries and China. The previous work on 'Chinese learner' literature has not given thorough, holistic and accurate account of students coming from China and 'Confucian heritage culture' (hereafter CHC) countries. The Western stereotype seems to contrast the Chinese learners to what an ideal student supposedly be without a critical understanding of the learning culture and culture of learning of the Chinese. The 'Chinese learner' literature is a response to Western literature characterizing CHC students as passive, rote learners, lacking critical thinking skills and using low-level cognitive strategies both in their own culture and overseas (Ninnes et al. 1999; Kumaravadivelu 2003; Chan 1999; Chow 1995; Bradley and Bradley 1984; Samuelowicz 1987). These students are not willing to take part in open discussions and thus do not respond favourably during class discussions (Chan 1999; Chow 1995; Kumaravadivelu 2003; Newell 1999); are quiet in classrooms and do not question their teachers or challenge their judgements, where course materials are designed to facilitate the memorization process and lessen the learning burden (Chow 1995; Chan 1999); learn in large, authoritarian classes in which they are prepared for external exams which test low-level cognitive goals (Biggs 1996); resist to speak up in class or express their opinions; respect the authority of the teacher (Durkin 2011; Turner 2013; Ryan 2010); prefer not to share their opinions in public (Wen and Clement 2003); prefer and expect close supervision and are more suited to group-oriented settings (Atkinson 1997; Carson 1992; Chan 1999; Chow 1995; Fox 1994; Kumaravadivelu 2003; Nelson 1995; Newell 1999; Oxford 1995); and characterize as passive due to their willingness to submit to authority that relates to their unwillingness to participate in class (Wen and Clement 2003).

These deficit and perceptions have been largely based on misunderstandings and/ or partial knowledge, not rigorous or even flawed research sample in terms of oversimplifying the categorization of 'Chinese students'. This has caused negative stereotype (Littlewood 2009; Ninnes et al. 1999) labels and defines CHC students' learning characteristics, values and beliefs as the opposites of Western academic values. Instead of taking these aspects negatively, they could be better appreciated if there are examined from the cultural differences perspective in comparison to the western academic virtues (Ryan 2010). The discussion will revisit past deficit theories and make sense of what should have been the more accurate interpretations from the deficit theories, thereafter examining the other side of the surplus theories with evidence advocating that the matter is evaluated too over simplistically and culturally biased.

Nakamura (1964) and Redding (1990) claimed that the Chinese exhibit five major characteristics in regard to Chinese thinking and behaviour, namely, (a) importance being placed on perception of concrete thoughts; (b) not having fully developed abstract thoughts; (c) emphasis placed on details and not universals; (d) the central focus being practicality and (e) concerns for reconciliation, agreement and stability. Nakamura (1964) characterized Chinese view in comparison with Western view. Three primary differences are applicable to the exploration of behavioural intention modeling among Chinese learners: (a) emphasis on the perception of the concrete; (b) practicality as a central focus and (c) concern for reconciliation, harmony and balance.

We shall examine deeper on the rooted stereotypes of the Chinese learners' characteristics in the literature that is classified as the deficit theories, categorizing them into six key themes, namely, (a) emphasis on the perception of the concrete; (b) practicality as a central focus; (c) concern for reconciliation, harmony and balance; (d) rote versus repetition style of learning; (e) classroom behaviour and (f) medium of instruction.

4.4.1 Emphasis on the Perception of the Concrete

Chinese people prefer to focus on concrete, tangible impetuses more than Westerners, who are more inclined to engage in abstract thought (Boisot and Child 1999; Frazee 1996; Tan and Akhtar 1998). Emphasis on essentials has been associated with Chinese orthography (Liu 1986a, b). Chinese script uses characters that embody single ideas, whereas English script is alphabetical. A pictorial language relies more heavily on the senses for the creation of its symbols which draws one's focus and concentration much more towards tangible, concrete objects (Redding 1993). The rote memorization required by Chinese language enables processing of concrete visual stimuli (Chan 1976). The Chinese script has been identified as one explanation for the consistently high scores of Chinese on spatial and numerical intelligence tests (Vernon 1982). It is also considered to be one of the factors that bind the meaning of words more closely to their visual identification, as measured by both the Stroop effect (Beiderman and Tsao 1979) and the affected meaning of semantic pairs (Hoosain and Osgood 1983). These mechanisms fundamentally act as some form of measurement of students' level of understanding of contents acquired through visual identification and impact.

Focusing on the concrete correlates negatively with the ability to articulate future events or outcomes. Hong Kong Chinese are less likely to extrapolate from currently perceived events to future consequences compared to Westerners (Wright et al. 1978). The Chinese focus more on the temporally concrete in perception, hence are more likely to place somewhat greater importance on the more concrete aspects of a product evaluation in comparison to Westerners (Malhotra and McCort 2001).

4.4.2 Practicality as a Central Focus

The Chinese thought process focuses on utilitarian motivation to a greater extent than does the Western counterparts (Nakamura 1964). This characteristic can be attributed to the poverty where most Chinese traditionally lived (Malhotra and McCort 2001). The imperial system of ancient China produced a society in which the masses were poor subsistence farmers. Frugality was a norm due to the small amount of expendable funds. Moreover, traditional Chinese society indoctrinated financial skills through the respectability of the pursuit of riches and by making surplus wealth easily confiscated by political superiors (Freedman 1979). This attitude towards money is reflective of a general pragmatism among the Chinese (Redding 1993) that is also highly utilitarian. The social fabric of China was based on Confucianism; it lacked a moral authority that would offer universal understandings of right and wrong (Lau 1982). Rather, all moral conduct was considered in the light of the family. Hence, a utilitarian familism developed, in which what benefited the family was good, regardless of the consequences to others (Malhotra and McCort 2001). Such influences, among others, have led Kahn (1979) to point out that the Chinese have been nurtured to be relatively serious in their handling of tasks. The Chinese espouse a more practical approach, downplaying emotional reactions in order to perform at their highest levels during significant endeavours or decision-making phases. This disposition may be largely due to the process in learning of language. The self-discipline ingrained in children by memorizing the Chinese orthography creates a better sense of self-control in Chinese people (Redding 1993).

4.4.3 Concern for Reconciliation, Harmony and Balance

There is a greater appreciation of harmony, intuitive thinking and balance in Chinese reasoning (Lin 1977; Nakamura 1964; Northrop 1946). In comparing the reasoning methods of Chinese and Americans, we could deduce that the Chinese perception is largely based on the overall pattern uniting objects, whereas Americans perceive on the basis of a characteristic shared by the objects (Bond 1991). Such reasoning can be associated with the concept of connectedness as one attempt to comprehend the interplay between the large arrays of forces that influence a decision. There is a close link between this pattern of reasoning and perception and the collectivist nature of Chinese culture (Bond and Hwang 1986; Hofstede 1980). Historically, living in a culture that imposes strong in-group allegiance has given the Chinese a need to balance personal desires with group demands (Triandis et al. 1988). The authoritarian decision-making strategies of groups (Tse et al. 1988) require that an individual balance the expectations of the leader with personal desires. This normative force dampens personal affective desires in the formation of intention (Malhotra and McCort 2001).

Chinese culture is based around self-effacement that derives from Confucian value of modest behaviour. Chinese students perceive as not worthy in comparison with their teachers. Chinese students prefer not to express their true opinions so as not to embarrass or offend others, as a strong belief in modesty (Chan 1999). There is also a strong emphasis on upholding honour (Kirkbride and Tang 1992). This concept is categorized into the two aspects of 'lien' (or 'face') and 'mien tsu' (or 'mianzi'), the former addressing the confidence that society has about a person's moral character and the latter concerning prestige arising from one's social status (Yau 1994).

Chan (1999, p. 299) further adds:

> 'Lien' is granted to those who deserve it by society, unlike 'mien tsu' which may be lost by misconduct or regained with appropriate conduct. In the classroom this may be manifested as students 'losing face' for poor performance or if the tutor's performance and behaviour fail to meet the students' expectations. The concept of 'ch'ih' or shame comes hand-in-hand with 'lien' and its existence is fundamental to the concept of face for the Chinese.

Emblematic classroom behaviour of Chinese learner, for example, of not voicing their opinions, indeed focuses on avert embarrassment and maintaining of the face of the individuals concerned. The preservation of traditional Chinese learning for the younger generation overseas is carried out by placing great importance on Chinese cultural heritage. This enables Chinese children to learn through concrete examples as well as cultivate a deeper knowledge of Chinese social values. This explains why many excel in mechanical subjects such as law and accounting, whereas the more intangible aspects like leadership and planning that require judgements in abstract thinking and personal interaction are challenging for many Chinese students to grasp (Bond 1992; Redding 1980). From the literature, it is apparent that the Chinese prefer to learn in a way that recognizes the intertwined cultural and social values that have been ingrained in them during their years of upbringing. Understanding the varying perspectives of the students' specific learning styles embedded with cultural aspects helps to better cater to these students and to learn more effectively the unique style of mainland Chinese students' learning behavioural patterns and approaches. By recognizing the unique style of mainland Chinese students' learning behavioural patterns and approaches, it becomes possible to look at how the curriculum can be designed to fit the students, thus facilitating them to learn to the best of their ability.

4.4.4   Rote Learning Versus Repetitive Learning: The Paradox of the Chinese Learner

Distinct characteristics of traditional Chinese learning process and teaching approach involve the role of memorization as a vital element and a traditional way of learning in CHC countries (McMahon 2011) and the emphasis on rote learning (Liu 2006). A review of the literature shows that Western observers confuse learning through memorization and repetition with rote learning and subsequently under-value Chinese students' learning strategies (McMahon 2011).

Memorization has played a prominent role in the Chinese education system (McMahon 2011).

Rote learning refers to learning without much thought or comprehension of the meaning in a rather perfunctory way that often results in the learner not able to understand the actual meaning of the material under study (Biggs 1994). The primary influence on Chinese learning largely comes from Confucius (Chan 1999). In modern Chinese society, Confucianism is a significant element of Chinese cultural identity, and the main writings continue to be taught in schools (Redding 1990). The acquisition of a vast store of knowledge through rote memorization is still a prevalent in Chinese education today, at the expense of creativity. Memorization is still largely used to teach pupils social and moral obligations (Chan 1999).

Yao (2000) reports that Confucianism is 'more a tradition generally rooted in Chinese culture and nurtured by Confucius and Confucians' (p. 17). Confucianism has gone through five stages across its historical perspectives, which are Confucianism in formation, Confucianism in adaption, Confucianism in transformation, Confucianism in variation and Confucianism in renovation (Yao 2000). Shi (2006) argued that Confucianism 'changed throughout a long history by adapting itself to new political and social demands and it is a multi- dimensional concept' (p. 124). Conventional educational approaches such as rote learning have remained largely unaffected because of the strength of the philosophy that is closely linked to education and learning. The stresses of learning and the need to excel academically leave the mainland Chinese students with limited choices, so as perhaps resort to rote learning of the essentials in order to pass the examination (Yee 1989), which is thought to lead to 'surface learning' as opposed to 'deep learning' (Marton et al. 1996). Such learning modes are believed to dominate the classroom behaviour of Chinese students in Hong Kong, China and Southeast Asia. Those students who are better able to repeat the information offered by the teacher are rewarded to reinforce their learning behaviours (Martinsons and Martinsons 1996).

Although rote learning has a potential to lead to 'surface learning', Lee (1996) contends Confucian tradition of learning is one of a deep approach and not a surface approach, which is a contradiction to the common understanding of Western observers that Chinese learners are rote learners. McMahon (2011) re-iterates that memorization is a vital part of learning in Confucian tradition and this should not be equated with the learning by rote as the process of memorization precedes and aids understanding, it does not replace it (p. 404). The literature reports, in Chinese classrooms, the learning of Chinese numbers, and sophisticated decomposition strategies rather than rote learning are actually being deployed (Biggs 1994). The learning of Chinese numbers entails lesser memory space compared with Western number names, allowing Chinese students to better focus their memory on higher-order learning strategies. The Chinese students are using memorization in reality to achieve learning at a much deeper level (Biggs 1996). Chinese teachers have described how they utilize the learning technique of memorization and repetition to help their understanding: 'Each time I repeat would have some new idea of understanding ... that is to say I can understand better ...' (Marton et al. 1996, p. 81). Chinese students in fact prefer high-level or deep learning strategies over the frequently misperceived rote learning. For many years, this caused the learning styles of mainland Chinese students to be misinterpreted as rote when in fact they were repetitive learning. But again, the specific instructional techniques to be adopted were not clearly and accurately identified with evidence-based outcomes. In such a situation, repetition is exercised to help the students to enable higher accuracy in the recall of information. Unlike rote learning, repetitive learning allowed the learner to relate meaning to the information learned. Chinese students adopt repetitive learning styles to understand issues taught so that they are able to remember the information much better during examinations that reiterates and justify their exam successes. More recent study by Kember (2016) suggests that there is an intermediate learning process between the surface memorization technique and deep understanding that contributes to the effectiveness of rote learning, in our case mainland Chinese students. This intermediate learning process combines both memorization and understanding. We could reiterate that due to cultural aspects and academic needs, Chinese students develop memorization skills that Western students do not. Chinese students in a culturally dislocated learning environment, say in Western universities, may be adopting varying learning strategies in comparison to the Western students that itself may cause these students to be unfairly labeled as 'insensitive rote learner' by Western academics.

4.4.5   Classroom Behaviour

Chinese students are usually quiet during lessons, classified as passive and superficial learners lacking critical thinking skills (Kumaravadivelu 2003; Ninnes et al. 1999; Ryan and Louie 2005) and prone to plagiarism (Ryan 2000; Kirkpatrick 2004). They are often seated in rows and adopt the rote learning approaches and receive specific instruction in letters, characters and numbers (Bond 1992). The students are taught never to question or challenge their teachers' instructions or judgements (Chan 1999). The literature also claims that as disobedience and poor performance could lead to reprimands and isolation designed to bring shame on the individuals concerned, discipline problems are not common in the classroom. Likewise, high achievers are readily rewarded and acknowledged by their teachers for their good performance.

Table 4.1 Eastern versus Western educational system

	Eastern	Western
Main purpose	Focus on loyal citizenry Develop literate citizenry Helps select future leaders Transmitter of past cultural heritage	Focus on individual Develop individual's full potential Transmitter of cultural heritage
Instruction mode	Teacher-centred Stresses recall of facts Use of rote learning Examinations as motivator Learner passive	Learner-centred Stresses understanding, application and ability Use of educational psychology Learner active
Curricular orientation	Past-present oriented Strict exams to develop academic knowledge Concepts first then skills	Present-future oriented Development of whole person Social interaction promoted

Adapted from Yee (1989)

Memorization was largely used as a strategy to teach the pupils social morals and obligations (Chan 1999). All supplementary course materials produced, such as lecture handouts and use of textbooks, are designed to facilitate the memorization process and lessen the learning burden. On the contrary, Western educators claimed that these materials were often not used appropriately by students who merely used them to rote learn (Martinsons and Martinsons 1996). In fact, students are encouraged to repeat prominent scholarly works word for word as part of their means of demonstrating acknowledgement and respect. In the West, the existing challenges associated with plagiarism would no doubt pose concerns for those adopting conventional Chinese learning styles. High-quality learning practices in the West typically revolve around the use of approaches where students are taught, for example:

- To use theoretical frameworks for conceptualizing the task
- To be cognitive in planning and keeping close track of their own progress
- That their outcomes are well-organized, systematic and integrated
- That learning is a pleasant process when they attain good results and answer the questions correctly. (Biggs 1994)

Table 4.1 provides a useful comparison of the key differences between Eastern and Western educational systems.

Chinese classrooms are usually large in size (50–60 students in them), teacher-centred, highly formal and perceived to be a strictly disciplined learning environment, compared to the West (Jin and Cortazzi 1998). The learning culture does not encourage students to ask questions, and more emphasis is inclined towards acquiring content knowledge from the teacher (McMahon 2011). It is unusual for a student to spontaneously participate in the discussion which makes it challenging to facilitate a classroom discussion, especially in a large, open class (Kumaravadivelu 2003; Chan 1999; Chow 1995).

Confucian value of modest behaviour influences mainland Chinese students to avoid speaking up in a large class (Redding 1980). The social norms of these Chinese students severely limit the expression of criticism, to avoid the individual losing face (Ryan and Louie 2005; Chow 1995). Their performance is often affected by criticism, which results in the deterioration or cessation of their achieving the desired outcomes. The inability to answer questions from fellow classmates may make them feel that they look ridiculous in front of the class. Research continues attempting to understand these Chinese students silence in class. In Yu (2016)'s article, he contends that self-construal, which is also manifested in other cultures, is the reason behind the silence in Chinese students in class. Students' minimum discourse performance in classrooms is the result of their semi-conscious act of internal modeling that entails reinforcing their identities on situational evaluations and conforming to social norms. In Zhang (2013)'s study of Chinese students' behaviour in an online learning environment, there is a reluctance of them interacting with the instructors. Instructors were viewed by students as authorities, major sources of knowledge and possessing high power. There is the presence of high-power distance in the Chinese learning culture, i.e. intimidation by the authority.

Mainland Chinese students prefer not to challenge another group's perspectives as they tend to value harmony in the learning environment (Zhang 2013). These students are also concerned about the possible retaliation when they do their own presentation (Zhang 2013). Problem-solving competencies are not emphasized as students' achievement is generally assessed through written examinations that are not designed to test ability to collaborate and solve problems pragmatically (Chan 1999). Chinese students tend to be typically more concrete and rational in evaluating ideas than their Western counterparts (Chan 1999). Due to the absence of creativity in their learning approach, they tend to less likely explore new and unaccustomed ways. The challenges are more pronounced when Chinese students pursue their studies at Western universities or in contemporary and fast-growing countries like Singapore, where Western-based education is facilitated through local institutions. Many overseas students prefer to choose subjects that enable them to better utilize their existing learning skills to overcome these issues. Mainland Chinese students are more suited to the additive and fine-tuning approaches to learning that are found in subjects such as physics, chemistry and engineering, which does not challenge the already existing knowledge or skills in them (Bond 1991).

These Chinese students prefer regular, sequential assignments on structured problems rather than the more ambiguous ones with no standard answers (Chow 1995). They show high level of discomfort with ambiguity and uncertainty, as they prefer highly structured, neat solutions similar to solving mathematical problems (Chow 1995). Group-oriented settings would be more suited for these Chinese students as they prefer and expect close guidance and supervision. These students prefer to work in a small group rather than independently. The Chinese classroom learning culture discourages active and critical inquiry (Chan 1999).

The assigned group leader is expected to announce the decision of the group. A key disadvantage of such group behaviour is that individuals tend to only communicate comfortably with each other after the relationship between themselves and the others in the group has been clearly described. This reiterates the reason for the difficulty in having the discussion groups commence, especially when a group leader is undecided, thus limiting the learning possibilities associated with group work and class activities (Yau 1994). Confucianism encourages the Chinese to respect hierarchical relationships between individuals so that teachers are expected to teach as well as guide students. Many would feel that ineffective teaching is taking place if they are continually asked in class to express their opinions or to solve a problem by themselves. Teachers are to decide what to be taught and are viewed as the ones with the authority and power. The students, on the other hand, are to accept information willingly and rarely question or challenge the teachers in the classroom. Spontaneous alliance is largely seen in Chinese learning behaviour, for example, group learning often takes place outside the classroom. The need to do well academically, coupled with intense competitiveness, is evident among the students due to social conditioning from family and peer members. However, this could also be attributed and explained by the intense competition for the limited education places available in China.

Although the authoritarian approach preponderates in the classroom in that there is only one right way, it was done by hand-holding, supported by considerable warmth and mutual respect and responsibility in teacher-student relations. The number of students seeking one-to-one interaction with the teacher as soon as the class is over, and with each other, was found to be far higher than with Western students, despite the apparent lack of interaction or spontaneity. The typical Chinese classrooms were discovered to be very different from the commonly recognized Western-based education format where they are characterized by (a) higher emphasis on group-related activities as they are student-centred; (b) learning relies greatly on interpersonal motivation between students; (c) the lecturer is the mentor and the student being mentored; and (d) much deeper analytical thinking with higher cognitive outcomes. The much larger class size, as compared to Western classrooms, prohibits the possibilities of the above issues to be addressed. The apparent emphasis on authoritarian teaching styles and the tendency to depend exclusively on examinations as a measure of academic performance are also likely to continue due to the class size.

Examinations are more commonly used to measure their performance (Bond 1992). The typical Chinese classroom would therefore appear to be highly dictatorial to maintain control and focus (Biggs 1994). Goals for examination success make teachers continuously under pressure to conform and students on exam stress. As benchmarks of academic progress and success, Chinese students are to pass large set-piece assessments that put them under intense pressure (McMahon 2011). Cortazzi and Jin 1996 relates the early years of these Chinese students learning of the basics of reading and writing where there is 'strong emphasis on memory, imitation and repetitive practice' (p. 173). Although the authoritarian education system and pressure to conform may lead the students to perform better that Western students do, 'Chinese students are not known for their creativity and original thinking' (Salili 1996, p. 100). The explanation of this could be related to the emphasis China places on its academic success committing material to memory (Wingrove 1993) instead of being able to perform critical analysis (McMahon 2011) or the learning processes that develops critical thinking competencies.

4.4.6 Medium of Instruction

The use of the mother tongue in teaching and learning is a crucial issue. The working language is often different from the mother tongue in most Asian countries. English is readily used in Singapore as it is the working language and medium for learning. In a cosmopolitan country like Singapore, there are no qualms that English is an imperative language in international business transactions. However, the problem of using a second language as a medium for learning should not be underestimated. If the students' English ability is not proficient enough, they will not be able to understand and therefore learn anything. The language proficiency of the Chinese students on their written and verbal communication has been a challenge for them. In a study by Schermerhorn (1987), 153 local undergraduates were provided two scenarios to be written in either English or Chinese. The completed work is then translated and back-translated by experts to perform a final check of equivalence. Students answered eight questions about the scenarios in the survey. Different answers surfaced from those who were questioned in Chinese and in English. From the analysis of the results, the analysis shows that language plays an essential role in conveying information between cultures.

4.5 Surplus Theories: Changes and Shifts of the Confucian Heritage Learning Culture

The myths about CHC learners have been debunked through the work of (Watkins and Biggs 1996, 2001; Rajaram 2010, 2013; Rajaram and Bordia 2011, 2013; Rajaram and Collins 2013) and many others (Chalmers and Volet 1997; Chan and Drover 1997; Coverdale-Jones and Rastall 2009; Geake and Maingard 1999; Hellmundt 2001; Jones 1999; Kember and Gow 1990; Littlewood 2009; Ninnes et al. 1999; O'Donoghue 1996; Volt and Ang 1998). The term 'surplus' theories of CHC learners (Ryan and Louie 2005) or 'cultural proficiency' theories (Ninness et al. 1999) attempts to counter these 'deficit' theories. Fundamentally, the surplus theories identify the goodness and positive aspects of the Chinese 'culture of learning' (Watkins and Biggs 2001) and explain the 'paradox of the Chinese learner' (Biggs 1996). Although the above-discussed notions and stereotypes of Chinese learners are still pervasive in literature, the rapid changes in China over the last decade have influenced and shifted the traditional cultural norms and values which have largely influenced the learning behaviour of Chinese learners. We could debate that the classification of the Chinese students needs to be clear and explicit, as one has to be mindful of the distinctive differences on their national, regional, economic, class and cultural backgrounds. Louie (2005) pointed out that these Chinese students have different cultural baggage, for example, the outlook, attitude and learning behaviour of a student whose parents are professors from Shanghai and another who are peasants from a village from Hunan are different. We must also challenge and question the ways both Western and Asian values are repeatedly described as discrete, homogeneous and unchanging. The broader such cultural and demographic boundaries extend, the less useful and more stereotyping the understanding will be shaped.

More recent studies by scholars (Chan and Rao 2009; Clarke and Gieve 2006; Rajaram and Bordia 2011; Rajaram 2010; Ryan and Slethaug 2010; Shi 2006; Yang 2009) have reported that Chinese learners prefer student-centred to teacher-centred approaches, where less supervision is required from the tutors, and they choose to participate in interactive and cooperative learning activities and are more willing to be on their own and not so dependent, although many studies are on the language skills courses rather than business-related courses.

Also, there are studies showing that Chinese students can adapt and change in a new learning environment. Cultural values of individuals can change because of acculturation (Hu et al. 2013). Saravanamuthu and Yap (2014)'s longitudinal study on Chinese learners in an Australian tertiary institution showed that achievement-motivated Chinese learners can adapt to the new learning strategies of the host countries. Chan and Rao (2009) argued against the stereotyped cultural impact on learning, whereas social learning was emphasized: 'It is the aspects of the social context, rather than cultural heritage per se that affects student learning … we need to consider teaching and learning, not just the chineseness of students or teachers' (p. 17–18). Clarke and Gieve (2006) emphasized that this entails a sense of cultural fixity and a notion of historicization where cultures are formed by a historical heritage rather than emerging through history and evolves dynamically. This was re-emphasized by Gu (2001), who argued that culture can be transformed only after a prolonged phase of confrontation, clashes and conflict between cultural traditions and modernization as cultural traditions are dynamic and ever developing. A recent study by Rajaram and Bordia (2011) showed that active instructional techniques (e.g. case study, individual research project, group project and classroom discussion) are perceived to be 'excellent avenues for quality learning in terms of knowledge and information acquisition' (p. 77). Further, they also discovered that 'comfort dislocation has no or minimal effect on perceived learning effectiveness' (Rajaram and Bordia 2011, p. 79). This reiterates the importance for educators to be creative, flexible and knowledgeable in their adoption of suitable and effective instructional techniques with greater autonomy and opportunities to penetrate through the barrier of cultural diversity.

4.6 Practical Implications on Challenges Faced: Western-Based Curriculum Versus Chinese Learning Culture and Style

Rote learning is a primary characteristic of conventional Chinese learning approach (Kumaravadivelu 2003; Liu 2006; Ryan and Louie 2005). Despite arguments against the method of repetitive memorization, Chinese students still learn through this force-fed teaching approach throughout primary and secondary education (Liu 2006). This learning style extends its influence right up to university education, where underprepared graduates struggle to deal with unexpected challenges.

Western teachers facilitating management education or training in China time and again come across students who are keen to accurately replicate the course materials in examinations and other forms of assessment. These students are often observed to be quiet listeners in class (Chan 1999; Martinsons and Martinsons 1996). This behaviour is mainly attributed to the influence of Confucian philosophy on education and learning, as Confucianism places high emphasis on community affiliations within a structurally oriented society. Although scholars have argued that the rapid changes in China over the past decade have influenced the values of Confucianism (Chan and Rao 2009; Hu 2003; Ryan and Slethaug 2010; Shi 2006; Yang 2009, Rajaram K 2013), some of the key aspects that describe the manner in which social relationships are maintained in Chinese societies are 'face', collectivism, harmony, conformity and power distance (McNaught 2012; Liu 2006). These values are manifested in the learning environments in the following ways:

- 'Respect for wisdom and knowledge. The authority of teachers who are purveyors of knowledge should not be challenged;
- 'Preservation of harmony. Individuals should conform to collective rather than developing distinctive values and beliefs; and
- 'Concern for face requires an individual to behave properly so that they will not bring shame to themselves and people to whom they are related'. (Liu 2006, p. 8)

Some studies have suggested that Western approaches to management education will not be effectively applied in China unless these cultural values are given due consideration (Biggs and Watkins 2001a, b; Warner 1991). Nonetheless, this can be claimed only as a partial truth. A better understanding of Chinese cultural values may encourage some local educators in Singapore teaching the Western-based curriculum to adjust their teaching styles and enhance the knowledge transfer process (Rajaram 2013). However, such knowledge provided by ad hoc, appear to be suitable, teaching methods does not spontaneously translate into necessary skills and competence for learners to confront the ever-changing environment. This can only be achieved by adopting a concrete framework and/or guideline of effective instructional techniques explicitly applied to address how knowledge can best be effectively transferred or ingrained in the minds of Chinese students.

Bu and Mitchell (1992) point out the major challenges faced by Western educators in developing management programmes geared towards Chinese managers. On a similar context, this could also be seen to be pertinent in terms of the challenges faced in the use of the western-based curriculum for mainland Chinese students on their pursuit of studies institutions collaborating with Western universities. Appropriate instructional techniques can be used to identify students' perceived learning effectiveness under the three broad categories of understanding, skills and processes. Many scholars (Bu and Mitchell 1992; Chan 1991; Chow 1995; McNaught 2012; Rajaram 2010; Ryan and Slethuag 2010; Shi 2006; Yang 2009) over the last decade have identified the following key challenges:

- The applicability of Western concepts to China: In general, management theories from the West originate from American research using examples from companies operating in very diverse economic, political and social environments. In order to address such problems, courses must not merely be pre-packaged portfolios of Western management courses but must take into consideration the varying operating situations of businesses. Much care and effort must be taken in designing and producing supporting materials for teaching, as the mere translation from English to Chinese is certainly not sufficient. Aside from selecting the most appropriate words for English terms, high emphasis and due consideration are given to ensure that these words have the same connotations in Chinese.
- Lack of student participation in classroom activities: The students' involvement in classroom activities, for example, sharing of opinions, contributing to discussions and challenging norms, are limited. The two-way communication which is highly advocated in management education, in many cases, is restricted. Although these students' receptiveness to learning is encouraging, their compliant and passive classroom behaviour may pose challenges for those used to more participative styles of teaching. To facilitate engagement and participation among Chinese students, (a) provide them clear instructions and allow them to define their respective roles at the outset and (b) allow them to think and reflect more about the topics to be discussed. Quietness and long silences in the classroom may not necessarily mean that students are not willing to participate but could be that they are pondering over the answers and may require further probing and encouragement from tutors.
- Limited use of typical management training techniques such as case studies, role-play and business games. As such it poses hazards for students not used to open discussions and expression of opinions due to their high reliant on abstract thinking. These approaches have to be introduced gradually with clear guidelines and adequate preparation time to be effective.
- Inefficiency of group discussions: Instructors are to have a good understanding on the psychology of the group. The openness of discussions may be limited by issues such as status, face and shame; hence, tutors are to be aware of the hidden messages and be sensitive to such constraints on their behaviour.

- Teacher-led classes: The status of the tutor is particularly important where the students need to be informed about the background and expertise of foreign experts. Teachers must assist students to be instrumental in shaping their own learning.

Although various challenges are identified in the learning styles by Chinese managers in general, the literature lacks concrete theories, integrating the cultural values and learning styles influencing the perceived learning effectiveness and effectiveness of learning. More importantly, no concrete evidence or informed grounded theories was found on mainland Chinese students pursuing Western education in Singapore, a continuous stream of large cohort of international students.

4.7 The Applicability of Western Concepts to China

In general, management theories from the West originate from American research using examples from companies operating in very diverse economic, political and social environments. In order to address such problems, the following strategies are recommended: (a) courses must not merely be pre-packaged portfolios of Western management courses but must take into consideration the varying operating situations of businesses; (b) much care and effort must be taken in designing and producing supporting materials for teaching, as the mere translation from English to Chinese is not adequate; and (c) besides selecting the most appropriate words for English terms, high emphasis and due consideration are to be given to ensure that these words have the same meaning in a Chinese language.

4.8 Students' Participation in Classroom Activities

There are mixed views on the Chinese students' involvement in classroom activities, for example, scholars have reported that the sharing of opinions, contributing to discussions and challenging norms are limited (Chan 1999; Chow 1995; Kumaravadivelu 2003; Ninnes et al. 1999; Ryan and Louie 2005). The two-way communication that is generally encouraged in management education, in many cases, would be restricted in Chinese classrooms. Although their receptiveness to learning is encouraging, their compliant and passive classroom behaviour may pose challenges for those used to more participative styles of teaching (Biggs 1994; Ryan and Louie 2005). From a contrary stance, Shi (2006) reported that the study in Shanghai showed that students 'show little difference from their Western counterparts by being active learners and preferring a more interactive relationship with their teachers' (p. 122); however, this cannot be generalized, and the study is conducted in China; hence, the dislocation issues vary in comparison to students pursuing a Western-based programme in another country.

However, other scholars have reported that there is a shift generally in Chinese students' learning behaviour in terms of being more acclimatized to participative learning approaches and prefer a two-way communication style of instructional techniques (e.g., Hu 2003; Ryan and Slethaug 2010; Shi 2006; Yang 2009). However, these reports may not be representatives of all Chinese students as they seem to be samples from specifically more developed provinces in China or those who came from a higher social status background where their exposure differs from an average Chinese student. The challenge is to question whether Chinese learners' behaviours can be generalized due to the varying progressive social, political and cultural exposure across the many provinces in China. It would be impossible to understand all the different cultural values, beliefs and norms of people from different provinces of China. However, it would be a great asset to understand the rapid changing influences so as to calibrate and customize the learning and teaching methodologies in line with these students' profile.

Hence, the following strategies are recommended to facilitate participation among Chinese students, especially those pursuing a Western-based education in a foreign country with complex cultural dislocation issues deep-rooted: (a) allow them the opportunity to define their roles at the outset, thus providing them unambiguous instructions; (b) this can be further enhanced by allowing the students to have more time to think about the topics under discussion (e.g. long silences in the classroom may not simply be indications that students are refusing to participate but that they may be thinking about the answers and require more probing and encouragement from tutors); (c) encourage by giving generous praises and having open acknowledgement to students who attempt to share their opinions/thoughts; and (d) incorporate participation as part of the assessment criteria and requirement which will automatically encourage as well as put pressure to open up and get accustomed to the participative learning culture.

4.9   Use of Typical Management Training Techniques

Active learning approaches—such as case studies, class discussions, group and individual projects, role-play and business games—could pose hazards for students not used to open discussions and expression of opinions, as these activities are heavily reliant on abstract thinking (Chan 1999; Chow 1995; Fox 1994; Kumaravadivelu 2003; Nelson 1995). On the other hand, there are also scholars who report that the Chinese learners are active and willing to participate in interactive and cooperative learning activities (Clarke and Gieve 2006; Slethaug 2010, Yang 2009). The study by Rajaram and Bordia (2013) showed mainland Chinese students learned more effectively by active instructional techniques, particularly by case studies and group projects. The rising trend and exposure to Western values and lifestyles of students are cited as influencing factors. This is an intensive study as the sample comprises a good mixture and large size of mainland Chinese students from 30 provinces in China. It is plausible that the inconsistencies in students' responses by various scholars can be linked to the student pool used, where these respondents may have had differing experiences with these instructional techniques. This is clearly reported:

> Some students may have experienced the case study technique in the passive style (predominantly lectures), while others experienced it in the active style (relatively autonomous or alone). In relation to the group projects, some students may have experienced high levels of guidance and direction, while others experienced assignments with low guidance and direction. This is especially so for group projects, as the amount of supervision, assistance and guidance provided varies largely depending on the instructors' style of managing them. If the students were subjected to closer supervision, obviously, there was a much higher possibility of expecting a different outcome compared to those given much lesser supervision. (Rajaram and Bordia 2013, p. 14)

There is a certain scope, style of active and participative learning in every management training technique that is crucial in engaging and transferring knowledge effectively to these mainland Chinese students in their pursuit of their studies outside China. Hence, it is crucial to understand how to incorporate the balance in adopting these management training techniques to teach them that results in optimal learning outcomes.

Rajaram (2010) reported that mainland Chinese students may not be comfortable in class discussions during the initial stage. This is largely due to their lack of exposure and language proficiency. After prolonged exposure with more active participation, their comfort level has improved. However, there were mixed responses in terms of subject of knowledge transfer for class discussions where it increases students' awareness of subject matter by relating to their past experiences (Rajaram and Bordia 2011), although some others highlighted that 'the amount of knowledge transfer was limited' (p. 75). Rajaram and Bordia (2011) reported that students were somewhat comfortable with the case-study technique, but 'they were not yet very confident or secure with this instructional approach' (p. 76). However, 'case study approaches facilitate mainland Chinese students to acquire information with greater ease by enabling them to refresh their acquired knowledge' (Rajaram and Bordia 2011, p. 75).

As for the individual project technique, Rajaram and Bordia (2011) highlighted that 'it allows students to present their ideas to a certain extent, in writing the report, thus allowing them to think independently' (p. 76). But three negative issues emerged, namely, their discomfort and insecure feeling, lack of confidence to deal with the project assignment on their own and having a less guided learning environment. This is supported by scholars who have reported that Chinese learners prefer to be guided and directed (Chan 1999; Chow 1995). There is no evidence to report on the receptivity on specific techniques like role-plays and business games on these students; however, we can state that there is a positive indication from scholars that these students prefer a student-centred approach to a teacher-centred approach (Ryan and Slethaug 2010; Yang 2009).

Shi (2006) classified mainland Chinese students as active learners who prefer a more interactive relationship with their teachers; however, the findings cannot be generalized as the study was conducted in China with only a certain cluster type of students. These active learning approaches have to be introduced progressively, with clear instructions and guidelines and adequate preparation time, to be effective. In order to help in the group work, it is essential to comprehend the psychology of the group. Issues such as status, 'face' and shame may limit the openness of discussions; thus, tutors need to be aware of the hidden messages behind what is disclosed by students and be sensitive to such constraints on Chinese learners' behaviour.

4.10 Teacher-Student Relationship and Active Versus Passive Teaching Approaches

Although scholars have argued that there is a shift in mainland Chinese students learning culture (Coverdale-Jones and Rastall 2009; Rajaram and Bordia 2011; Ryan and Slethaug 2010; Shi 2006), some fundamental learning behavioural aspects still remain, at least until they have been subjected to longer exposure. Chinese students did not think that having their own opinions was vital for a good learner (Shi 2006). Mainland Chinese students' unwillingness to participate in class can be related to their willingness to submit to authority (Wen and Clement 2003). These are social-cultural values and norms, which are embedded in individuals and influence their learning attitudes and behaviours. However, even though it is unusual for the students to put across their disagreements openly to their professors, they do not acknowledge the information provided blindly. From Shi (2006)'s study, it was reported that mainland Chinese students 'wanted their teachers to be light-hearted and use various teaching activities. On the other hand, students also expected teachers to help them pass tests and provide them with detailed and clear notes' (Shi 2006, p. 138).

The close association between behaviour and belief of Chinese students is evident with the following pressures: (a) to conform, (b) to preserve harmony and (c) to avoid loss of face and shame, which implies that the Chinese have preferences for certain styles of teaching and learning. The more participative approaches, which are more commonly used in Western teaching, may therefore pose a challenge for Chinese learners. However, Leung et al. (2008) presented a contrary view:

> When mainland Chinese students had been observed attempting to memorize material, they were not necessarily using a surface approach as characterized in the original Western studies. The memorization was not necessarily rote learning but could be combined in various ways with attempts to reach understanding. This then could explain the evidence of good performance of Chinese students. They were attempting to reach understanding, which is consistent with successful learning outcomes. At the same time, though, they were memorizing key material. This could often be of benefit for assessment, as examinations and tests often reward those who have memorized material. (p. 253–254)

Substantive evidence of the intention to both comprehend and memorize has also been found in mainland Chinese students (Marton et al. 1996) and Japanese students (Hess and Azuma 1991). It is quite prevalent among Asian students (Leung et al. 2008). There is a high possibility that the approaches combining understanding and memorization (Kember and Gow 1990; Marton et al. 1996) may be more familiar in Asia. As Kember (1996) has speculated that influences on their adoption may emerge from learning a character-based language, learning in a second language or being brought up in a society that conventionally has shown high levels of filial piety (Ho 1986).

Asian students tend not to express their feelings openly, mainly due to their culture and training. However, with the evolving changes in students' exposure, the younger generation of Asian students is more outspoken as the inhibition in their expression of feelings is somewhat fading. Recent studies have argued that these perceptions have often been based on partial knowledge or misunderstandings of mainland Chinese students but have given rise to negative stereotypes (Littlewood 2009; Ninnes et al. 1999). As Rajaram (2010) wrote:

> The mainland Chinese students generally reported that they learned more effectively active instructional techniques, with the exception of lectures as the passive instructional technique. This may be due to the increasing trend and exposure to Western values and lifestyles in the learning and teaching actions of courses back in China. As China progresses to become internationally recognized by opening its doors to other countries, there is bound to be an increase of Western exposure influencing the country's educational approach and, importantly, influencing how mainland Chinese students are being taught and their learning styles, as well. (p. 298)

As countries open up their trading and movement barriers to the more and more globalized economy, higher education became internationally tradable (Daquila 2013). As more countries seek to progress economically, many more universities/colleges will allocate instructors to educate individuals in a foreign country or from foreign countries at home. Rodrigues (2004, pp. 608–9) further states:

> When conducting teaching programs, instructors often identify a set of programs learning expectations, as well as a set of instructional techniques which they believe best helps accomplish the learning expectations. But applying the same technique or techniques can be effective with a group of students holding similar pedagogical and/or holding a homogeneous cultural orientation, but not necessarily with a group holding diverse (heterogeneous) pedagogical preferences and/or cultural orientations.

An instructional technique that is effective with students from one culture is not effective with students from another. This is because, as many scholars (e.g. Holland 1989; Kolb and Fry 1975; Witkins et al. 1977) believe, culture shapes the learning styles of the students, and the fundamental differences in learning style lead to differing pedagogical preferences. Asian and Western learners embrace differing pedagogical preferences. Some scholars (Pun 1989a, b; Jarrah 1998; Ladd and Ruby 1999) suggest that Western learners accept involvement and learning through their own exploration, and Chinese learners expect the teacher to lead, guide and provide learning points. Therefore, culturally, some students desire greater control and personal responsibility in the learning process, whereas others prefer that the teacher provides the required structure.

Rodrigues (2004, p. 609) highlights that:

> Therefore, some students prefer passive (P-like) instructional techniques, such as lecturing, wherein relatively low control and personal responsibility for learning is given to them, and some prefer active (A-like) instructional techniques, such as individual problem-solving projects, wherein relatively high control and personal responsibility for learning is given to them.

Students' frustration may be one of the outcomes if an inappropriate instructional technique is adopted. To be effective in cross-cultural teaching, the instructors need to apply the correct type of instructional techniques by which the students learn best and gain optimal knowledge. The selection of the instructional techniques depends on where the instructors are going to be teaching or countries from which the foreign students came.

Mainland Chinese students have certain distinctive cultural values due to their cultural background. Their optimal learning and gaining of knowledge largely depend on the use of correct mix of instructional techniques. Due to the Western-based educational curriculum in Singapore, there are noticeable differences in the instructional methodologies used in China and in Singapore. The only way that the students' learning can be optimized is by ensuring that they are being taught through the instructional techniques that best help them to learn and acquire knowledge.

In modern Chinese society, Confucianism is a critical element of Chinese cultural identity, and the main writings continue to be taught in schools, where children are encouraged to memorize the classics (Redding 1990). Together with the emphasis on the family, Confucianism ensures that socialization shows the way to a high level of education, skills attainment, earnestness about one's tasks, jobs, family and commitments. Chinese societies are frequently described as didactic and trainer-centred when assessed in terms of teaching styles arising from the Confucian ethic (Kirkbride and Tang 1992).

Biggs's (1994) review of the typical Chinese classrooms in fact shows them to be very different from the universally perceived format where they are characterized by the following:

- They are student-centred with much importance on group-related activities.
- Learning is based on interpersonal motivation between students.
- The teacher is the mentor and the student is the mentee.
- High critical and analytical thinking outcomes take place.

A learning institution needs to find congruence between the Western-based education and the teaching style, cultural background, values, learning patterns and styles of these mainland Chinese students. This study focused on the developmental framework that addresses the pedagogic needs of mainland Chinese students pursuing Western-based education. In order to implement this framework, there is a need to identify, combine and empirically test all the aspects. Based on Hofstede's (1980) and Hofstede and Bond's (1988) model, three cultural dimensions—namely, power distance, uncertainty avoidance and the philosophy of Confucianism—will be used as the main pillars from the cultural dislocation perspective. Ten instructional techniques commonly used by business professors in universities identified by Rodrigues (2004) are leveraged on. This framework was adopted to comprehend the level of importance that these Chinese students place on these instructional techniques, based on their perceived learning effectiveness outcomes in a cultural dislocation context, away from China, in our case in Singapore. The categorization of the ten instructional techniques is as follows:

Four active (A-like) techniques
- Case studies
- Individual research projects
- Group projects
- Classroom discussions

Six passive (P-like) techniques
- Lectures by instructor
- Reading textbooks
- Guest speakers
- Videos shown during lessons
- Classroom presentations by students
- Computerized learning assignments

Further deep understanding is required to unravel the indefinite learning aspects of the mainland Chinese before Western or local educators teaching Western education can fully appreciate varying instructional techniques to learning that enables them to adopt and many times customize to use it accurately with the suitable fit, respectively.

4.11 Gaps in Current Knowledge of Learning Styles of Mainland Chinese Learners

The primary research question formulated to address the gap in the literature is 'How do Chinese values, background, learning patterns and styles influence their choice of instructional techniques based on their perceived learning effectiveness?' The challenges in teaching the mainland Chinese students outside of mainland China and in a multiracial learning environment are addressed. To be specific, the impact of the cultural dislocation issues on teaching these students will be examined.

Management, as a discipline, was not previously taught in China, and much of the knowledge base for this education has been introduced from the West. The linear attempt to transfer explicit management knowledge from the West to Chinese students is based on false assumptions about the nature of knowledge and therefore is unlikely to be effective. There needs to be an interaction between Chinese and Western ideas in order to have effective engagement with the Chinese students. The challenges Western educators experience in teaching mainland Chinese students are as follows: (a) a lack of abstract thinking; (b) constraints on behaviour caused by face issue; (c) excessive emphasis on concrete examples and (d) lack of creativity and the need to compromise in group situations. There are distinct educational differences that are to be addressed for Chinese students to reach their fullest potential in courses offered overseas universities conducted in Singapore. The primary goal of the study is to appreciate and comprehend the influence of cultural dislocation inferences in pursuing a Western-based education, in our case, mainland Chinese students. To be specific, the influence of Chinese cultural values, background, learning patterns and styles on the pursuit of Western-based business education is addressed. The motivation of this study is largely due to the minimal or weak research evidence that has been conducted on mainland Chinese students pursuing a Western-based education in Singapore.

There is a close correlation between the Chinese culture, their learning styles and instructional methodologies adopted to transfer knowledge. It is emphasized that rote learning is intensely rooted in Chinese traditions that acts as a key influencing element. Confucian-based learning culture constitutes a formidable obstacle in shifting from knowledge transmission to learning facilitation. Thus, this study aims to discuss and presents theoretical evidence on how the Chinese culture has an impact on their learning styles with grounded justifications and arguments. Extensive literature on the entwined relationships of educational and cultural aspects strengthens the underlying intention for the development of the emerging conceptual framework. The curriculum development and teaching style could be viewed as the outcomes of cultural impact (Selvarajah 2006).

Apart from language and translation, other critical cultural gaps have to be identified and addressed—for example, not only in the adaptation of the training materials for relevancy but also in the style of delivery in meeting students' educational needs. Ford (2004) examines the behavioural aspects in the manner information is received and processed by individuals and on how the behavioural notions are encompassed in the general learning processes. Richards and Ross (2004) point out how culture influences learning and teaching styles. This is further validated in the integrated frameworks of Hofstede's (2001) cultural dimensions and Gibb's (1996) enterprising approach that examines the teaching and learning styles. The themes from this integrated framework provided useful referencing bases in the development of the conceptual framework, especially when examined from the perspective of facilitating offshore programmes in a cross-cultural context.

Thus, the following gaps are distinctively identified in the current literature:

(a) The cultural dislocation and learning cultural challenges involved in the adaptability of mainland Chinese students pursuing a Western-based education in another cultural setting, i.e. Singapore.
(b) No single and concrete framework exists to specifically address the learning effectiveness of mainland Chinese students in their pursuit of Western-based education in preparing them to achieve good academic grades and be able to deliver quality outcomes as future managers.

(c) The specific behavioural patterns and learning styles of mainland Chinese students, focusing on the effectiveness on their learning in contrast to their preferred instructional techniques.

There has been ardent interest in research on the learning approaches in a Chinese context due to the broad anecdotal evidence of Hong Kong and mainland Chinese students' use of rote learning (McKay and Kember 1997), which has been perceived as an inappropriate and ineffective learning approach for Western-style higher education (Leung et al. 2008). However, when this aspect was examined in overseas universities, it was discovered that Chinese students performed well compared to their Western counterparts, for example, results from the International Association for the Evaluation of Educational Achievement, 1988 as a validating source. This rote learning phenomenon has evolved to be acknowledged as the paradox of the Chinese learner (Leung et al. 2008). Hence this directs us to reflect on the question: 'If Chinese students really did predominantly use approaches to learning associated with negative outcomes, how and why could they still perform well compared to Western students?' Some researchers are beginning to argue that the Western studies have misunderstood the Chinese learners due to cultural biases and assumptions (Wu 2015; Zhang 2013; Rajaram 2013). This re-emphasizes the urgency and importance of examining the appropriate instructional techniques that facilitate mainland Chinese students to acquire knowledge effectively, thus enabling them to understand the information taught to their best academic potential.

Incontrovertibly, a new generation of Chinese leaders is emerging, and they are, to some extent, different from those of the past in terms of work values. The new generation group of Chinese leaders scored significantly higher on individualism, characterized by self-enhancement and openness to change, than did the current and older generation groups (Jaw et al. 2007). With 10 over years since then with so much of evolution and advancement of China, we could be convinced that the Chinese leaders have evolved in their openness and new ways of thinking. It is highly probable that the current generation of mainland Chinese students do not share the same preferred learning style with the previous generations. Thus, it is essential to offer an integrated framework that investigates the relationships on how the cultural dislocation aspects namely, familiarity, comfort and knowledge transfer influence the students' learning effectiveness when measured across varying instructional techniques. This becomes absolutely necessary, especially when there is no clear empirical validation as to how these cultural dislocation attributes and inferred learning effectiveness variables react when examined through the lens of the instructional techniques.

The profile of undergraduate students was chosen as they form the largest cohort among the cluster of mainland Chinese students in the pursuit of their studies in Singapore. That decision was further validated as they form one of the largest percentages among the international students' profile. This study will add to and enrich the existing findings in Singapore, which endeavours to be a global educational hub. The new knowledge of the Chinese cultural dislocation aspects and appropriate instructional modes to attain an optimal learning effectiveness through adoption of the correct mix of instructional techniques, hence creating an effective learning process and climate, provides beneficial inputs to all higher education institutions that attract a large proportion of mainland Chinese students. The study serves as a one-stop platform to understand and better nurture this group of international students, as they are the future managers who are expected to take up leadership positions in various organizations and ministries in Singapore and globally. By having the students to learn effectively through equipping them the required contents knowledge, enhancing their cultural awareness, competencies and skills, it enables them to contribute competently as future leaders.

References

Atkins, T. V., & Ashcroft, L. (2004). Information skills of undergraduate business students: A comparison of UK and international students. *Library Management, 25*(1/2), 39–55.

Atkinson, D. (1997). A critical approach to critical thinking in TESOL. *TESOL Quarterly, 31*(1), 9–37. https://doi.org/10.2307/3587975

Ball, M. A., & Mahony, M. (1987). Foreign students, libraries, and culture. *College and Research Libraries, 48*(2), 160–166.

Barmeyer, C. I. (2004). Learning styles and their impact on cross-cultural training: An international comparison in France, Germany, and Quebec. *International Journal of Intercultural Relations, 28*(6), 577–594. https://doi.org/10.1016/j.ijintrel.2005.01.011

Baron, S., & Strout-Dapaz, A. (2001). Communicating with and empowering international students with a library skills set. *Reference Services Review, 29*(4), 314–326. https://doi.org/10.1108/00907320110408447

Berry, J. W. (1976). *Human ecology and cognitive style: Comparative studies in cultural and psychological adaptation* (Vol. 3). New York: Wiley.

Biederman, I., & Tsao, Y. C. (1979). On processing Chinese ideographs and English words: Some implications from Stroop-test results. *Cognitive Psychology, 11*(2), 125–132.

Biggs, J. (1991). Approaches to learning in secondary and tertiary students in Hong Kong: Some comparative studies. *Educational Research Journal, 6*, 27–39.

Biggs, J. (1994). Asian learners through Western eyes: An astigmatic paradox. *Australian and New Zealand Journal of Vocational Educational Research, 2*(2), 40–63.

Biggs, J. (1996). Western misperceptions of the Confucian heritage learning culture. In D. Watkins & J. Biggs (Eds.), *The Chinese learner: Cultural, psychological, and contextual influences* (pp. 45–67). Hong Kong, China: Comparative Education Research Centre.

Biggs, J. B., & Watkins, D. (2001a). Insights into teaching the Chinese learner. In D. Watkin & J. B. Biggs (Eds.), *Teaching the Chinese learner: Psychological and pedagogical perspectives* (pp. 277–300). Hong Kong: Comparative Education and Research Centre and Australian Council for Educational Research.

Biggs, J. B., & Watkins, D. (2001b). The paradox of the Chinese learner and beyond. In D. Watkins & J. B. Biggs (Eds.), *Teaching the Chinese learner: Psychological and pedagogical perspectives* (pp. 3–23). Hong Kong: Comparative Education and Research Centre and Australian Council for Educational Research.

Bohlin, N., & Brenner, P. (1996). The learning organization journey: Assessing and valuing progress. *The Systems Thinker, 7*(5), 1–5.

Boisot, M., & Child, J. (1999). Organizations as adaptive systems in complex environments: The case of China. *Organization Science, 10*(3), 237–252.

Bond, M. H. (1991). *Beyond the Chinese face: Insights from psychology*. USA: Oxford University Press.

Bond, M. H. (1992). *Beyond the Chinese face: Insights from psychology*. Hong Kong: Oxford University Press.

Bond, M. H., & Hwang, K.-K. (1986). The social psychology of Chinese people. In M. H. Bond (Ed.), *The psychology of the Chinese people* (pp. 213–266). New York: Oxford University Press.

Bradley, D., & Bradley, M. (1984). *Problems of Asian students in Australia: Language, culture and education*. Canberra: AGPS.

Bu, N., & Mitchell, V. F. (1992). Developing the PRC's managers: How can western experts become more helpful? *Journal of Management Development, 11*(2), 42–53. https://doi.org/10.1108/EUM0000000001394

Cagiltay, K., & Bichelmeyer, B. (2000). Differences in learning styles in different cultures: A qualitative study. *Cognitive Style, 23*, 1–23.

Carson, J. (1992). Becoming biliterate: First language influences. *Journal of Second Language Writing, 1*(1), 37–60. https://doi.org/10.1016/1060-3743(92)90019-L

Cassidy, S. (2004). Learning styles: An overview of theories, models and measures. *Educational Psychology, 24*(4), 419–444.

Chalmers, D., & Volet, S. (1997). Common misconceptions from South-East Asia studying in Australia. *Higher Education Research & Development, 16*(1), 87–99.

Chan, J. (1976). Is Raven's Progressive Matrices test culture-free or culture-fair? Some research findings in Hong Kong context. In *Third international association for cross-cultural psychology congress*, Tilburg.

Chan, S. (1991). *Asian Americans: An interpretative history*. Boston: Twayne.

Chan, S. (1999). The Chinese learner: A question of style. *Education & Training, 41*(6/7), 294–304. https://doi.org/10.1108/00400919910285345

Chan, D., & Drover, G. (1997). Teaching and learning for overseas students: The Hong Kong connection. In D. McNamara & R. Harris (Eds.), *Overseas students in higher education* (Issues in teaching and learning) (pp. 46–61). London: Routledge.

Chan, C. K. K., & Rao, N. (2009). *Revisiting the Chinese learner: Changing education, changing context*. Hong Kong: Springer and the Comparative Education Research Centre, University of Hong Kong.

Chen, M. L. (2009). Influence of grade level on perceptual learning style preferences and language learning strategies of Taiwanese English as a Foreign Language Learners. *Learning and Individual Differences, 19*, 304–308.

Chow, I. H. S. (1995). Management education in Hong Kong: Needs and challenges, International. *Journal of Educational Management, 9*, 10–15.

Chris, S. H., & Arthur, E. P. (2014). Chinese students' participation: The effect of cultural factors. *Education + Training, 56*(5), 430–446.

Civil Service College. (2017). *Singapore four principles of governance*. Retrieved September 25, 2017, from https://www.cscollege.gov.sg/Knowledge/Ethos/Ethos%20November%202004/Pages/Singapore%20Four%20Principles%20Of%20Governance.aspx

Clark, R., & Gieve, S. N. (2006). On the discursive construction of 'the Chinese learner'. *Language, Culture and Curriculum, 19*(1), 54–73.

Coffield, F., et al. (2004). *Learning styles and pedagogy in post-16 learning*. Learning and Skills Research Centre. http://www.lsda.org.uk/files/PDF/1543.pdf

Cortazzi, M., & Jin, L. (1996). Cultures of learning: Language classrooms in China. In H. Coleman (Ed.), *Society and the language classroom* (pp. 169–206). Cambridge: CUP.

Cortazzi, M., & Jin, L. (2001). Large classes in China 'good' teachers and interaction. In J. Biggs & D. Watkins (Eds.), *Teaching the Chinese learner* (pp. 115–134). Hong Kong: Comparative Education Research Centre.

Coverdale-Jones, T., & Rastall, P. (Eds.). (2009). *Internationalising the University: The Chinese context*. Houndsmills: Palgrave Macmillan.

Daniel, H. K. (1993). The LMK between individual and organisational Learning, Sloan Management Review Association

Daquila, T. C. (2013). Internationalizing higher education in Singapore: Government policies and the NUS experience. *Journal of Studies in International Education, 17*(5), 629–647.

De Vita, G. (2002). Cultural equivalence in the assessment of home and international business management students: A UK exploratory study. *Studies in Higher Education, 27*(2), 221–231. https://doi.org/10.1080/03075070220120038

Durkin, K. (2011). Adapting to Western norms of critical argumentation and debate. In L. Jin & M. Cortazzi (Eds.), *Researching Chinese learners: Skills, perceptions, and intercultural adaptations* (pp. 274–291). London: Palgrave Macmillan.

Edwards, D. (1982). Project marking: Some problems and issues. *Teaching at a Distance, 21*, 28–34.

Ehrman, M., & Oxford, R. (1990). Adult language learning styles and strategies in an intensive training setting. *Modern Language Journal, 74*(3), 311–327.

Ehrman, M. E., Leaver, B. L., & Oxford, R. L. (2003). A brief overview of individual differences in second language learning 1. *System, 31*(3), 313–330.

Felder, R. M., & Silverman, L. K. (1998). Learning and teaching styles in engineering education. *Engineering Education, 78*(7), 674–681.

Ford, N. (2004). Towards a model of learning for educational informatics. *Journal of documentation, 60*(2), 183–225.

Fox, H. (1994). *Listening to the world*. Urbana: National Council of Teachers of English.

Frazee, V. (1996). Keeping up on Chinese culture. *Personnel Journal, 1*(1), 16.

Freedman, M. (1979). *The study of Chinese society: Essays by Maurice Freedman, selected and introduced by G. William Skinner*. Sanford: Stanford University Press.

Garcha, R., & Russell, P. Y. (1993). Bibliographic instruction for international students in academic libraries. *Library Review, 42*(6), 14–22. https://doi.org/10.1108/00242539310045426

Geake, J., & Maingard, C. (1999). NESB postgraduate students at a new university: Plus ca change plus c'est la meme chose. In Y. Ryan & O. Zuber-Skerritt (Eds.), *Supervising postgraduates from non-English speaking backgrounds* (pp. 48–60). Buckingham: The Society for Research into Higher Education and Open University Press.

Gibb, A. A. (1996). Entrepreneurship and small business management: Can we afford to neglect them in the twenty-first century business school? *British Journal of management, 7*(4), 309–321.

Gu, M. (2001). *Education in China and abroad: Perspectives from a lifetime in comparative education*. Hong Kong: Comparative Education Centre.

Hellmundt, S. (2001, December). *The Internationalisation of the Tertiary Curriculum: Strategies to Link Critical Theory and Intercultural Understandings*. Paper presented at the Australian Association for Research in Education Conference, Fremantle.

Hess, R., & Azuma, H. (1991). Cultural support for schooling: Contrasts between Japan and the United States. *Educational Researcher, 20*(9), 2–8. https://doi.org/10.3102/0013189X020009002

Ho, D. Y. F. (1986). Chinese patterns of socialization: A critical review. In M. H. Bond (Ed.), *The psychology of the Chinese people* (pp. 1–35). Oxford: Oxford University Press.

Hofstede, G. (1980). *Culture's consequences*. Beverly Hills: Sage.

Hofstede, G. (2001). *Culture's consequences: Comparing values, behaviors, institutions and organizations across nations*. Thousand Oaks: Sage.

Hofstede, G., & Bond, M. H. (1988). The Confucian connection: From cultural roots to economic growth. *Organizational Dynamics, 16*(4), 5–21.

Holland, R. P. (1989). Learner characteristics and learner performance: Implications for instructional placement decision. In B. J. R. Shade (Ed.), *Culture, style and the educative process* (pp. 167–183). Springfield: Charles C. Thomas.

Hoosain, R., & Osgood, C. E. (1983). Processing times for English and Chinese words. *Perception & Psychophysics, 34*(6), 573–577.

Hu, G. W. (2003). English language teaching in China: Regional differences and contributing factors. *Journal of Multilingual and Multicultural Development, 24*(4), 290–318. https://doi.org/10.1080/01434630308666503

Hu, C., Chand, P., & Evans, E. (2013). The effect of national culture, acculturation, and education on accounting judgments: A comparative study of Australian and Chinese culture. *Journal of International Accounting Research, 12*(2), 51–77.

Huang, F., Hoi, C. K. W., & Teo, T. (2018). The influence of learning style on English learning achievement among undergraduates in mainland China. *Journal of Psycholinguistic.* https://doi.org/10.1007/s10936-018-9578-3

Jarrah, F. (1998). New courses will target transition to university. *China Morning Post,* 23 April, 28.

Jaw, B. S., Ling, Y. H., Yu-Ping Wang, C., & Chang, W. C. (2007). The impact of culture on Chinese employees' work values. *Personnel Review, 36*(1), 128–144.

Jin, L., & Cortazzi, M. (1998). Dimensions of dialogue: Large classes in China. *International Journal of Educational Research, 29,* 739–761.

Jones, J. (1999). From silence to talk: Cross cultural ideas on students' participation in academic group discussion. *English for Specific Purposes, 18*(3), 243–259.

Kahn, R. L. (1979). Aging and social support. *Aging from birth to death: Interdisciplinary perspectives, 1,* 77–91.

Kamhi-Stein, L. D. (1998). Profiles of underprepared second-language readers. *Journal of Adolescent & Adult Literacy, 41*(8), 610–619.

Kember, D. (1996). The intention to both memorise and understand: Another approach to learning? *Higher Education, 31,* 341–354.

Kember, D. (2016). Understanding and teaching the Chinese learner: Resolving the paradox of the Chinese learner. In *The psychology of Asian learners* (pp. 173–187). Singapore: Springer.

Kember, D., & Gow, L. (1990). Cultural specificity of approaches to study. *British Journal of Educational Psychology, 60*(3), 356–363. https://doi.org/10.1111/j.2044-8279.1990.tb00952.x

Kirkpatrick, A. 2004. "Some thoughts on the Chinese learner and the teaching of writing.

Kirkbride, P. S., & Tang, S. F. (1992). Management development in the Nanyang Chinese societies of south-east Asia. *Journal of Management Development, 11*(2), 54–66.

Kolb, D. A., & Fry, R. (1975). Toward an applied theory of experiential learning. In C. Cooper (Ed.), *Studies of Group Process* (pp. 33–57). New York: Wiley.

Kumaravadivelu, B. (2003). Problematizing culture stereotypes in TESOL. *TESOL Quarterly, 37*(4), 709–716. https://doi.org/10.2307/3588219

Lacina, J. G. (2002). Preparing international students for a successful social experience in higher education. *New Directions for Higher Education, 117,* 21–28. https://doi.org/10.1002/he.43

Ladd, P. D., & Ruby Jr., R. (1999). Learning style and adjustment issues of international students. *Journal of Education in Business, 74*(6), 363–367.

Lau, S. K. (1982). *Society and politics in Hong Kong.* Hong Kong: Chinese University Press.

Lee, W. O. (1996). The cultural context for Chinese learners: Conceptions of learning in the Confucian tradition. *The Chinese learner: Cultural, psychological and contextual influences, 34,* 63–67.

Leung, D. Y. P., Ginns, P., & Kember, D. (2008). Examining the cultural specificity of approaches to learning in universities in Hong Kong and Sydney. *Journal of Cross-Cultural Psychology, 39*(3), 251–266. https://doi.org/10.1177/0022022107313905

Lin, Y. (1977). *My country and my people.* Hong Kong: Heinemann.

Littlewood, W. (2009). Participation-based pedagogy: How congruent is it with Chinese cultures of learning? In P. Cheng & J. X. Yan (Eds.), *Cultural identity and language anxiety* (pp. 179–202). Guilin: Guangxi Normal University Press.

Liu, I. M. (1986a). Chinese cognition. In M. H. Bond (Ed.), *The psychology of the Chinese people* (pp. 73–105). New York: Oxford University Press.

Liu, I. M. (1986b). Chinese cognition. In M. H. Bond (Ed.), *The psychology of the Chinese people.* Hong Kong: Oxford University Press.

Liu, S. (2006). Developing China's future managers: Learning from the West? *Education & Training, 48*(1), 6–14.

Louie, K. (2005). Gathering cultural knowledge: Useful or use with care? In J. Carroll & J. Ryan (Eds.), *Teaching international students: Improving learning for all* (pp. 17–25). London: Routledge Falmer.

Low, L. (2001). The Singapore developmental state in the new economy and polity. *The Pacific Review, 14*(3), 411–441.

Malhotra, N. K., & McCort, J. D. (2001). A cross-cultural comparison of behavioral intention models-Theoretical consideration and an empirical investigation. *International Marketing Review, 18*(3), 235–269.

Martinsons, M. G., & Martinsons, A. B. (1996). Conquering cultural constraints to cultivate Chinese management creativity and innovation. *Journal of Management Development, 15*(9), 18–35.

Marton, F., Dall'Alba, G., & Tse, L. K. (1996). Memorizing and understanding: The keys to the paradox? In D. A. Watkins & J. B. Biggs (Eds.), *The Chinese learner: Cultural, psychological and contextual influences* (pp. 69–83). Hong Kong: Comparative Education Research Centre and The Australian Council for Educational Research.

McKay, J., & Kember, D. (1997). Spoon feeding leads to regurgitation: A better diet can result in more digestible learning outcomes. *Higher Education Research & Development, 16*(1), 55–67.

McMahon, P. (2011). Chinese voices: Chinese learners and their experiences of living and studying in the United Kingdom. *Journal of Higher Education Policy and Management, 33*(4), 401–414.

McNaught, C. (2012). SOTL at cultural interfaces: Exploring nuance in learning designs at a Chinese university. *International Journal for the Scholarship of Teaching and Learning, 6*(2), 1–7.

Ministry of Education. (2017, March 7). *Many paths, new possibilities: Nurturing our students' aptitudes & enhancing their access to opportunities.* Retrieved from https://www.moe.gov.sg/news/press-releases/many-paths%2D%2Dnew-possibilities%2D%2Dnurturing-our-students-aptitudes-and-enhancing-their-access-to-opportunities

Ministry of Trade and Industry Singapore. (1986, February). *Report of the economic committee.* Retrieved from https://www.mti.gov.sg/ResearchRoom/Documents/app.mti.gov.sg/data/pages/885/doc/econ.pdf

Ministry of Trade and Industry Singapore. (1991, December 1). *The strategic economic plan: Towards a developed nation.* Retrieved from https://www.mti.gov.sg/ResearchRoom/Documents/app.mti.gov.sg/data/pages/885/doc/NWS_plan.pdf

Morey, D., & Frangioso, T. (1998). Aligning an organization for learning – The six principles of effective learning. *Journal of Knowledge Management, 1*(4), 308–214.

Nakamura, H. (1964). *Ways of thinking of Eastern people.* Honolulu: University of Hawaii Press.

Naserieh, F., & Sarab, M. R. A. (2013). Perceptual learning style preferences among Iranian graduate students. *System, 41*(1), 122–133.

Natowitz, A. (1995). International students in US academic libraries: Recent concerns and trends. *Research Strategies, 13*(1), 4–16.

Nelson, G. (1995). Cultural differences in learning styles. In J. Reid (Ed.), *Learning styles in the ESL/EFL classroom* (pp. 3–18). New York: Heinle & Heinle.

Newell, S. (1999). The transfer of management knowledge to China: Building learning communities rather than translating Western textbooks? *Education + Training, 41*(6/7), 286–294.

Ninnes, P., Aitchison, C., & Kalos, S. (1999). Challenges to stereotypes of international students' prior educational experience: Undergraduate education in India. *Higher Education, Research and Development, 18*(3), 323–342. https://doi.org/10.1080/0729436990180304

Northrop, F. S. C. (1946). *The meeting of east and west.* New York: Macmillan.

O'Donoghue, T. (1996). Malaysian Chinese students' perceptions of what is necessary for their academic success in Australia: A case study at one university. *Journal of Further and Higher Education, 20*(2), 67–80.

Oxford, R. (1995). A cross cultural view of learning styles. *Language Teaching, 28,* 201–215.

Oxford, R. L. (2003). *Language learning styles and strategies: An overview*. Retrieved November, 2015, from http://web.ntpu.edu.tw/~language/workshop/read2.pdf

Oxford, R. L., & Anderson, N. (1995). A cross-cultural view of learning styles. *Language Teaching, 28*(4), 201–215.

Pun, A. S. L. (1989a). *Developing managers internationally: Culture free or culture bound.* Symposium presentation at the Conference on International Personnel and Human Resource Management, Hong Kong, 13 December.

Pun, A. S. L. (1989b). Action learning in the Chinese culture: Possibility or pitfall. In *Manchester international human resource development conference*, Manchester.

Rajaram, K. (2010). *Culture Clash: Teaching western-based business education to mainland Chinese students in Singapore*. PhD thesis, University of South Australia.

Rajaram, K. (2013). Followers of Confucianism or a New Generation? Learning culture of mainland Chinese: In pursuit of western based business education away from mainland China. *International Journal of Teaching & Learning in Higher Education, 25*(3), 369–377.

Rajaram, K., & Bordia, S. (2011). Culture Clash: Teaching Western-based management education to mainland Chinese students in Singapore. *Journal of International Education in Business, 4*(1), 63–83.

Rajaram, K., & Bordia, S. (2013). East versus west: Effectiveness of knowledge acquisition and impact of cultural dislocation issues for mainland Chinese students across ten commonly used instructional techniques. *International Journal for the Scholarship of Teaching and Learning, 7*(1), 1–21.

Rajaram, K., & Collins, J. B. (2013). Qualitative identification of learning effectiveness indicators among mainland Chinese students in culturally dislocated study environments. *Journal of International Education in Business, 6*(2), 179–199.

Redding, S. G. (1980). Management education for Orientals. In B. Garrat & J. Stopford (Eds.), *Breaking down barriers: Practice and priorities for international management education*. Farnborough: Westmead.

Redding, G. (1990). *The spirit of Chinese capitalism*. New York: Walter de Guyter.

Redding, S. G. (1993). The Chinese family business. In *The spirit of Chinese capitalism* (pp. 143–181). New York: Walter de Guyter.

Reid, J. M. (1987). The learning style preferences of ESL students. *TESOL quarterly, 21*(1), 87–111.

Richards, N., & Lee Ross, D. (2004). Offshore teaching and learning: An exploratory Singaporean study. *International Journal of Educational Management, 18*(4), 260–265.

Riding, R. J., & Read, G. (1996). Cognitive style and pupil learning preferences. *Educational Psychology, 16*(1), 81–106.

Rodrigues, C. A. (2004). The importance level of ten teaching/learning techniques as rated by university business students and instructors. *Journal of Management Development, 23*(2), 169–182. https://doi.org/10.1108/02621710410517256

Ryan, J. (2000). *A guide to teaching international students*. Oxford: Oxford Centre for Staff and Learning Development.

Ryan, J. (2010). "Chinese learners": Misconceptions and realities. In J. Ryan & G. Slethaug (Eds.), *International education and the Chinese learner* (pp. 37–56). Hong Kong: Hong Kong University Press.

Ryan, J., & Louie, K. (2005, November). Dichotomy or complexity: Problematising concepts of scholarship and learning. In *34th Annual philosophy of education society of Australasia conference*.

Ryan, J., & Slethaug, G. (2010). *International Education and the Chinese Learner* (pp. 13–89). Hong Kong: University Press.

Sadeghi, N., Kasim, Z. M., Tan, B. H., & Abdullah, F. S. (2012). Learning styles, personality types and reading comprehension performance. *English Language Teaching, 5*(4), 116–123.

Salili, F. (1996). Accepting personal responsibility for learning. In D. Watkins & J. Biggs (Eds.), *The Chinese learner: Cultural, psychological and contextual influences* (pp. 85–106). Hong

Kong: Comparative Education Research Centre and Australian Council of Educational Research.

Samuelowicz, K. (1987). Learning problems of overseas students: Two sides of a story. *Higher Education Research and Development, 6*, 121–134.

Saravanamuthu, K., & Yap, C. (2014). Pedagogy to empower Chinese Learners to adapt to western learning circumstances: A longitudinal case-study. *Cambridge Journal of Education, 44*(3), 361–384. https://doi.org/10.1080/0305764X.2014.914154

Schermerhorn, J. R. (1987). Organizational features of Chinese industrial enterprise: Paradoxes of stability in times of change. *The Academy of Management Executive, 1*(4), 345–349.

Selvarajah, C. (2006). Cross-Cultural study of Asian and European student perception: The need to understand the changing educational environment in New Zealand. *Cross-cultural management: An International Journal, 13*(2), 142–155.

Senge, P. (1990). *The fifth discipline*. The Art of Practice of the Learning Organization, Doubleday.

Shade, B. J. (1989a). Culture and learning style within the Afro-American community. In *Culture, style and the educative process* (pp. 16–32). Springfield: Charles C. Thomas.

Shade, B. J. (1989b). Culture: The key to adaptation. In B. J. R. Shade (Ed.), *Culture, style and the educative process* (pp. 9–15). Springfield: Charles C. Thomas Publisher.

Shi, L. (2006). The successors to Confucianism or a new generation? A questionnaire study on Chinese students' culture of learning English'. *Language, Culture and Curriculum, 19*(1), 122–147.

SkillsFuture Singapore and Workforce Singapore. (2017, November 9). Retrieved from http://www.ssg-wsg.gov.sg/about.html?_ga=2.63711594.414705368.1498703964-53519 9895.1498703964

Slethaug, G. (2010). Something happened while nobody was looking: The growth of international education and the Chinese learner. In *International education and the Chinese learner* (pp. 15–36). Hong Kong: Hong Kong University Press.

Sun, P. P., & Teng, L. S. (2017). Profiling perceptual learning styles of Chinese as a second language learners in university settings. *Journal of Psycholinguistic Research, 46*, 1529–1548.

Tan, D., & Akhtar, S. (1998). Organizational commitment and experienced burnout: An exploratory study from a Chinese cultural perspective. *International Journal of Organizational Analysis, 6*(4), 310–333.

Tian, X., & Qian, D. (2014). Online learning and Chinese student: Still searching for the right blend. *Currents in Teaching & Learning, 6*(2), 4–16.

Triandis, H. C., Bontempo, R., Villareal, M. J., Asai, M., & Lucca, N. (1988). Individualism and collectivism: Cross-cultural perspectives on self-ingroup relationships. *Journal of personality and Social Psychology, 54*(2), 323.

Tse, D. K., Lee, K. H., Vertinsky, I., & Wehrung, D. A. (1988). Does culture matter? A cross-cultural study of executives' choice, decisiveness, and risk adjustment in international marketing. *The Journal of Marketing, 52*, 81–95.

Turner, Y. (2006). Chinese students in UK business school: Hearing the student voice in reflective teaching and learning. *Higher Education Quarterly, 60*, 27–51.

Turner, Y. (2013). Pathologies of silence? Reflecting on international learner identities amidst the classroom chatter. In J. Ryan (Ed.), *Cross-cultural teaching and learning for home and international students* (pp. 15–26). London: Routledge.

Vernon, P. E. (1982). *The abilities and achievements of Orientals in North America*. New York: Academic Press.

Volt, S., & Ang, G. (1998). Culturally mixed groups on international campuses: An opportunity for inter-cultural learning. *Higher Education Research and Development, 17*(1), 5–23.

Warner, M. (1991). How Chinese managers learn. *Journal of General Management, 16*(4), 66–84.

Watkins, D. (2000). Learning and teaching: A cross-cultural perspective. *School Leadership and Management, 20*(2), 161–173.

Watkins, D. A., & Biggs, J. B. (Eds.). (1996). *The Chinese learner: Cultural, psychological and contextual influences*. Hong Kong/Melbourne: Comparative Education Research Centre, The University of Hong Kong/Australian Council for Educational Research.

Watkins, D., & Biggs, J. B. (2001). The paradox of the Chinese learner and beyond. In D. Watkins & J. B. Biggs (Eds.), *Teaching the Chinese learner*. CERC: Hong Kong.

Wayman, S. G. (1984). The international student in the academic library. *Journal of Academic Librarianship, 9*(6), 336–341.

Wen, W. P., & Clement, R. (2003). A Chinese conceptualisation of willingness to communicate in ESL. *Language, Culture and Curriculum, 16*(1), 18–38.

Wingrove, N. (1993). It's not always piracy say Hong Kong engineers. *Research Technology Management, 6*(36), 4–5.

Wintergerst, A. C., DeCapua, A., & Verna, M. A. (2003). Conceptualizing learning style modalities for ESL/EFL students. *System, 31*(1), 85–106.

Witkin, H. A., & Berry, J. W. (1975). Psychological differentiation in cross-cultural perspective. *ETS Research Report Series, 1975*(1).

Witkin, H. A., Dyk, R. B., Fattuson, H. F., Goodenough, D. R., & Karp, S. A. (1962). *Psychological differentiation: Studies of development*. New York: Wiley.

Witkins, H. A., Moore, C. A., Goodenough, D. R., & Cox, P. W. (1977). Field-dependent and field-independent cognitive styles and their educational implications. *Review of Educational Research, 47*(1), 1–64. https://doi.org/10.3102/00346543047001001

Wright, G. N., Phillips, L. D., Whalley, P. C., Choo, G. T., Ng, K. O., Tan, I., et al. (1978). Cultural differences in probabilistic thinking. *Journal of Cross-Cultural Psychology, 9*(3), 285–299.

Wu, Q. (2015). Re-examining the "Chinese learner": A case study of mainland Chinese students' learning experiences at British Universities. *Higher Education, 70*(4), 753–766.

Yang, Z. (2009). The effect of mother tongue transfer on English writing. *Teaching and Management, 11*(3), 16–20.

Yao, X. (2000). *An introduction to Confucianism*. Cambridge: CUP.

Yau, O. (1994). *Consumer behavior in China*. London: Routledge.

Yee, A. (1989). Cross cultural perspectives on higher education in East Asia: Psychological effects upon Asian students. *Journal of Multilingual and Multicultural Development, 10*(3), 213–232. https://doi.org/10.1080/01434632.1989.9994375

Yu, H. (2016). Why are they silent?: Unilateralism in the classroom discourse of Chinese higher education (Symposium: Worlds of representation). *Society, 53*(6), 625–628.

Zhang, Y. L. (2013). Power distance in online learning: Experience of Chinese learners in US higher education. *The International Review of Research in Open and Distributed Learning, 14*(4), 238–254.

Zhang, J., & Evans, M. S. (2013). An empirical study on the multidimensional learning styles of Chinese EFL students. *International Proceedings of Economic Development and Research, 68*, 61–69.

Part II
Applications to Universities and Higher Education Institutions

Chapter 5
Teach and Engage Mainland Chinese Students: Impact of Instructional Techniques Across Perceived Learning Effectiveness, Comfort, Familiarity and Knowledge Transfer

The chapter presents the interworkings between perceived learning effectiveness, comfort, familiarity and knowledge transfer across the cultural dislocation aspects and active/passive instructional techniques. Next, the quantitative analysis of the following is presented with supporting discussions, namely, (a) perceived learning effectiveness across different instructional techniques; (b) correlations among perceived learning effectiveness, comfort, familiarity and knowledge transfer; (c) perceived learning effectiveness and comfort; (d) perceived learning effectiveness and familiarity; (e) perceived learning effectiveness and ease of knowledge transfer; and (f) active versus passive instructional techniques. The chapter concludes with a section on implications and recommendations inline to mainland Chinese students' cultural dislocation aspects and the nuances in delivering knowledge to them effectively to achieve quality education.

Universities and higher education institutions require adequate measurements of learning effectiveness evaluated from varying aspects to set out processes to achieve quality educational deliverables. The usage of the correct set of instructional techniques requires a good understanding of the learning culture and culture of learning in context. Facilitating with the correct mix of instructional techniques allows optimal level of knowledge transfer to occur and allows students to bring out their fullest potential in terms of their performance. Studies have found that correlation between the presentations of learning materials and adopting the correct mix of instructional techniques with a good understanding on learning principles will have an impact on students' learning behaviour, the culture of learning and learning culture (Rajaram 2010, 2013). Rajaram and Collins (2013) advocate when an institution adopts

---

This chapter is improved from Rajaram, K. (2013). Learning in foreign cultures: Self-reports learning effectiveness across different instructional techniques. *World Journal of Education, 3*(4), 71–95 and Rajaram, K., & Bordia, S. (2013). East versus west: Effectiveness of knowledge acquisition and impact of cultural dislocation issues for mainland Chinese students across ten commonly used instructional techniques. *International Journal for the Scholarship of Teaching and Learning, 7*(1), 1–21.

© Springer Nature Singapore Pte Ltd. 2020
K. Rajaram, *Educating Mainland Chinese Learners in Business Education*,
https://doi.org/10.1007/978-981-15-3395-2_5

inappropriate instructional techniques not in congruence with its learning philosophy, mission and directions, they bound to receive unsatisfactory learning outcomes. Scholars such a Tan (2011), Rajaram and Bordia (2011) and Rajaram (2013) believe that one of the primary challenges in today's international business education is to have instructors comprehend the complexities involved in the learning culture and culture of learning embedded with cultural dislocation aspects in varying contexts enabling them to adopt appropriate and effective instructional strategies.

5.1   The Interworkings Between Learning Effectiveness, Comfort, Familiarity and Knowledge Transfer

In our research study, we have shown the linkage between the terms 'power distance' to comfort, 'uncertainty avoidance' to familiarity and 'philosophy of Confucianism' to knowledge transfer. Basically, for power distance, the level of hierarchical structure involved in a professional relationship and the effectiveness of the work structure are measured on the range of comfort and discomfort that one experiences; as for the uncertainty avoidance, the ambiguity, unsure feeling and vagueness that occur in varying situational context are measured on the range of familiarity and not so. Here, we use a basic logic of higher familiarity correlates to lesser ambiguity and vice versa. Lastly, for 'philosophy of Confucianism', the values and beliefs emerging from the philosophy of Confucius are measured on the effects of the learning process and the culture it shapes.

Comfort
Learners from a collective and a higher power distance culture prefer to be in a more structured, with more levels of consensus to be reached and information coming from an expert or a person of authority in that field to facilitate their learning and acquire knowledge more effectively. In other words, these students feel discomfort if they are placed in a learning environment where there is higher involvement of peers' evaluation in comparison to the instructor's involvement, who is viewed as an expert and higher in the hierarchy. In general, Chinese learning culture is categorized to be in the range of high power distance. These students do not challenge the teacher's teaching and generally obey those in an authoritative or higher position in the hierarchy. Shi (2006) in his study reported that mainland Chinese students 'did not think having their own opinions was important for a good learner' (p. 138). However, the question that we were intrigued about was to examine if these students' comfort level on the instructional techniques affects their perceived learning effectiveness.

Familiarity
Lecture as an instructional technique is the most preferred by mainland Chinese students due to their exposure to this approach since their high school days. Participative, interactive and competitive activities may not be compatible with Chinese social values (Kumaravadivelu 2003; Chan 1991; Carson and Nelson 1996; Nelson 1995; Oxford 1995). However, Shi's (2006) study involving 400 middle school students in Shanghai revealed that students prefer a more interactive rela-

tionship with teachers. So, we were interested to examine if students' familiarity to instructional techniques has any effect on their perceived learning effectiveness and preference in accepting how they were taught.

Knowledge Transfer

Different ways by which knowledge is transferred to students have varying impacts on the effectiveness of students' learning. Evidence in the literature states that mainland Chinese students need close supervision and directions to carry out their assigned academic tasks (Chan 1999; Chow 1995; Newell 1999; Oxford 1995). It was also emphasized that they prefer the more passive way of learning, where a higher level of supervision is provided (Chan 2006; Kumaravadivelu 2003; Wen and Clément 2003). In contrary, there are other scholars (Ryan and Slethaug 2010; Chan and Rao 2009; Shi 2006; Yang 2009; Rajaram 2013) who reported that mainland Chinese students prefer a student-centred approach to a teacher-centred approach, and they are willing to participate in interactive and cooperative learning activities. We were intrigued to examine mainland Chinese students' learning experiences in a culturally dislocated learning context, pursuing a Western-based education outside China, in our case, Singapore.

In all of the above three elements, we were interested if the paradox of whether the outcomes of our research could be debated with some concrete evidence in a setting from a cultural dislocation context by examining with a large sample size with a well-balanced profile from varying potential possibilities, for example, specifically varying provinces of China (both advanced and not so advanced ones), students from more prestigious background and those from a poorer rural family, different institutions from varying clusters of provinces and so on. This enabled us to make some concrete conclusions at the eventual stage of our results analysis.

5.1.1   Cultural Dislocation Aspects

Three of Hofstede's cultural dimensions, namely, power distance, uncertainty avoidance and the philosophy of Confucianism, are used to frame the cultural dislocation context adopted in this book. Further to that, we have adapted Morey and Frangioso's (1998) learning effectiveness principles through incorporating learning constructs of understanding, skills, processes and inferred learning effectiveness elements (self-reported).

The cultural dislocation constructs—comfort (in terms of power distance), familiarity (in terms of uncertainty avoidance) and knowledge transfer (based on the philosophy of Confucianism)—were based on Hofstede's (1980) and Hofstede and Bond's (1988) cultural dimensions.

Concepts and terms such as 'power distance', 'uncertainty avoidance' and 'Confucian learning principles' are scarcely in the daily vocabulary of business students studying overseas. Therefore, these concepts were translated to students using words and terms which were more familiar to them and for which precedents existed in the cultural dislocation literature. Table 5.1 reports how the three dislocation aspects are operationalized and summarizes how students reported each of the ten instructional techniques examined.

Table 5.1 Dislocation aspects, operational measures and research precedents

Dislocation aspect (what theory claims)	Operational measures (what students were asked to report)	Precedents (previous use of similar terms)
Power distance	Comfort	Chan (1999, pp. 300–301) Nield (2004, pp. 190)
Uncertainty avoidance	Familiarity	Chan (1999, pp. 302–303) Chow (1995, pp. 12–13) Shi (2006, pp. 137–138)
Confucianism	Knowledge transfer	Bu and Mitchell (1992, pp. 47–48) Tweed and Lehman (2002, pp. 85–86) Tweed and Lehman (2002, pp. 148–149)

Adapted from Rajaram (2013)

Power distance defines how people perceive and deal with inequities on the distribution of power. Some instructional techniques deliberately minimize the power distance between learner and instructor (or among learners), while other techniques accentuate the power disequilibrium. Instruction by its very nature requires one to navigate the skilful challenges to make students get into their comfort zones. Instructors' involvement affects students' varying comfort levels, and students' comfort level affects their perception of learning effectiveness. In Shi (2006)'s study of 167 mainland Chinese students with English majors specializing in English language and literature, students were found to prefer a student-centred learning approach to a teacher-centred approach. Although they were willing to participate in interactive and cooperative language learning activities, they still expect teachers' guidance to help them pass tests and provide them with detailed and clear notes (Shi 2006). Within reason, the question that needs to be addressed should be: Do greater instructor's involvement results in higher level of comfort and would that contribute to a higher level of perceived learning effectiveness? To have this logic examined, we carried out a study that requires students to report their comfort level with each of the ten instructional techniques as a proxy measure of power distance.

Uncertainty avoidance refers to the ease in dealing with conflicts and antagonism in equivocal situations. Within these ten commonly used instructional techniques, there are varying opportunities for potential conflict, aggression and ambiguity between instructor and learners or among learners themselves. This can be validated by Shi (2006)'s study where the mainland Chinese learners prefer their teachers to be lighthearted and adopt different instructional activities; on the other hand, students also expected teachers to help them pass tests and provide them with thorough and clear notes. The question for us to ponder is whether these uncertainties are more avoidable among familiar instructional techniques, whereas other techniques that are fraught with ambiguity, aggression or conflict are unfamiliar, and their uncertainty is to be avoided in favour of greater perceived learning effectiveness.

A distinctive learning style emerges among people sharing a common historical and geographical setting because in general they collectively adapt to a unique set of environmental demands (Shade 1989). In contrary, this conception is challenged by scholars (Ryan and Slethaug 2010; Chan and Rao 2009; Rajaram 2010; Yang 2009; Littlewood 2009) emphasizing that the choice of learning styles/approaches is primarily driven by the assessment methods rather than a certain cultural heritage and values. On the other hand, the cultural background could be highly influential to the students' learning style at least during the phase where the adaption of a new culture is taking place.

Characteristic learning styles of a nation and culture are also institutionalized and reinforced through its childrearing practices and education systems, for example, 'mainland Chinese students did not perceive that having their own opinions was vital to be a good learner (Shi 2006).' Wen and Clément (2003) debated that mainland Chinese students' reluctance to participate in class can be associated to their willingness to be submissive to authority. The social and cultural values/norms that are implanted in individuals' behaviour influence their learning attitudes and behaviours. The cultural backgrounds of learners do influence their levels of knowledge acquisition, particularly in terms of academic learning (Tweed and Lehman 2002). Hence, knowledge transfer is held as a pivotal dimension of Confucianism.

Each society has a unique set of social cultural values that influences and guides managerial belief and actions in workplace practices and business relationships (Adler et al. 1989). Similar logic can be applied to classroom environments where a specific cultural group of students presents a specific trend of learning behaviours and styles. Many studies (Ryan and Slethaug 2010; Littlewood 2009; Chan and Rao 2009; Jin and Cortazzi 2006; Yang 2009; Shi 2006; Ryan and Louie 2007; Kumaravadivelu 2003; Hu 2002) have been conducted on mainland Chinese learners; however, there is limited research evidence that covers cultural dislocation notions influencing instructional approaches and its effects on perceived learning effectiveness in pursuit of Western-based programmes in a developed cosmopolitan countries.

5.1.2   Active/Passive Instructional Techniques

Rodrigues (2004) categorized ten instructional techniques into six passive and four active techniques. The four active techniques are 'case studies', 'individual research projects', 'classroom discussions' and 'group projects', and the six passive techniques are 'lectures by instructor', 'reading textbooks', 'guest speakers', 'videos shown in the classroom', 'classroom presentations by students' and 'computerized learning'.

A possible way of understanding the categorization could be from the level, intensity and frequency of the instructors and students' participation in classroom that is required for the technique. Passive techniques require lesser instructor to student or student-to-student interactions. It, more often or not, tends to be a much more one-way information delivery. The active techniques, on the other hand, tend to facilitate more participation and exchange of perspectives between the instructor and students or among students themselves. Student may be frustrated if their learning process through using inappropriate instructional techniques causes discomfort and inconvenience. We could define an inappropriate instructional technique to be one that is unfamiliar, causing discomfort or one, which students do not value, or benefit in their perception. For the techniques adopted to be effective in cross-cultural context, the following aspects need to be considered: (a) where—the location and in what cultural context the teaching is to be facilitated, (b) the varying cultural backgrounds (in our case, which part of China, i.e. advanced or rural state, northern, southern, Western or Eastern parts) of students and (c) the type of subject that needs to be taught.

There are perceptible differences, although not clear at a superficial level, on the instructional methodologies adopted in China and Singapore. To optimize mainland Chinese students learning in Singapore, it requires careful identification of a correct mix of instructional techniques that best help them shift from their rooted Confucian values to Western-based educational curricula and business practices.

Scholars (Ryan and Louie 2005; Kumaravadivelu 2003; Chan 1999; Chow 1995) reported that mainland Chinese students prefer to learn by rote and passive learning. Conversely, other scholars (Rajaram 2010; Littlewood 2009; Chan and Rao 2009; Rajaram and Bordia 2011; Hu 2002; Yang 2009; Jin and Cortazzi 2006) debated that the mainland Chinese students have shifted their preference towards a more active learning approaches. Shi (2006) testified the Chinese students 'show little difference from their western counterparts by being active learners and prefer a more interactive relationship with teachers' (p. 122). Nevertheless, we need to acknowledge that mainland Chinese students' preference in instructional approach is not the same to their perception of perceived learning effectiveness and learning effectiveness using the instructional approach.

5.2   Quantitative Analysis

5.2.1   Perceived Learning Effectiveness Across Different Instructional Techniques

The hypothesis that 'passive techniques are rated higher in importance than active techniques in terms of learning effectiveness in pursuing a western-style education' is partially supported. The general principle is illustrated by certain passive techniques but not all the ten instructional techniques. Table 5.2 reports the students' self-reported learning effectiveness ratings across ten instructional techniques.

Four passive techniques, 'lectures', 'videos', 'guest speakers' and 'classroom presentations', are rated higher than two of the active techniques ('classroom discussions' and 'individual research projects'). As the hypothesis supports only four out of six passive techniques, the relationship does not operate at all instances. This is evident from two of the four active techniques, 'case study' and 'group project', that were rated as effective instructional techniques. The highest rated techniques are from an active cluster ('case study'), as well as from a passive cluster ('lectures') scoring a mean score of 3.77. The second highest ranked is group project, with a score of 3.67. This emphasizes clearly that the hypothesis is not supported for

Table 5.2 Perceived Learning effectiveness across ten instructional techniques

Ten instructional techniques[a]	Overall students' self-reported learning effectiveness ratings[b]
Case studies *(A)*	3.77
Lectures by instructor *(P)*	3.77
Group projects *(A)*	3.67
Videos *(P)*	3.63
Guest speakers *(P)*	3.56
Classroom presentations *(P)*	3.53
Classroom discussions *(A)*	3.46
Individual research projects *(A)*	3.46
Computerized learning *(P)*	3.36
Reading textbooks *(P)*	3.35

[a]*A* active, *P* passive; [b]Ratings are computed on the average of: 'Strongly disagree' = 1; 'Disagree' = 2; 'Neutral' = 3: 'Agree' = 4; 'Strongly Agree' = 5
Adapted from Rajaram and Bordia (2013)

two active techniques that are rated higher than the passive techniques. The hypothesis is not valid at all times but, rather, is only partially supported by fulfilling some specific aspects of the relationship.

The active techniques of 'case study' and 'group projects' are rated as most effective, with only the passive technique of 'lecture' being ranked in the most effective category. This is contradictory to Neild's (2004) study that mainland Chinese students prefer passive teaching methods. The active techniques of 'case studies' and 'group projects' are among the highest rated techniques for their effectiveness. One possible explanation could be that the students who participated have had more exposure to Singapore education (Western-based education system) and are already adapted to these techniques for a much-prolonged period.

5.2.2 Correlations Among Perceived Learning Effectiveness, Comfort, Familiarity and Knowledge Transfer

Greater learning effectiveness is generally associated with lesser comfort (Vygotsky 1997, 2004), greater familiarity and greater ease of knowledge. Means for the ten techniques (as rated by all 400 students, Table 5.4) were intercorrelated. Table 5.3 reports these correlations. All correlations are statistically significant, even though these data are now means for the ten techniques aggregated across all students.

Clearly, perceived learning effectiveness, comfort, familiarity and knowledge transfer are significantly interlocking concepts (Table 5.3) which correlate with perceived learning effectiveness in that order (comfort = 0.6,1; familiarity = 0.56; and knowledge transfer = 0.53). The result suggests that in culturally dislocated settings, learning effectiveness is mediated first by comfort, then by familiarity and third by actual knowledge transfer.

Table 5.3 Correlations among pereceived learning effectiveness, comfort, familiarity and knowledge transfer

	LE	Com	Fam	KT
Perceived Learning effectiveness	–			
Comfort	.614**	–		
Familiarity	.564**	.759**	–	
Knowledge transfer	.526**	.660**	.769**	–

**(P < 0.01); *(P < 0.05); n = 10
Adapted from Rajaram (2013)

5.2.3   Perceived Learning Effectiveness and Comfort

Comfort had the highest association ($r = 0.614$) with perceived learning effectiveness. Techniques which the Chinese student participants have rated as 'comfortable' ('lectures', 'case studies', 'group projects', etc.) were also reported high in perception of learning effectiveness, while less 'comfortable' techniques ('reading textbook', 'computerized learning', 'classroom discussions') also have a low reported perceptions of learning effectiveness. Figure 5.1 shows these results for all ten techniques.

Overall, students rated 'lectures' and 'case studies' as the most effective learning techniques, followed by 'group projects', 'classroom presentations', 'videos', 'guest speakers', 'classroom discussions' and 'individual research projects', while 'computerized learning' and 'reading textbook' were seen as the least effective. Similarly, students reported that they were most comfortable with 'lectures', followed by 'case studies', 'group projects', 'classroom presentations', 'videos', 'guest speakers', 'classroom discussions', 'computerized learning' and 'reading textbooks', while they were least comfortable with 'individual research projects'.

5.2.4   Perceived Learning Effectiveness and Familiarity

Familiarity had the second highest correlation ($r = 0.564$) with perceived learning effectiveness (Fig. 5.2) indicating that the techniques most familiar to these students also were assumed to yield the greatest learning outcomes (e.g. 'lectures', 'case studies' and 'group projects'). While techniques less familiar to the students were related to lower perceived learning outcomes (e.g. 'videos', 'guest speakers', 'classroom presentations' and more markedly 'reading textbook' and 'computerized learning').

Reading and extracting information and understanding concepts from textbooks are generally challenging for most students globally regardless of the educational system. However, in today's world with highly saturated with technology, students' rating on 'computerized learning' came as a surprise. One possible explanation could be a lack of exposure to advanced and contemporary educational technological platforms back in their home country (China). Furthermore, these students came from different regions of China where different stages of modernization and techno-

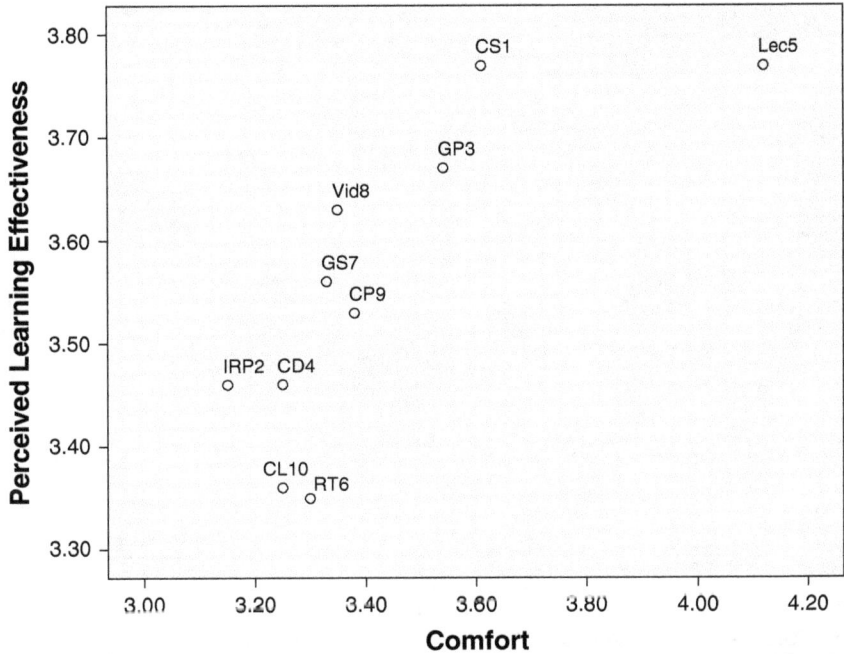

('Lec5' – Lecture; 'CS1' – Case study; 'GP3' – Group project; 'Vid8' – Video; 'GS7' – Guest
speakers; 'CP9' – Classroom presentations; 'IRP2' – Individual research project; 'CD4' – Classroom
discussion; 'CL10' – Computerized learning; 'RT6' – Reading textbooks)

Fig. 5.1 Perceived Learning effectiveness and comfort for ten instructional techniques. (Adapted
from Rajaram 2013)

logical advancement could have been experienced. Another possible explanation
could be the manner in which this instructional technique is design and executed
may not have fit well into the learning context of these students.

Overall, students reported that they were most familiar with 'lectures', followed
by 'group projects', 'case studies', 'reading textbooks', 'classroom discussions',
'individual research', 'computerized learning', 'class presentation' and 'guest
speakers', while they were least familiar with 'videos'. Not surprisingly, assessment
ratings of familiarity were closely linked ($r = 0.759$) to comfort.

5.2.5   Perceived Learning Effectiveness and Ease of Knowledge Transfer

Perceived Learning Effectiveness and Ease of Knowledge Transfer
Ease of knowledge transfer (from teacher to student) also correlated significantly
($r = 0.526$) with perceived learning effectiveness, especially (Fig. 5.3) for 'lectures'
and' case studies', and to a lesser degree for 'group projects' and 'videos'. In con-

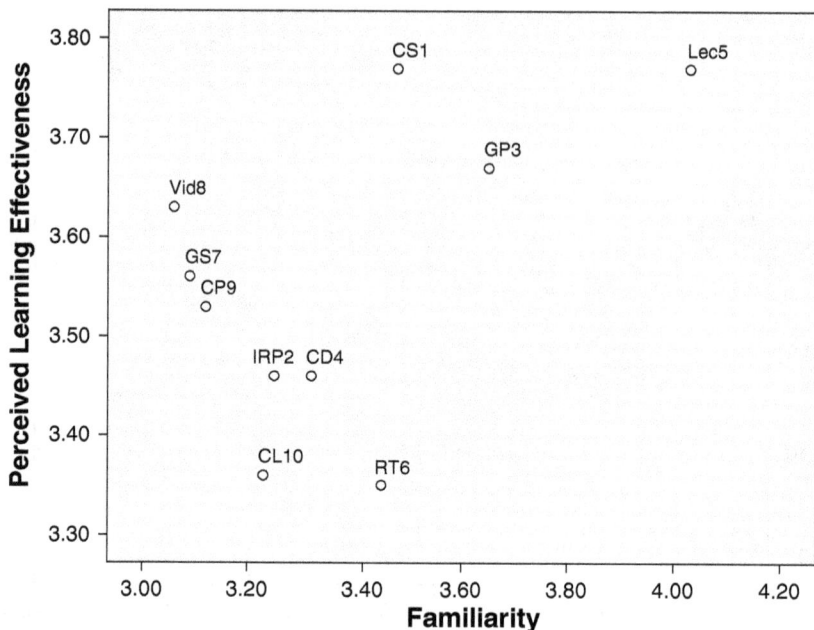

('Lec5' – Lecture; 'CS1' – Case study; 'GP3' – Group project; 'Vid8' – Video; 'GS7' – Guest speakers; 'CP9' – Classroom presentations; 'IRP2' – Individual research project; 'CD4' – Classroom discussion; 'CL10' – Computerized learning; 'RT6' – Reading textbooks)

Fig. 5.2 Perceived Learning effectiveness and familiarity for ten instructional techniques. (Adapted from Rajaram 2013)

trast, students judged 'classroom projects', 'individual research projects' and 'reading texts' to be less effective for knowledge transfer and also low in perceived learning effectiveness.

Overall, they reported the greatest ease of knowledge transfer for 'lecturers', followed by 'case studies', 'group projects', 'classroom discussions', 'videos', 'computerized learning', 'guest speakers', 'reading textbooks', 'individual research projects' and with 'classroom presentations' least of all.

On the face of it, perceived learning effectiveness and knowledge transfer would seem to be the same concept. Students were asked to differentiate learning effectiveness and knowledge transfer in the interview. For knowledge transfer, students were to distinguish among the ten instructional techniques in terms of 'easier, faster gaining and learning of knowledge'. In contrast, learning effectiveness was a more complex construct characterized by about a dozen specific phrases including 'enhanced scope of knowledge', 'quality of learning', 'efficient, effective learning', 'control over learning', 'gain more knowledge', 'increased awareness', 'enhanced effectiveness' and 'applicability of learning'.

Students reported that two instructional techniques, 'classroom discussions' and 'computerized learning', enabled them to acquire knowledge with reasonable ease,

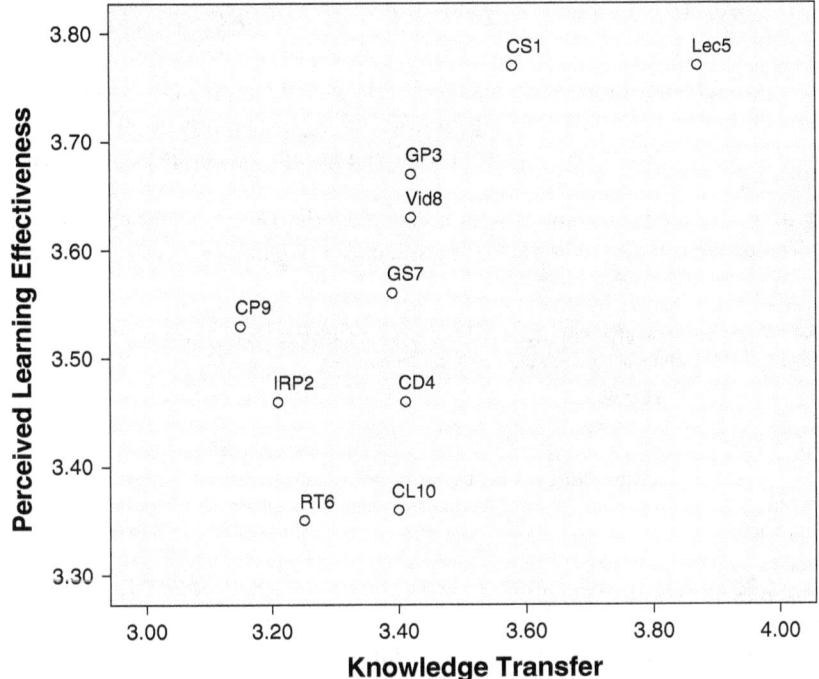

('Lec5' – Lecture; 'CS1' – Case study; 'GP3' – Group project; 'Vid8' – Video; 'GS7' – Guest speakers; 'CP9' – Classroom presentations; 'IRP2' – Individual research project; 'CD4' – Classroom discussion; 'CL10' – Computerized learning; 'RT6' – Reading textbooks)

Fig. 5.3 Perecived Learning effectiveness and knowledge transfer for ten instructional techniques. (Adapted from Rajaram 2013)

but did not bring about perceived learning effectiveness. Students' qualitative reports (that were conducted as an explorative study in earlier stage of the research) show that the said two techniques deterred them from acquiring knowledge. This may be largely due to the mismatch on ways these instructional techniques are being facilitated to fit the students' perceived engagement in terms of ease of acquiring of knowledge. For example, Shi (2006) reported that the Chinese learners 'did not think having their own opinions was essential for a good learner' (p. 138). This may be one of the reasons why class discussions and computerized learning may be rated highly in terms of ease of acquiring knowledge. Both require students to share their perspectives, in terms of verbal sharing for 'class discussions' and written expression of thoughts for 'computerized learning', for example, through discussion boards, forums and e-dialogue sessions. Similarly, the students rated 'individual research projects' and 'classroom presentations' as least effective for knowledge transfer but mid-range for overall perceived learning effectiveness. Other factors, namely, instructor's delivery style, level of student autonomy and instructors' cultural backgrounds that may contribute to perceived learning effectiveness warrant future research.

5.2.6   Active Versus Passive Instructional Techniques

Table 5.4 presents the comparative analysis of perceived learning effectiveness versus comfort, familiarity and knowledge transfer ratings. It reports the students' ratings for four aspects of ten instructional techniques grouped according to Rodrigues' (2004) scheme of active and passive

Apparent differences in ratings within the categories of active and passive were found. The active category was viewed by students as significantly less comfortable

Table 5.4 Comparative analysis of perceived learning effectiveness versus comfort, familirity and knowledge transfer ratings across ten instructional techniques

Instructional techniques active	Perceived Learning effectiveness means rating (standard deviations)	Comfort means rating (standard deviations)	Familiarity means rating (standard deviations)	Knowledge transfer means rating (standard deviations)
Case studies	3.77 (0.64)	3.61 (0.76)	3.48 (0.81)	3.58 (0.93)
Individual research projects	3.46 (0.58)	3.15 (0.95)	3.25 (0.99)	3.21 (1.00)
Group projects	3.67 (0.90)	3.54 (1.10)	3.65 (0.79)	3.42 (0.98)
Classroom discussions	3.46 (0.70)	3.25 (1.05)	3.32 (0.96)	3.41 (1.02)
Mean of active techniques	3.59 (0.70)	3.39 (0.96)	3.43 (0.89)	3.41 (0.98)
Passive				
Lectures by instructor	3.77 (0.73)	4.12 (0.89)	4.03 (0.94)	3.87 (0.95)
Reading textbooks	3.35 (0.82)	3.30 (1.04)	3.45 (0.91)	3.25 (0.91)
Guest speakers	3.56 (0.83)	3.33 (1.01)	3.09 (1.14)	3.39 (1.06)
Videos	3.63 (0.70)	3.35 (1.03)	3.06 (1.16)	3.41 (0.99)
Classroom presentations	3.53 (0.79)	3.38 (1.02)	3.12 (1.12)	3.15 (1.17)
Computerized learning	3.36 (0.75)	3.25 (1.08)	3.23 (1.14)	3.40 (0.99)
Mean of passive techniques	3.53 (0.77)	3.46 (1.01)	3.33 (1.07)	3.41 (1.01)
Overall means (SD) for ten techniques	**3.56 (0.55)**	**3.43 (0.31)**	**3.37 (0.298)**	**3.39 (0.21)**
Significant differences among techniques	$F = 25.58$, $df = 9$, $p < .001$	$F = 43.27$, $df = 9$, $p < .001$	$F = 48.60$, $df = 9$, $p < .001$	$F = 24.50$, $df = 9$, $p < .001$
Significant differences between active and passive categories	$t = -0.44$, $df = 393$ $p = ns$	$t = -2.23$, $df = 395$ $p < .026$	$t = 3.60$, $df = 398$ $p < .001$	$t = -0.35$, $df = 394$ $p = ns$

Means and standard deviation ratings are computed where strongly disagree = 1; disagree = 2; neutral = 3; agree = 4; strongly agree = 5
Adapted from Rajaram (2013)

and as pointedly more unfamiliar than the passive category of instructional techniques. Top rated and bottom rated techniques appear within both active and passive categories.

Some past literature found that mainland Chinese students who attain good learning outcomes are very closely supervised and guided, although these findings were argued to be Western biased (Biggs 1994; Marton et al. 1996; Tang 1996). In contrast, there are studies (Ryan and Slethaug 2010; Clark and Gieve 2006; Chan and Rao 2009; Shi 2006; Yang 2009) that reported that Chinese learners are highly proactive, self-monitor their studies, learn from their mistakes and relate to their past experiences, incorporating those learning reflections to their studies, prefer a student-centred approach to a teacher-centred approach and are willing to participate in interactive and cooperative learning activities. The predominant view in the past literature maintains that mainland Chinese students prefer passive teaching methods such as lectures, demonstrations, handouts, displays, films and videos. The more participative teaching methods such as experiential exercises, case studies, role play and simulations are least preferred. The preference was shaped by the cultural influence and students' prolonged exposure to the non-active and non-participative style of educational system since their high school. In contrast to the past research, the results from our current study show no particular preference of passive to the active instructional techniques. This is an important finding that creates awareness and informs instructors of how they could adopt the correct mix of instructional techniques to formulate the learning design of their respective courses to achieve optimal learning for their students.

One possible explanation for the difference between the current study and the past studies of mainland Chinese students preferring passive techniques was mostly conducted decades ago. It could also be that past studies' samples were taken from lesser developed provinces in China with other intertwined social demographic factors, whereas the students in the current study were pursuing their education in Singapore, a culturally modernized environment with a much high level of Western educational influence. Furthermore, to our best knowledge, none of these researches studied the perceived learning effectiveness across the commonly used instructional techniques.

The results show preferences that range across the 'active' and 'passive' activities categorized by Rodrigues (2004). The results could be due to (1) mainland Chinese students are different from Rodrigues' international study groups; (2) active and passive distinctions do not exist; (3) differences among the techniques do exist, but not as Rodrigues has characterized them; or (4) students have changed and developed in their preferences as they experienced, became familiar with and then adapted to Singaporean assessment strategies. Cluster analysis of the ten instructional techniques on the four learning aspects collectively confirms what the previous three figures hint at only individually; gross active/passive classification is too simplistic and fails to capture that Chinese students see these instructional techniques in ways that are more complex.

Figure 5.4 shows that students perceive three such cluster groups. 'Lectures' approach remains most prominent students' perception of effective teaching meth-

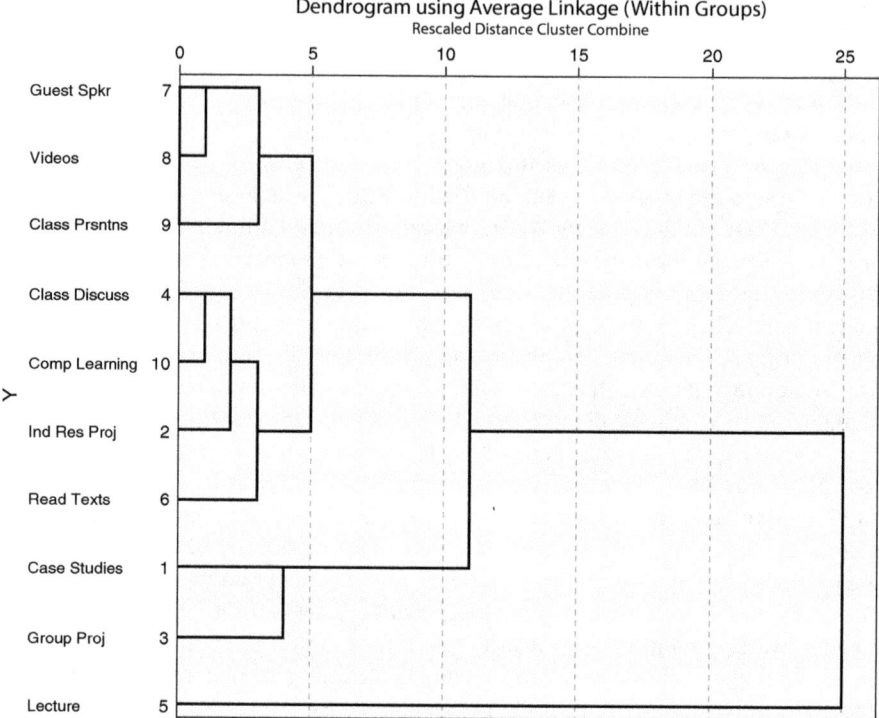

Fig. 5.4 Mainland Chinese students' groupings of ten instructional techniques on simultaneous criteria of learning effectiveness, comfort, familiarity and knowledge transfer. (Adapted from Rajaram 2013)

ods for learning. Least preferred (top) are the closely linked techniques of 'guest speakers', 'videos' and 'classroom presentations'; next group is 'classroom discussions', 'computerized learning', 'individual projects' and 'reading textbooks', while 'case studies' and 'group projects' are seen as a second most preferred cluster. 'Lectures' (bottom most) are rated as the most effective, comfortable, familiar and easiest route of knowledge transfer.

From this perspective, differences among the clusters of instructional techniques are statistically significant for all four learning aspects—learning effectiveness ($df = 3$, $F = 31.02$, $p < 0.001$), comfort ($df = 3$, $F = 113.49$, $p < 0.001$), familiarity ($df = 3$, $F = 28.80$, $p < 0.001$) and knowledge transfer ($df = 3$, $F = 5.59$, $p < 0.047$).

Many studies (Biggs 1994; Chow 1995; Chan 1997, 1999; Clark and Gieve 2006; Chan and Rao 2009; Coverdale-Jones and Rastall 2009, Littlewood 2009; Ryan and Slethaug 2010; Shi 2006; Tang 1996; Turner 2006; Wen and Clément 2003) have been conducted to provide evidence on instructional preferences for mainland Chinese learners. However, no studies (till Rajaram 2010, 2013, Rajaram and Bordia 2011 and Rajaram and Collins 2013 studies) have been conducted on the perceived effectiveness of specific (yet commonly used) groups of instructional techniques that explicitly focus on a holistic coverage (a) to include a well-balanced and mixed sample size which include students from varying cultural, social backgrounds, differing business programmes, age and gender (b) in an environment that is cosmopolitan, Western-influenced yet rooted in Confucian culture and conducts a Western-based education.

The students' preferences on instructional approaches can be influenced by their previous exposure, the type of assessment incorporated, long-established cultural and social values and norms (at least in the interim phases until they are fully adapted to the new learning cultures) and personality type. We need to acknowledge that how these students' learning differs depending on what type of learners they are, for example, visual, cognitive, aural or kinaesthetic and on the learning design, processes involved in adopting the correct mix and customization of these instructional techniques to help the students acquire knowledge information.

5.3 Implications and Recommendations

A clear and deep understanding of mainland Chinese students' cultural aspects and the nuances in delivering knowledge to them effectively is required to achieve quality education for them, respectively. The primary issues are (a) identifying and understanding the commonly adopted instructional techniques to teach this profile of students and (b) finding out the most appropriate mix of instructional techniques that best suits these mainland Chinese students aligning to their learning preferences and styles of learning. This study serves as a connecting link to address the elements of cultural dislocation and perceived effectiveness of learning for mainland Chinese students.

These findings enable instructors to utilize a range of instructional techniques based on grounded evidence in enhancing their engagement with students and on their quality of teaching delivery. The study prompts the following recommendations:

(a) Instructors are to be creative and sensitive to students' learning needs where they should adopt a mix of instructional techniques (whether 'active' or 'passive'). Even if these instructional techniques are not necessarily preferred, i.e. causing discomfort and are unfamiliar, but it could be a case of them adopted primarily through customization to enable students to learn effectively.
(b) Evidence shows that mainland Chinese students may prefer passive instructional techniques but do not necessarily learn most effectively or with optimal acquisition of knowledge.
(c) Instructors should not generalize or incline towards only a specific cluster of instructional techniques.

It is vital to realize that no one instructional technique leads to optimal learning among mainland Chinese students. The varying learners' characteristics should be recognized, and appropriate instructional techniques should be adopted in varying situations based on students' cultural values/beliefs (i.e. students coming from varying provinces of China), prior knowledge, practical examples and maturity level. In summary, the ability to be equipped with a clear and thorough understanding of the cultural dislocation elements and its effect on the instructional techniques assists instructors to design, develop and deliver business curricula effectively.

References

Adler, N. J., Campbel, N., & Laurent, A. (1989). In search of appropriate methodology: From outside the People's Republic of China looking in. *Journal of International Business Studies, 20*, 61–74.

Biggs, J. (1994). Asian learners through western eyes: An astigmatic paradox. *Australian and New Zealand Journal of Vocational Educational Research, 2*(2), 40–63.

Bu, N., & Mitchell, V. F. (1992). Developing the PRC's managers: How can Western experts to be more helpful? *Journal of Management Development, 11*(2), 42–53.

Carson, J. G., & Nelson, G. L. (1996). Chinese students' perceptions of ESL peer response group interaction. *Journal of Second Language Writing, 5*(1), 1–19.

Chan, S. (1991). *Asian Americans: An interpretive history.* Twayne Publishers.

Chan, S. (1997). Migration, cultural identity and assimilation effects on entrepreneurship for the overseas Chinese in Britain. *Asia Pacific Business Review, 3*(4), 211–222.

Chan, S. (1999). The Chinese learner—A question of style. *Education & Training, 41*(6/7), 294–304.

Chan, K. (2006). Consumer socialization of Chinese children in schools: Analysis of consumption values in textbooks. *Journal of Consumer Marketing, 23*(3), 125–132.

Chan, C. K. K., & Rao, N. (2009) Revisiting the Chinese Learner. *CERC Studies in Comparative Education, 25.*

Chow, I. H. S. (1995). Management education in Hong Kong: Needs and challenges. *International Journal of Educational Management, 9*(5), 10–15.

Clark, R., & Gieve, S. N. (2006). On the discursive construction of the Chinese learner. *Language, Culture and Curriculum, 19*(1), 54–73.

Coverdale-Jones, T., & Rastall, P. (Eds.). (2009). *Internationalizing the university: The Chinese context.* Houndmills: Palgrave Macmillian.

Hofstede, G. (1980). *Culture's consequence. International differences in work-related values.* Newbury Park: Sage.

Hofstede, G., & Bond, M. H. (1988). The Confucius connection: From cultural roots to economic growth. *Organizational Dynamics, 16*(4), 5–21.

Hu, G. W. (2002). English language teaching in the People's Republic of China. In R. E. Silver, G. W. Hu, & M. Iino (Eds.), *English language education in China, Japan, and Singapore* (pp. 1–77). Singapore: National Institute of Education.

Jin, L., & Cortazzi, M. (2006). Changing practices in Chinese cultures of learning, language. *Culture and Curriculum, 1*(1), 5–20.

Kumaravadivelu, B. (2003). Problematizing cultural stereotypes in TESOL. *TESOL Quarterly, 37*(4), 709–719.

Littlewood, W. (2009). Participation-based pedagogy: How congruent is it with Chinese cultures of learning? In P. Cheng & J. X. Yan (Eds.), *Cultural identity and language anxiety* (pp. 179–202). Guilin: Guangxi Normal University Press.

Marton, F., Dall'Alba, G., & Tse, L. K. (1996). Memorizing and understanding: The keys to the paradox. In *The Chinese learner: Cultural, psychological and contextual influences* (pp. 69–83).

Morey, D., & Frangioso, T. (1998). Aligning an organisation for learning—The six principles of effective learning. *Journal of Knowledge Management, 1*(4), 308–314.

Neild, K. (2004). Questioning the myth of the Chinese learner. *International Journal of Contemporary Hospitality Management, 16*(3), 189–196.

Nelson, G. (1995). Cultural differences in learning styles. In J. Reid (Ed.), *Learning styles in the ESL/EFL classroom* (pp. 3–18). Boston, MA: Heinle & Heinle.

Newell, S. (1999). The transfer of management knowledge to China: Building learning communities rather than translating Western textbooks? *Education + Training, 41*(6/7), 286–294.

Oxford, R. (1995). A cross cultural view of learning styles. *Language Teaching, 28*, 201–215.

Rajaram, K. (2010). *Culture Clash: Teaching western-based business education to mainland Chinese students in Singapore* (Unpublished doctoral dissertation). University of South Australia, Adelaide, Australia.

Rajaram, K. (2013). Followers of Confucianism or a new generation? Learning culture of mainland Chinese: In pursuit of western based business education away from mainland China. *International Journal of Teaching & Learning in Higher Education, 25*(3), 369–377.

Rajaram, K., & Bordia, S. (2011). Culture clash: Teaching Western-based management education to mainland Chinese students in Singapore. *Journal of International Education in Business, 4*(1), 63–83.

Rajaram, K., & Bordia, S. (2013). East versus west: Effectiveness of knowledge acquisition and impact of cultural dislocation issues for mainland Chinese students across ten commonly used instructional techniques. *International Journal for the Scholarship of Teaching and Learning, 7*(1), 1–21.

Rajaram, K., & Collins, J. B. (2013). Qualitative identification of learning effectiveness indicators among mainland Chinese students in culturally dislocated study environments. *Journal of International Education in Business, 6*(2), 179–199.

Rodrigues, C. A. (2004). The importance level of ten teaching/learning techniques as rated by university business students and instructors. *Journal of Management Development, 23*(2), 169–182.

Ryan, J., & Louie, K. (2005, November). *Dichotomy or complexity: Problematising concepts of scholarship and learning*. In 34th annual Philosophy of Education Society of Australasia Conference.

Ryan, J., & Louie, K. (2007). False dichotomy? 'Western' and 'Confucian' concepts of scholarship and learning. *Educational Philosophy and Theory, 39*(4), 404–417.

Ryan, J., & Slethaug, G. (2010). *International education and the Chinese learner* (pp. 13–89). Hong Kong: Hong Kong University Press.

Shade, B. J. R. (1989). Culture: The key to adaptation. In B. J. R. Shade (Ed.), *Culture, style and the educative process* (pp. 9–15). Springfield: Charles C. Thomas Publisher.

Shi, L. (2006). The successors to Confucianism or a new generation? A questionnaire study on Chinese students' culture of learning English. *Language, Culture and Curriculum, 19*(1), 122–147.

Tan, J. (2011). *Revisiting the Chinese learner: Changing contexts, changing education*. Taylor & Francis.

Tang, C. (1996). Collaborative learning: The latent dimension in Chinese students' learning. In D. A. Watkins & J. B. Biggs (Eds.), *The Chinese learner: Cultural, psychological and contextual influences* (pp. 183–205). Hong Kong: Comparative Education Research Center.

Turner, Y. (2006). Chinese students in U.K. business school: Hearing the student voice in reflective teaching and learning. *Higher Education Quarterly, 60*, 27–51.

Tweed, R. G., & Lehman, D. R. (2002). Learning considered within a cultural context: Confucian and Socratic approaches. *American Psychologist, 57*(2), 89–99.

Vygotsky, L. S. (1997). Interaction between learning and development. In M. Gauvain & M. Cole (Eds.), *Readings on the development of children* (2nd ed., pp. 79–91). Cambridge, MA: Harvard University Press.

Vygotsky, L. S. (2004). Imagination and creativity in childhood. *Journal of Russian and East European Psychology, 42*(1), 7–97.

Wen, W.-P., & Clément, R. (2003). A Chinese conceptualisation of willingness to communicate in ESL. *Language Culture and Curriculum, 16*(1), 18–38.

Yang, Z. (2009). The effect of mother tongue transfer on English writing. *Teaching and Management, 11*(3), 16–20.

Chapter 6
Learning Design: Effective Adaptation of Instructional Techniques to Enhance the Learning Process

The chapter presents the analysis and discussion on the findings of the learning design in terms of the effective adaptation of instructional techniques to engage mainland Chinese students to achieve optimal learning and knowledge acquisition. The first part of the discussion focuses on the mainland Chinese students' ratings of perceived learning effectiveness, comfort, familiarity and knowledge transfer for the ten instructional techniques. The second part focuses on the discussion on the ten instructional techniques on its outcomes on the relational effect between perceived learning effectiveness and comfort, familiarity, ease of knowledge transfer and other influences on learning outcome. The chapter concludes with an implications and recommendations section that addresses the importance of rethinking and redesigning the teaching and learning strategy by adopting the correct mix and through customizing the instructional techniques to achieve effective learning for these mainland Chinese students. Learning culture and culture of learning plays a vital role in addressing the cross-cultural teaching and learning issues in a business education context.

6.1 Discussion

Learning culture plays a vital role in how one should rethink and redesign the learning strategy in adopting the correct mix of instructional techniques. Identifying and using the correct mix of instructional techniques require adequate awareness and knowledge. We need to be mindful of the rooted values and norms that affect students' preference, comfort and ease in making the delivered knowledge to be transferred.

This chapter is improved from Rajaram, K. (2013). Learning in foreign cultures: Self-reports learning effectiveness across different instructional techniques. *World Journal of Education, 3*(4), 71–95 and Rajaram, K., & Bordia, S. (2011). Culture clash: Teaching Western-based management education to mainland Chinese students in Singapore. *Journal of International Education in Business, 4*(1), 63–83.

© Springer Nature Singapore Pte Ltd. 2020
K. Rajaram, *Educating Mainland Chinese Learners in Business Education*,
https://doi.org/10.1007/978-981-15-3395-2_6

Having a thorough understanding on the broader categorization of the types of instructional techniques would be helpful in having them customized explicitly to attain effectiveness when adopting them to teach these mainland Chinese learners. Leveraging on Rodrigues (2004) work, we have categorized the ten commonly used instructional techniques into four active-like (A-like) and six passive-like (P-like), having them to be characterized as two large clusters. These ten instructional techniques could be seen as the most commonly used and fundamental ones adopted by instructors across varying disciplines, where the research experimental context is focused on. The passive instructional techniques require much lesser personal responsibility from students for learning, and the autonomy in terms of control could be classified as low. Other students may learn better through active instructional techniques which require higher self-regulation, personal responsibility with higher autonomy in terms of control. We need to tackle two key aspects, firstly, the culture of learning in which these mainland Chinese students have been educated all these while that dominates their learning styles. Secondly, identify the context of learning culture and how it is advocated by the institution or emphasized. There would be ripple effects on how these students have been influenced by the norms and beliefs that were advocated and ingrained, as such they are likely to perceive certain instructional techniques to be more favourable than others for their learning. However, there is much more caution and complexities involved before we could simply claim that learning culture and their perceived preference on these instructional techniques are the only reasons that lead to their optimal learning or knowledge acquisition. Students' comfort and preferred instructional techniques do not directly correlate to effective learning outcomes, rather it could be a case where instructional techniques that cause discomfort and those that may not be preferred by the students could be the more effective ones in terms of transferring of knowledge and learning.

Past literature tends to portray mainland Chinese students as preferring passive teaching methods (Nield 2004) to participative teaching methods. Mainland Chinese students were also viewed as rote-learners, where 'rote' means 'learning something in order to be able to repeat it from memory, rather than in order to understand it'. These claims were challenged by other scholars (Littlewood 2009; Rajaram 2010; Rajaram and Bordia 2011; Ryan and Louie 2007; Ryan and Slethaug 2010) who advised readers not to stereotype Chinese students' learning approaches as they are not discrete, homogeneous and unchanging. The clusters of students could be further categorized into clusters such as whether they are from the more rural (backward) or modern provinces, the family background and their values and exposure, the learners' exposure over their schooling years till their pursuit of their studies in Singapore.

A study by Rajaram and Bordia (2013) on perceived learning effectiveness of instructional techniques indicates that mainland Chinese students rated active instructional techniques better in terms of their perceived learning effectiveness. The shift could be due to varying reasons such as the increasing exposure to globalized contexts, evolution of learning environments, climates and increasingly more Western style of techniques being adopted that influences how students learn and acquire knowledge. The results were benchmarked against 'lecture' approach, which these students were accustomed to largely in Chinese education. When measured across the combined score of the social-cultural dislocation variables, namely, comfort,

Table 6.1 Contrasts between Rodrigues' active/passive classifications and mainland Chinese student ratings of effectiveness, comfort, familiarity and knowledge transfer for ten instructional techniques current

Current study results	Rodrigue's (2004) classification	
Effective, comfort, familiar, ease of knowledge transfer	Active	Passive
Highest		Lectures
High	Case studies	
	Group projects	
Moderate	Individual research projects	Computerised learning
	Classroom discussions	Reading texts
Mediocre		Classroom presentations
		Guest speakers
		Videos

Extracted from Rajaram, K., (2013)

familiarity and knowledge transfer, it was discovered that the active instructional techniques were once again rated higher than the passive instructional techniques (please see Table 6.1). Moreover, all three variables scored high individually when measured across the active instructional techniques.

6.1.1   Interview Results and Discussion

Past literature shows lecture is the most preferred technique of teaching for mainland Chinese students, largely grounding them to the learning culture that is closely tied to it. Evidence shows that the learning approaches, i.e. 'case study', 'individual research project', 'group project' and 'classroom discussions', are being rated highly by mainland Chinese learners in terms of perceived learning effectiveness and the process of learning.

6.1.1.1   Case Study

Case study is an instructional technique that refers to an in-depth descriptive and/or explorative analysis of an organization, event, group and/or individual to explore the root causes of underlying concepts and principles. In our context, we classified the types of case studies into exploratory, illustrative and critical. Exploratory case studies are generally resonated as pilot studies. The scope tends to be addressing compelling research questions and methods for a larger and more complex study. Illustrative case studies are descriptive in nature and focus on a specific situation, context, set of circumstances and social relations and processes that are embedded within them. These cases are effective largely when instances where new angle of discussion is shared where most are not aware of. Critical case studies are scoped in line to a unique event and/or challenge commonly held assumptions due to a lack of deep and critical understanding.

Field evidence shows that the mainland Chinese students largely feel comfortable in acquiring knowledge through the case study approach. They perceive it to be an effective approach to facilitate critical and analytical thinking that enables them to acquire useful and relevant knowledge. The students also indicated that the part of group discussions among inter- and/or intragroups allows them to feel secured in reassuring their perspectives with their peers, bouncing ideas and having them developed before deciding on the final solution. However, key observations to reach such effectiveness in the adoption of case studies require some level of customized teaching approaches and learning design.

6.1.1.2 Individual Research Project

Students perceive learning through the individual research project technique to be limiting or constrained in terms of sharing information among their peers but finds it positive in terms of presenting their own thoughts in writing and enabling them to learn to think independently. This could be validated explicitly by the third and fourth stages of the sequential four-stage process through which the Chinese students' learning happens: (1) memorizing; (2) understanding; (3) applying and (4) questioning or modifying (Tweed and Lehman 2002). Tan (2011) described that a Chinese international student rote learns while adopting deep and achieving approaches concurrently, which explains the part of their independent thinking aspect. Evidence inform us that an individual research project is ranked under moderate category in terms of student ratings of effectiveness, comfort, familiarity and knowledge transfer. Mainland Chinese learners prefer to be guided and directed and to follow and obey their teachers without doubt, questions or challenges (Chan 1999; Samuelowicz and Bain 2001; Tuener and Acker 2002). Hence it was not surprising that there are fundamental challenges that the students experienced with the 'individual research project' technique, namely, feelings of discomfort and insecurity due to ambiguity in dealing with the project assignment on their own and having a less guided learning environment.

6.1.1.3 Group Project

Evidence indicates that a group project is perceived to be rated high in terms of students' ratings of effectiveness, comfort, familiarity and knowledge transfer. This is in contrary to the study by Phuong-Mai et al. (2006), where they claimed that Chinese learners find group work uncomfortable that is related to their high uncertainty avoidance culture orientation. From our study, the evidence shows that if the group work, if designed with a deep understanding and awareness of the social-cultural aspects (i.e. classroom formality, face saving, group harmony, competition and respect for authority), then it can work well with the mainland Chinese students, as they feel comfortable and secure with the 'group project' instructional technique. Moreover, the constructivist approach of self-regulatory learning, with active interactions with other group members, debating and so on, has to be reviewed and taken into due consideration to have the learning design of the group project customized. Chinese students tend to prefer structured learning with thorough and explicit instruction and objectives rather than open-ended discussions (Wang 2012). However, these students are familiar with group and collaborative learning, for they enjoy group work where they can discuss academic issues (Li and Campbell 2008). Nonetheless, Tiong and Yong (2004) described the Chinese students' preference is for collaborative learning in a more informal setting, for example, after class instead of during class, formal situations among their peers and instructors where they become hesitant. In line with the informal setting, the collective nature of the group work instructional technique enables these students to be more comfortable as they largely perceive it to a more secured and safer environment to share their inputs; in our case, discussions for the group work tend to be mostly outside class in non-formal settings. This also enables them to engage with those who they have already become more familiar, perhaps having built rapport with.

6.1.1.4   Classroom Discussion

Research evidence shows that typically Chinese classroom activities are dominated by lectures with limited questioning or class discussions as these students generally prefer not to express their opinions in public (Chan 1999; Gao et al. 1996; Wang 2012). Our interview results validated the finding of this behavioural style of Chinese students as a majority of interviewees reported that the 'classroom discussion' approach was uncomfortable and they were not confident in learning via this instructional approach. The results could be explained and justified in some logical ways with prior grounded evidence. Gao et al. (1996) pointed out and reported that in Chinese culture, not everyone is entitled to speak; a spoken 'voice' is equated with experience, seniority, authority, expertise and knowledge. Hence, this influences the free flow and exchange of ideas and questioning of knowledge and authority that lacks in the Chinese educational system (Cho et al. 2008). In the study by Wang (2012), it was found that Chinese students thrice before acting tend to use indirect communicating style due to their concerns about what to say and how to say it; they expressed concern about being mocked at when making a wrong or valueless statement and the issue of being less fluent in articulating their views that may waste other students' time. In Confucian heritage culture, sharing all that is in one's mind, speaking loudly and posing irrelevant questions are labeled as poor manners and a lack of respect (Valiente 2008).

6.1.1.5   4 Active Instructional Techniques

Rajaram and Bordia's (2013) study validates the results of this study where learning effectiveness for 402 mainland Chinese students is reported to be high when measured through the adoption of active instructional techniques of 'case studies' and 'group projects'. The results could be explained as there has been an increasing exposure to

Western values and lifestyles of the people in China in the past decade, which contradict with Rodrigues' (2004) study findings. The inconsistencies were examined and accounted for by the difference in the students' sample used, where the participants may have had differing experiences with the instructional techniques, largely because of how it has been structured and delivered. Some students may have experienced the 'case study' technique in a more passive style (predominantly lectures), while others may have experienced it in a more active style (relatively autonomous or alone). In relation to the 'group projects', some students may have experienced high levels of guidance and direction, while others may have experienced assignments with low guidance and direction. This is especially so for 'group projects', as the amount of supervision, assistance and guidance provided largely depends on the instructors' style of managing them. If the students were subjected to closer supervision, obviously, there was a much higher possibility of expecting a different outcome compared to those given much less supervision. One other explanation for the inconsistencies between our interview results and Rodrigues' (2004) study may be due to individual differences of learners and how that influences their learning process. Though the student participants came from a culture of stronger uncertainty avoidance (Hofstede 1991), they may have a personality that is weak in uncertainty avoidance as shown by their decision to study in a foreign country. Moreover, Singapore measures weak in uncertainty avoidance (Hofstede 1991). These students may be influenced by the Singapore culture as the majority of the participants have been in their course programme in Singapore for at least 2 years. Even though foreign students are accustomed to 'lectures' (Ladd and Ruby 1999), they adjust to new learning techniques after some reasonable amount of time and exposure (Jarrah 1998; Cornet 1983). Applying this rationale, it is very likely that the students who participated in this study had adjusted, at least to an adequate extent to these active instructional techniques. Hence, this helps to explain the closeness of the ratings, especially between the active and passive techniques which fall in the mid-range category.

Moreover, new insights surfaced for the other six passive instructional techniques, 'lectures by instructors', 'reading textbooks', 'guest speakers', 'videos shown in class', 'classroom presentations by students' and 'computerized (online) learning assignments.

6.1.1.6 Lectures by Instructors

In a Chinese classroom context, the general accepted view of an instructor tends to be inclined towards teacher-centric, where the expectations are to teach, to provide knowledge and to set rules. Passive teaching approaches are inclined towards a more one-way delivery, for example, lectures by instructors (Nield 2004). The learning social-cultural values of these Chinese students are ingrained since their years of junior education in China. Chinese classrooms are highly formal and teacher-centric and entail strict disciplined learning environments, with large number of students (compared to the West) (Jin and Cortazzi 1998). Chinese students are obedient and submissive to authority (Kumaravadivelu 2003); they are not encouraged to ask questions and look upon their teachers as the embodiment of knowledge where there is an emphasis on them to acquire knowledge (contents) from the teacher (Liu 1998). Evidence from our study also points towards students feeling greater sense of security and comfort via the lecture approach. This could be largely attributed towards how these students were nurtured in their junior and high school education and the learning culture that was advocated to them all these years in their pursuit of their education.

6.1.1.7 Reading Textbooks and Computerized (Online) Learning Assignments

Our evidence shows the two passive teaching approaches, namely, reading textbooks and computerized learning assignments, do not seem to be perceived as an effective instructional technique from the mainland Chinese students' point of view. These students are unable to relate to the applied knowledge delivered, especially having to comprehend the contents. This was found to be linked to the fact due to the one-way information flow with minimal face-to-face contact, from a practical point of view when the two instructional techniques were used. Students mentioned that close guidance and supervision are required to have them feel more comfortable and secure with learning. Shi (2006)'s study described that the Chinese students' negative attitude towards the quality of contents and relevancy of the textbooks increased as they grow older. The explanation provided is that these students have probably realized that the contents gathered in the textbooks are outdated, more exam-oriented and not aligned to the contemporary context. The analysis from the data collected in Shi (2006)'s study pointed out that these students did not hold a reverent attitude on the contents of their textbooks as Hu (2002) claimed; rather a majority of them had thought the contents could not be always correct. Chinese students displayed a low social presence in the online environment (Tu 2001). Chinese learners are categorized into the high-context communication (HCC) group (Chen and Starosta 1998) that means these students gather more information from the physical context and internalize the concept of the individual during correspondence, communicating and paying lesser attention to direct verbal content. Cheung (2004) reported that CMC (computer-mediated communication) provided restricted cues in such aspects and hence did not suit these Chinese learners so well. Moreover, Tu (2001) pointed out that language barriers also played a vital part in the limited social presence of the Chinese students.

6.1.1.8 Classroom Presentations, Videos Shown in Class and Guest Speakers

Students perceived these three approaches to be lesser effective as not much learning happens although students find them engaging and entertaining at times. When we investigated further, it came to our knowing that the process in having the students think critically and reflect deeply and having an engaged conversation with the instructor or peers is very minimal and is all three of these instructional techniques.

Furthermore, all three techniques tend to largely be a one-way process rather than an interactive one that becomes a contributing factor in terms of the level of impact on its effectiveness.

As for the classroom presentations, the Chinese learners are not comfortable due to their lack of language proficiency and limited exposure to express their thoughts in a formal setting. Most Chinese students were not exposed much and accustomed to minimal speaking opportunities at school where listening to their teachers is their common classroom experience (Liu and Littlewood 1997). The Chinese learners were not prepared for the dialogic nature of classroom dialogue and exchanges, which created challenges in comprehending, listening and interacting (Holmes 2004). The barrier of communication for this cluster of students could be related to their language proficiency in academic listening and oral presentation that is characterized as 'second language anxiety' (Foss and Reitzel 1991) and 'foreign language classroom anxiety' (Jackson 2002). The Chinese students' low proficiency in English is associated with lower confidence to engage verbally, in our case in class presentations (Liu and Littlewood 1997; Jackson 2002).

The instructional technique video is also perceived as not an effective approach in terms of learning. This could be explained through a couple of reasons, for example, the Chinese students are not able to resonate and relate the videos screened largely due to relevancy of 'context' that causes difficulties in them understanding its contents covered. The context here could be defined from the students' comprehension aspect, level of guidance provided and the learning approach adopted. Students reported that the contents in the video are articulated in a manner they could not relate easily as it is not of local context. They also find it challenging to understand what is being communicated due to their lack of fluency in the language, also because there are no subtitles that help them to follow through. The immediate discussion follow-up after the video screening puts the students under pressure to deal with questions without much guidance, where this creates much discomfort.

These Chinese students are blinded by their discomfort where they do not see actual value in terms of leveraging on guest speakers as an instructional technique. They reported that they could not relate much to what they were sharing and had difficulty in understanding due to the high proficiency and speed adopted to communicate. The students described that they find the guest speaker often put them on the spot that makes them intimidated as they engage in open questions, at times directing them on students. The students feel the discomfort that affects their preference in adopting it as an instructional technique due to the above-stated issues although the contrary of guest speakers is supposedly to be a platform that enables rich sharing of experiences and anecdotes.

6.1.2 Comfort

The ten instructional techniques show varying outcomes on the relational effect between learning effectiveness and comfort. These mainland Chinese students find it comfortable in acquiring knowledge from passive styles of instruction through

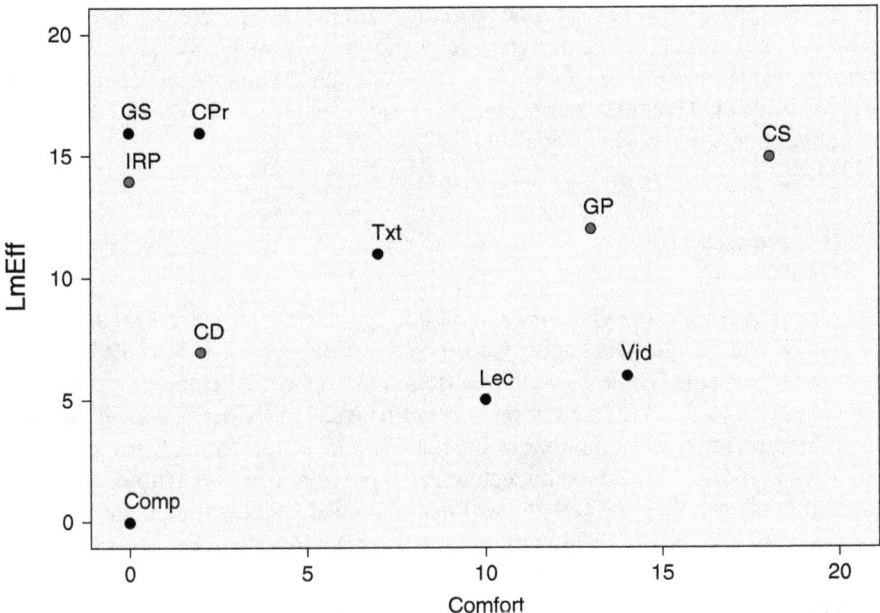

Fig. 6.1 Learning effectiveness vs comfort of ten commonly used instructional techniques (Extracted from Rajaram and Bordia 2011) (Notes *LmEff* learning effectiveness, *GS* guest speakers, *CPr* classroom presentations, *IRP* individual research project, *CD* classroom discussion, *Comp* computerized learning, *Txt* reading textbook, *Lec* lecture, *GP* group project, *Vid* videos, *CS* case study)

content-based learning. Figure 6.1 presents the scatter plots on learning effectiveness and comfort agreement for all ten instructional techniques. The qualitative study performed via the interviews with 20 students validates that there is no distinct difference between the active and passive techniques on learning effectiveness and the relationship between learning effectiveness and comfort. A 'case study' emerged as the most comfortable instructional technique rated as having the highest learning effectiveness effect, whereas 'computerized learning assignments' emerged as the least comfortable with minimal learning effectiveness effect. 'Guest speakers' and 'classroom presentations' were reported as the least comfortable but on the contrary were rated high in learning effectiveness.

From the results, we could report that the learning effectiveness of these mainland Chinese students has no direct effect of whether they are comfortable with the type of instructional technique (active versus passive) adopted. This claim is validated through the Spearman correlation analysis where there is no or minimal cause and dependency effect relationship between comfort and the learning effectiveness for the reports of these 20 students about the ten instructional techniques. Higher order of effective learning happens when one is placed outside his/her comfort zone. Despite the challenges, these students have to deal with, due to cultural dislocation elements, their emotional discomfort which could be seen as the driving force to bring them out of their comfort zone enabling learning to be promoted. In a Western-based education, the learning design largely tends to have students outside their comfort zone for learning to spontaneously occur. With an adequate prolonged exposure to these situational contexts, these mainland Chinese students will be able to fit better into a Western-based business education.

### 6.1.3	Familiarity

The interview results show that the more familiar the students were with the type of instructional techniques, the higher is the positive influence of the learning effectiveness on the students. Three instructional techniques, namely, 'lectures', 'case study' and 'group project', were rated as the most effective. The evidence stating that 'lectures' been rated the most familiar technique could be supported by literature, where it has been reported that generally lecture is the predominant instructional technique adopted in China. Nield (2004) claimed that mainland Chinese are taught in lecture approach largely since their high school days; hence, it is one of the more popular, familiar and likely the preferred form of teaching approach.

A possible reason of students' familiarity of 'case studies' and 'group projects' is students' minimum of 2 years of exposure to the Western-based methodologies. These mainland Chinese students are accustomed to learning mainly through the lecture techniques, but over time they do get accustomed to new instructional techniques. Instructional techniques such as 'reading textbooks', 'classroom discussions', 'individual research projects', 'computerized learning assignments' and 'classroom presentations' fell in the mid-range category of familiarity. 'Guest speakers' and 'videos' were the two techniques that were identified as the least familiar techniques. One possible explanation could be that these instructional techniques might not have been integrated with much emphasis or adopted on high-frequency levels during their high school days back in China.

### 6.1.4	Ease of Knowledge Transfer

Ease of knowledge transfer influences the effectiveness of learning. The easier it is for the students to acquire knowledge through an instructional technique makes it more effective and seamless for students to learn. 'Lectures' was rated the most effective in terms of students' ease of acquiring knowledge, highly because of the high level of guidance, specific instructions and information provided that make students feel secured psychologically. The high level of familiarity and exposure to the lecture technique since their high school days might be another key influencing element where the processes involved were appreciated much more easily and, therefore, assist in the accelerated process of gaining of knowledge.

Similarly, for the two other techniques, namely, 'case studies' and 'group projects', they comprise of elements which contribute to these students' easier gaining and learning of knowledge. Both these techniques facilitate opportunities for students to exercise critical thinking, to share views and thoughts and to be explorative but still with a sense of security through guidance and support offered by their peers, group mates or instructors.

Instructional techniques, namely, 'videos', 'classroom discussions', 'computerized learning', 'guest speakers' and 'reading textbooks', fell in the mid-range category with scores ranging from 3.25 to 3.41. 'Individual research projects' and 'classroom presentations' were rated as the least effective in terms of transfer of knowledge. A possible explanation could be due to the lesser guided and more independency nature involved and minimal guidance provided in these techniques. We could report from the literature that mainland Chinese students prefer to learn in a more collective than an individualistic learning environment. Another possibility lies in the fact that both techniques require students to be very explorative and independent and work with limited instructions and guidance, where these aspects lower the perception of ease of knowledge transfer for mainland Chinese students.

6.1.5   Other Influences on Learning Outcome

It is imperative for us to comprehend thoroughly the other possible and potential aspects of cultural dislocation elements that affect these students' learning outcome. The primary distinctive Chinese cultural differences in comparison to other cultures are often attributed to the Confucianism values that are deeply rooted in the Chinese history. The differences that arise affect how the Chinese education is formulated. Chinese culture is based around self-effacement which evolves from the Confucian value of modest behaviour. Hence, the Confucian value of modest behaviour largely influences mainland Chinese students to avoid speaking up or vocally share their thoughts in a large class setting. Mainland Chinese students when asked to facilitate an open discussion in front of a large audience, their self-effacement value is threatened. These mainland Chinese generally prefer not to express true opinions so as to not embarrass or offend others. Therefore, the mainland Chinese social norms severely limit the expression of criticism or speaking up against the norms. These Chinese students in classrooms will behave so as to avoid embarrassment and maintain the 'face' of individuals concerned.

Mainland Chinese learners prefer more guidance and scaffolding process in their learning. In the study by Chi et al. (2017) on Chinese learners in a higher education context, four environment factors were examined, namely, course challenge, faculty guidance, academic climate and interpersonal relationships, among which faculty guidance was found to have the greatest impact on intellectual development of students.

Literature states that there are differences in how mainland Chinese students think that affects how they learn. The distinct differences in Chinese learners' thinking can be categorized as:

(a) Mainland Chinese learners prefer palpable and concrete information to be provided in comparison to their Western counterparts who are more readily engaged in abstract thoughts (Boisot and Child 1999; Frazee 1996; Tan and Akhtar 1998).

(b) Mainland Chinese tend to have a more utilitarian motivation in their thinking process than the Westerners (Nakamura 1964).
(c) There is a greater appreciation of harmony, intuitive thinking and balance in Chinese reasoning (Lin 1977; Nakamura 1964; Northrop 1946).

Evidence shows that mainland Chinese learners prefer a certain mix of instructional techniques over the others. However, we need to realize and acknowledge that the preferred instructional techniques may not necessarily be the more effective ones when measured in terms of effectiveness of their learning. We should acknowledge that these students would experience a level of discomfort based on varying reasons in their pursuit of a Western-based education due to the cultural dislocation elements. For example, they may not be comfortable to speak up and give feedback to another with ease in a classroom context or when they are exposed to an increased number of abstract concepts. The evidence from our study has, however, shown that comfort as a cultural dislocation element has minimal impact on the students' perception of optimal knowledge acquisition. Despite the varying types of instructional techniques (active or passive) or the level of perceived comfort, familiarity or knowledge transfer, learning effectiveness can still be achieved. Mainland Chinese learners may resist and will take time to fully accept unfamiliar instructional approaches. However, if these instructional techniques are delivered and operationalized in a mindful approach with awareness and sensitivity, then that eases these students into familiarity, from the initial stages itself, where optimal learning can be achieved.

Due to the rapid evolving changes that influence the Chinese culture, the learning preference of Chinese learners is also progressively changing (Rajaram and Bordia 2013; Wang et al. 2016). From a survey conducted on Chinese learners, they found that the learners prefer not only traditional learning approaches but participative learning approaches as well (Wang et al. 2016).

6.2   Implications and Recommendations

The book aims in helping readers to have a deeper understanding of cross-cultural teaching and learning issues in a business education context.

The findings caution against overgeneralizing the use of different instructional techniques. The following are recommendations for more appropriate and contextualized applications of instructional techniques for mainland Chinese students' effective learning:

First, to maximize course appeal and effectiveness and optimize students' learning, various factors should be taken into consideration: previous exposure, combinations of techniques and students' comfort and familiarity with the teaching techniques.

Second, students' preference or comfort level with teaching techniques should not be the only consideration when an instructor chooses an optimal teaching technique. Students may be comfortable being taught with a particular technique but that does not necessarily mean that this technique best facilitates effective learning.

'Chinese students may prefer passive instructional techniques but not necessarily learn effectively with optimal knowledge acquisition' (Rajaram and Bordia 2011, p.80).

Third, instructors must be able to understand the different learners' characteristics and apply correct instructional techniques based on learners' prior knowledge, experience, educational, family and social background, cultural exposure, beliefs/values, maturity level and type of learners (auditory, visual or kinaesthetic).

Fourth, the class size and the style of delivery approach (e.g., seminar style, workshop and lecture) affect the level of interaction and the practical operational issues. Therefore, due consideration needs to be given in course planning.

Fifth, there is a need to shift away from the traditional one-way lecture style towards more participative and interactive activities to encourage student engagement and promote critical and reflective thinking.

Lastly, tutors need to understand that no one category of instructional techniques ('active' or 'passive') can guarantee effective learning among the mainland Chinese students. Rather, it is essential to first understand the composition of these mainland Chinese students in terms of their varying demographics like age group, gender, type of business programmes, provinces where students pursued their prior education, social background and any prior Western exposure, so as to facilitate effective learning through employment of the most suitable instructional techniques.

The following section presents the evidence-based findings with supported discussions and proposes recommendations tested for its effectiveness measured against the intended learning outcomes for each of the instructional techniques that are evidence-based extracted from observation field notes through years of experiences and encounters:

We performed a comparative analysis of students' performance on facilitation using case study, comparing the reports of before and after implementation of the improvised recommended approach adopted. Table 6.2a presents the findings of the analysis.

Table 6.2a Comparative analysis of students' case study performance before and after the improvised approach

Case study		
	Prior to the implementation of the improvised approach adopted for case study (n = 398)	**After the implementation of the improvised approach adopted for case study (n = 398)**
	Mean score (Total rating score = 3)	
Assessment criteria		
Comprehension of contents	1.83	2.77
Application of contents	1.91	2.82
Ability to effectively integrate and exchange thoughts	2.31	2.78
Average	2.02	2.79

Table 6.2b Comparative analysis of students' case study performance before and after the improvised approach

Instructional technique	Recommendations to customize the instructional technique 'case study' (i.e. improvised approach) to fit into the mainland Chinese learning culture
Case study	To provide more scaffolded guidance, for example, to have the case study dissected in smaller clusters for it to be interpreted with much ease
	To have the case studies explained possibly using visuals or short videos for students to resonate the context and have a clearer understanding. This enables students to build up their confidence, reassuring the directions and guidance provided by the tutor
	To build culturally sensitive and well thought-through case studies that students could possibly relate their past acquired knowledge and limited experiences. For example, a case study that focuses on Western-based context or related issues has to be now put in perspective from a localized understanding so that students are able to appreciate it with an optimal level of comprehension. To illustrate specifically, in the discussion, the interlinks with possible implications, consequences to China or South East should be discussed. By doing so, it helps the students to better relate and appreciate the issues from their own cultural context that enables the discussions to be expanded to the Western context to present the effects, differences and intertwined aspects
	To form smaller groups of 4–5 students in each and assign roles such as a leader, scribe and devil advocate to ensure the discussion that happens within are productive. Ensure students are equipped with the relevant learning resources, such as supporting journal, practice-oriented, newspaper articles, Internet resources and reference textbooks for an organized, guided and fruitful discussion
	The instructors should also explore to see if some sort of scaffolding learning support systems could be deployed to capture individual contributions before an engagement through a group discussion is facilitated as students may require a more structured approach to reach the eventual learning outcomes that are largely due to its cultural context
	If the profile of students in the class is diverse, then the groups are to be organized in a well-balanced manner in terms of composition of team members which enables these students to easily integrate and exchange their thoughts comfortably
	Allow the students to form their own groups, with guidelines of team-forming criteria that focus on diversity. This gives the students the autonomy and be accountable in forming their own team with members who they are more comfortable and familiar with yet fulfilling the diversity criteria. Such approach will potentially assist to smoothen the team synergy and cohesiveness which enables students to engage in more fruitful and productive discussions. However, tutors are encouraged to intervene by disrupting this monotony at appropriate junctures to inject diversity of thoughts and challenges gradually as they ease out of the uncertain learning climate

From the results presented in Table 6.2a it is evident that the improvised approach for the case study (Table 6.2b) made a positive impact as there was an improvement in the mean scores across all four assessment criteria for the control group prior and after implementation of improved approach. For all the four assessment criteria 'comprehension of contents', 'application of contents' and 'ability to effectively integrate and exchange thoughts', there was a significant positive improvement in the range of 15.67–31.33%. There was also a 25.67% overall positive impact which positively reaffirmed and validated the adoption of improvised approach. We could conclude that the improvised approach of the case study facilitation has enabled these mainland Chinese students to think and apply what they learnt in a holistic context that has enabled them to achieve higher average scores.

Next, we performed a comparative analysis of students' performance on adopting individual research project as an instructional technique, comparing the reports of before and after implementation of the improvised recommended approach adopted. Table 6.3a presents the findings of the analysis.

From the results, it is evident that the improvised approach for the individual research project (Table 6.3b) made an affirmative impact as there was an improvement in the mean scores across all four assessment criteria for the control group prior and after implementation of improved approach. For all the four assessment criteria 'defining the problem', 'devise strategies to solve the problem', 'assess implementation feasibility' and 'evaluate outcomes', there was a moderate positive improvement in the range of 7–11%. There was also a 9.33% overall positive impact which positively reaffirmed and validated the adoption of improvised approach. We could

Table 6.3a Comparative analysis of students' individual research project performance before and after the improvised approach

Individual research project		
	Prior to the implementation of the Improvised approach adopted for case study (n = 398)	**After the implementation of the improvised approach adopted for case study (n = 398)**
	Mean score (Total rating score = 3)	
Assessment criteria		
Defining the problem	2.23	2.51
Devise strategies to solve the problem	2.12	2.42
Assess implementation feasibility	2.32	2.53
Evaluate outcomes	2.14	2.47
Average	2.20	2.48

Table 6.3b Comparative analysis of students' individual research project performance before and after the improvised approach

Instructional technique	Recommendations to customize the instructional technique 'individual research project' (i.e. improvised approach) to fit into the mainland Chinese learning culture
Individual research project	To provide scaffolded guidance and explicit instructions in terms of mentoring them to understand the requirements and assessment criteria of the assignment. This allows students to have a clear understanding on the scope of what they are expected of
	To facilitate interventions through group consultations or individualized coaching based on the needs that are to be incorporated in phases, possibly in the form of reviews and feedback. To address the cultural norms of these students, it will be a necessity to reinforce that they are provided sufficient directions from the instructor who is perceived to be the subject matter expert.
	To encourage and guide on how to be engaged in peer conversations to exchange fruitful thoughts and feedback but also to emphasize the importance of independent thinking and deep analysis

Table 6.4a Comparative analysis of students' group project performance before and after the improvised approach

Group project		
	Prior to the implementation of the improvised approach adopted for group project (n = 398)	**After the implementation of the improvised approach adopted for group project (n = 398)**
	Mean score (Total rating score = 3)	
Assessment criteria		
Defining the problem	2.25	2.31
Devise strategies to solve the problem	2.12	2.56
Assess implementation feasibility	2.21	2.45
Evaluate outcomes	2.13	2.52
Average	2.18	2.46

conclude that the improvised approach of the individual research project facilitation has enabled these Chinese students to scope the problem more clearly, think and apply through developing solutions based on what they have learnt in a holistic context that has enabled them to achieve higher average scores.

Next, we performed a comparative analysis of students' performance on adopting group project as an instructional technique, comparing the reports of before and after implementation of the improvised recommended approach adopted. Table 6.4a presents the findings of the analysis.

From the results, it is evident that the improvised approach for the group project (Table 6.4b) made a positive impact as there was an improvement in the mean scores across all four assessment criteria for the control group prior and after implementation of improved approach. For the assessment criterion 'Define the problem', there was only a small improvement within a range of 2%. As for the assessment criteria 'Devise strategies to solve the problem', 'Assess Implementation Feasibility' and 'Evaluate Outcomes', there was a significant positive improvement in the range of 8–14.67%. There was also a 9.33% overall positive impact which positively reaffirmed and validated the adoption of improvised approach of group project. We could conclude that the improvised approach has enabled students to think more critically through a guided process and effectively apply what they learnt in a holistic context that has enabled them to achieve higher average scores.

We performed a comparative analysis of students' performance on facilitation using class discussion, comparing the reports of before and after implementation of the improvised recommended approach adopted. Table 6.5a presents the findings of the analysis.

Table 6.4b Comparative analysis of students' group project performance before and after the improvised approach

Instructional technique	Recommendations to customize the instructional technique 'group project' (i.e. improvised approach) to fit into the mainland Chinese learning culture
Group project	To facilitate the students to form their own groups, with a few ground rules to maintain diversity and work with individuals whom they are comfortable with. This is recommended as their cultural inclination is high on uncertainty avoidance as well as on discomfort in unfamiliarity context. This arrangement allows them to work with individuals who they are comfortable with. Nonetheless, the tutor can revisit and examine how the students could possibly be dispersed if the general concern is to address the issue of diversity in terms of difference on the ethnicity, year of study, gender, personality and learning values
	To reiterate the importance of identifying the roles and responsibilities of the team members, i.e. group leader, rotating role of devil's advocate and scribe. Advocate the responsibility and accountability to devise their own meeting schedule and how they intend to progress with their work systematically
	To instil values through advocating and highlighting the concrete negative consequences of plagiarism and collusion
	To ensure the group size is moderated and students are equally distributed. A general guideline of having a group of 4–5 students for a 3–4 months project assignment that requires approximately 3000 words is acceptable. The primary objective is to have a correct group size assigned that enables members in the group to participate and be involved in the tasks effectively

Table 6.5a Comparative analysis of students' class discussion performance before and after the improvised approach

Class discussion	Prior to the implementation of the improvised approach adopted for class discussion (n = 382)	After the implementation of the improvised approach adopted for class discussion (n = 385)
	Mean score (Total rating score = 3)	
Assessment criteria		
Comprehension of contents	1.96	2.21
Application of contents	1.75	2.18
Ability to effectively integrate and exchange thoughts	2.05	2.34
Confident in expressing thoughts	1.58	2.15
Average	1.84	2.22

Table 6.5b Comparative analysis of students' class discussion performance before and after the improvised approach

Instructional technique	Recommendations to customize the instructional technique 'class discussions' (i.e. improvised approach) to fit into the mainland Chinese learning culture
Class discussions	Assign the students questions to brainstorm before initiating the class discussions. To have students formed in smaller groups that enables them to express their opinions more confidently and openly. Provide an avenue for them to write down their thoughts before engaging them to articulate. A recommended approach could be having them to write down their individual thoughts first within an allocated time, thereafter allowing some dedicated time for group discussion, followed by class discussion. The space and time provided for them to be familiar and build up better understanding leads them to be more engaged and more spontaneous in a larger context during the class discussion
	Ask for volunteers, and have the more vocal students to express their opinions first. This allows the break of silence and facilitates the momentum of participation from others
	Encourage and give praises appropriately for taking courage to share their thoughts and attempting, even if the answers may not necessarily be correct. This facilitates a 'safe' and nonjudgmental learning climate for them to be engaged with. This makes them want to contribute naturally and share more forthcomingly as the discussion progresses
	Do not ridicule their sharing despite the level of quality rather acknowledge that as a good attempt, but inform them tactfully that the answer could be improved through non-confrontational feedback and highlighting that it is not correct. This is important as it will make them lose face and embarrassed, affect their confidence and would probably make them shy away even more as they will not want to contribute anymore

From the results, it is evident that the improvised approach for the class discussion made (Table 6.5b) a positive impact, as there was an improvement in the mean scores across all four assessment criteria for the control group prior and after implementation of improved approach. For all the four assessment criteria 'comprehension of contents', 'application of contents', 'ability to effectively integrate and exchange thoughts' and 'confident in expressing thoughts', there was a significant positive improvement in the range of 8.33–19%. There was also a 12.67% overall positive impact that positively reaffirmed and validated the adoption of improvised approach. We could conclude that the improvised approach of the class discussion facilitation has enabled these mainland Chinese students to have their confidence enhanced, reflect more critically and think and apply what they learnt in a holistic context that has enabled them to achieve higher average scores.

We performed a comparative analysis of students' performance on facilitation using lectures, comparing the reports of before and after implementation of the improvised recommended approach adopted. Table 6.6a presents the findings of the analysis.

From the results, it is evident that the improvised approach for the lectures made a positive impact (Table 6.6b), as there was an improvement in the mean scores across all four assessment criteria for the control group prior and after implementation of

Table 6.6a Comparative analysis of students' performance before and after the improvised approach of lectures

Lectures		
	Prior to the implementation of the improvised approach for lectures (n = 396)	**After the implementation of the improvised approach for lectures (n = 398)**
	Mean score (Total rating score = 3)	
Assessment criteria		
Comprehension of contents	1.53	2.47
Application of contents	1.61	2.53
Ability to effectively integrate and exchange thoughts	1.32	2.33
Confident in expressing thoughts	1.58	2.38
Average	1.51	2.43

Table 6.6b Comparative analysis of students' performance before and after the improvised approach of lectures

Instructional technique	Recommendations to customize the instructional technique 'lectures' (i.e. improvised approach) to fit into the mainland Chinese learning culture
Lectures	Mainland Chinese students expect more of a one-way communication and dissemination of information from their instructors. To navigate this, we should incorporate interactive lectures where students are engaged and encouraged in varying forms to participate and contribute their thoughts in short phases in between the lectures that eventually enhances reflective and critical thinking. In terms of questioning technique, instructors could adopt asking open-ended questions and direct and easy questions that may require them to recap and reiterate what have been taught. Students could then be allowed to refer to their notes for reference and answer the questions asked. These successful attempts will progressively enhance their confidence to share and contribute on a more forthcoming manner.
	Do facilitate the interactive lectures in a slow pace, and articulate the sentences in a clear, simple manner for them to comprehend. Majority of these students may find it challenging to keep up with the fast pace and the manner in which these sentences are presented.
	Use creative approaches, for example, clickers or 'K^mAlive'—learning support system that monitors, captures and has the ability to assess 'real-time' contributions in class (Founder/creator, Kumaran Rajaram, PhD—Nanyang Technological University I Nanyang Business School) to engage the students through reflective and interactive quizzes to ensure they understand the concepts taught

improved approach. For all the four assessment criteria 'comprehension of contents', 'application of contents', 'ability to effectively integrate and exchange thoughts' and 'confident in expressing thoughts', there was a significant positive improvement in the range of 26.67–33.67%. There was also a 30.67% overall positive impact that positively reaffirmed and validated the adoption of the improvised approach. We could conclude that the improvised approach of the lecture facilitation has enabled these Chinese students to comprehend the contents delivered much better, able to relate and reflect more critically and to think and apply what they learnt in a holistic context that has enabled them to achieve higher average scores (Table 6.6a).

From the results it is evident that the improvised approach for the reading textbooks (Table 6.7b) as an instructional approach made a positive impact, as there was an improvement in the mean scores across all four assessment criteria for the control group prior and after implementation of improved approach. For all the three assessment criteria 'comprehension of contents', 'application of contents', and 'ability to effectively integrate and exchange thoughts', there was a positive improvement in the range of 7.67–8.67%. There was also about 8% overall positive impact that positively

Table 6.7a Comparative analysis of students' performance before and after the improvised approach of reading textbooks

Reading textbooks		
	Prior to the implementation of the improvised approach for reading textbooks (n = 396)	**After the implementation of the improvised approach for reading textbooks (n = 398)**
	Mean score (Total rating score = 3)	
Assessment criteria		
Comprehension of contents	1.89	2.15
Application of contents	1.94	2.18
Ability to effectively integrate and exchange thoughts	1.98	2.21
Average	1.94	2.18

Table 6.7b Comparative analysis of students' performance before and after the improvised approach of reading textbooks

Instructional technique	Recommendations to customize the instructional technique 'reading textbooks' (i.e. improvised approach) to fit into the mainland Chinese learning culture
Reading textbooks	Tutors are to assist in identifying the key parts that require specific reading, guiding students and facilitating an easy channel to have them seek clarifications, if required
	Some of the more complex and challenging parts of the reading sections are to be revisited through class discussion and guided by the instructors
	To carefully select and recommend reference textbooks that are simpler in terms of content structure and easier to read and understand in terms of language interpretation. This approach adopted ensures that the language does not become a key issue in interpreting and digesting the contents covered
	Textbooks are to be also carefully selected in terms of the context, for example, if there is an Asian perspective version, adopting that allows easier relating and connecting to the issues that need to be taught. But again, to keep diversity intact, the supplementary readings can include those that cover the Western examples as well

reaffirmed and validated the adoption of improvised approach. We could conclude that the improvised approach of the reading textbooks facilitation has enabled these mainland Chinese students to comprehend the contents delivered much better, able to relate and reflect more critically and to think and apply what they learnt in a holistic context that has enabled them to achieve higher average scores (Table 6.7a).

From the result it is evident that the improvised approach for the guest speakers made a positive impact, as there was an improvement in the mean scores across all four assessment criteria for the control group prior and after implementation of improved approach. For all the three assessment criteria 'comprehension of contents', 'application of contents' and 'ability to effectively integrate and exchange thoughts', there was a positive improvement in the range of 9.67–12%. There was also about 10.67% overall positive impact that positively reaffirmed and validated the adoption of improvised approach. We could conclude that the improvised approach of the guest speakers' facilitation has enabled these Chinese students to comprehend the contents delivered much better, able to relate and reflect more critically and to think and apply what they learnt in a holistic context that has enabled them to achieve higher average scores (Tables 6.8a and 6.8b).

Table 6.8a Comparative analysis of students' performance before and after the improvised approach of guest speakers' facilitation

Guest speakers		
	Prior to the implementation of the improvised approach for guest speakers' facilitation (n = 396)	**After the implementation of the improvised approach for guest speakers' facilitation(n = 398)**
	Mean score (Total rating score = 3)	
Assessment criteria		
Comprehension of contents	2.12	2.43
Application of contents	2.05	2.34
Ability to effectively integrate and exchange thoughts	2.01	2.37
Average	2.06	2.38

Table 6.8b Comparative analysis of students' performance before and after the improvised approach of guest speakers' facilitation

Instructional technique	Recommendations to customize the instructional technique 'guest speakers' (i.e. improvised approach) to fit into the mainland Chinese learning culture
Guest speakers	To ensure the guest speaker is able to understand, relate and connect to these mainland Chinese students' learning behavioural, social and cultural characteristics and their challenges
	The guest speaker is to be someone inspiring and has the ability to engage the students with not only practical experiences and content knowledge but able to relate to these students in an engaging and nonintimidating approach as what they perceived it to be

From the results it is evident that the improvised approach for the videos (Table 6.9b) made a positive impact, as there was an improvement in the mean scores across all three assessment criteria for the control group prior and after implementation of improved approach. For all the three assessment criteria 'comprehension of contents', 'application of contents' and 'ability to effectively integrate and exchange thoughts', there was a positive improvement in the range of 8.67–12.67%. There was also about 11.33% overall positive impact that positively reaffirmed and validated the adoption of improvised approach. We could conclude that the improvised approach of the videos' facilitation has enabled these mainland Chinese students to comprehend the contents delivered much better, able to relate and reflect more critically and to think and apply what they learnt in a holistic context that has enabled them to achieve higher average scores (Table 6.9a).

Table 6.9a Comparative analysis of students' performance before and after the improvised approach of the adoption of videos

Videos

	Prior to the implementation of the improvised approach of the adoption of videos (n = 396)	After the implementation of the improvised approach of the adoption of videos(n = 398)
	Mean score (Total rating score = 3)	
Assessment criteria		
Comprehension of contents	2.23	2.61
Application of contents	2.18	2.44
Ability to effectively integrate and exchange thoughts	2.11	2.47
Average	2.17	2.51

Table 6.9b Comparative analysis of students' performance before and after the improvised approach of the adoption of videos

Instructional technique	Recommendations to customize the instructional technique 'videos' (i.e. improvised approach) to fit into the mainland Chinese learning culture
Videos	The videos are to be carefully selected, i.e. the level of contents and language is not overly challenging to comprehend
	There should be an organized, guided group and/or class discussions after the video screening to ensure the students are able to comprehend, relate, interpret and apply the contents adequately well to achieve the intended learning outcomes
	The effectiveness of the video contents in terms of the relevance, updatedness and the localized context is to be examined carefully so that it engages students at the appropriate level on the depth of thinking
	The duration of the videos has to be moderately short yet engaging and interesting filled with quality contents. It should avoid being lengthy as it will negatively affect students' engagement and learning effectiveness. Video clips that evoke and provoke a good level of discussion and reflective interaction with the students are recommended

From the results it is evident that the improvised approach for the class presentations (Table 6.10b) made a positive impact, as there was an improvement in the mean scores across all four assessment criteria for the control group prior and after implementation of improved approach. For all the four assessment criteria 'comprehension of contents', 'application of contents', 'ability to effectively integrate and exchange thoughts' and 'confident in expressing thoughts', there was a positive improvement in the range of 6.33–13.33%. There was also about 11% overall positive impact that positively reaffirmed and validated the adoption of improvised approach. We could conclude that the improvised approach of the class presentations' facilitation has enabled these main Chinese students to comprehend the contents delivered much better, able to relate and reflect more critically and to think and apply what they learnt in a holistic context that has enabled them to achieve higher average scores (Table 6.10a).

From the results it is evident that the improvised approach for the computerized learning assignments (Table 6.11b) made a positive impact, as there was an improvement in the mean scores across all four assessment criteria for the control group prior and after implementation of improved approach. For all the four assessment criteria 'comprehension of contents', 'application of contents', 'ability to effectively integrate and exchange thoughts' and 'confident in expressing thoughts', there was a positive improvement in the range of 11.67–13.33%. There was about 12.67% overall positive impact that positively reaffirmed and validated the adoption of the improvised approach. We could conclude that the improvised approach of the computerized learning assignments' facilitation has enabled these Chinese students to comprehend the contents delivered much better, able to relate and reflect more critically and to think and apply what they learnt in a holistic context that has enabled them to achieve higher average scores (Table 6.11a).

Table 6.10a Comparative analysis of students' performance before and after the improvised approach of class presentations

Class presentations		
	Prior to the implementation of the improvised approach of class presentations (n = 396)	**After the implementation of the improvised approach of class presentations(n = 398)**
	Mean score (Total rating score = 3)	
Assessment criteria		
Comprehension of contents	2.01	2.41
Application of contents	2.16	2.35
Ability to effectively integrate and exchange thoughts	2.03	2.39
Confident in expressing thoughts	1.98	2.38
Average	2.05	2.38

Table 6.10b Comparative analysis of students' performance before and after the improvised approach of class representations

Instructional technique	Recommendations to customize the instructional technique 'class presentations' (i.e. improvised approach) to fit into the mainland Chinese learning culture
Class presentations	To have short informal presentations progressively to get the students familiar with the contents and presentation techniques that help them to improve their confidence level
	Instructors need to be tolerant and patient by adopting nurturing approaches to guide these students in helping them build their confidence and presentation skills progressively. Initially the students may be totally unwilling or even refuse to participate by exemplifying a non-motivated, non-receptive and not forthcoming behaviour. This is largely due to them fearing of being embarrassed in front of others and fearing of losing face plus the deep-rooted learning of cultural values and norms that they have been exposed to and the learning environment they are cultivated from. However, after being exposed to prolonged, encouraging and friendly learning environment, it enables them to progressively build on their confidence. Further to that, this exposure would also develop them to their fullest potential on their presentation skills and ability to be critical and reflective thinkers that facilitate easier verbal articulation of thoughts

Table 6.11a Comparative analysis of students' performance before and after the improvised approach of computerized learning assignments

Computerized learning assignments		
	Prior to the implementation of the improvised approach of computerized learning assignments(n = 396)	**After the implementation of the improvised approach of computerized learning assignments(n = 398)**
	Mean score (Total rating score = 3)	
Assessment criteria		
Comprehension of contents	1.96	2.31
Application of contents	2.05	2.43
Ability to effectively integrate and exchange thoughts	2.12	2.52
Average	2.04	2.42

Table 6.11b Comaparative analysis of students' performance before and after the improvised approach of computerized learning assignments

Instructional technique	Recommendations to customize the instructional technique 'computerized learning assignments' (i.e. improvised approach) to fit into the mainland Chinese learning culture
Computerized learning assignments	Instructors need to create a group-based learning platform that resembles a community or peer grouped learning climate that makes students feel more secured and confident. The individualized nature involved in a computerized learning needs to be shifted to more of a group-oriented one that aligns to their preference and the learning culture of these students
	Tutors are to empathize and understand the norms of these students' learning culture, hence contextualizing the process to facilitate easier knowledge transfer and learning. This could be explicitly addressed by ensuring the computerized learning is tailor-made to address the common challenges faced by these mainland Chinese students, for example, to address the language proficiency issues, the automated voice embedded that may need to be articulated slowly and clearly, more visuals for easier understanding of phrases and so on
	The approach should be more guided and directed where the involvement of the instructor is essential for students to feel secure that they have been guided
	The instructors should not assume that all students will be technology savvy in general; perhaps they are only exposed to a limited level on this type of learning; hence instructors are required to assist students to shift towards their 'comfort' zone of learning progressively by making them enjoy this computerized learning process. Some of the strategies include creating awareness, highlighting interesting and engaging aspects in the learning system and reinforcing the key message that help is always rendered progressively

References

Boisot, M., & Child, J. (1999). Organizations as adaptive systems in complex environments: The case of China. *Organization Science, 10*(3), 237–252.

Chan, S. (1999). The Chinese learner–a question of style. *Education + Training, 41*(6/7), 294–305.

Chen, G. M., & Starosta, W. J. (1998). A review of the concept of intercultural sensitivity. *Human Communication, 1*, 1–16.

Cheung, W. Y. (2004). Engaging students in a virtual classroom: The use of bulletin boards in teaching and learning for Chinese learners. *Journal of Technology in Human Services, 22*(3), 41–67. https://doi.org/10.1300/J017v22n03_03

Chi, X., Liu, J., & Bai, Y. (2017). College environment, student involvement, and intellectual development: Evidence in China. *Higher Education, 74*(1), 81–99.

Cho, C. H., Roberts, R. W., & Roberts, S. K. (2008). Chinese students in US accounting and business PhD programs: Educational, political and social considerations. *Critical Perspectives on Accounting, 19*(2), 199–216.

Cornet, C. E. (1983). *What you should know about teaching and learning styles*. Bloomfield: Phi Delta Kappa Educational Foundation.

Foss, K. A., & Reitzel, A. (1991). A relational model for managing second language anxiety. In E. Horwitz & D. J. Young (Eds.), *Language anxiety from theory and research to classroom implication* (pp. 129–140). Englewood Cliffs: Prentice-Hall.

Frazee, V. (1996). Keeping up on Chinese culture. *Personnel Journal, 1*(1), 16.

Gao, G., Ting-Toomey, S., & Gudykunst, W. B. (1996). Chinese communication processes. In M. H. Bond (Ed.), *The handbook of Chinese psychology*. Hong Kong: Oxford University Press.

Hofstede, G. (1991). *Cultures and organizations: Software of the mind*. London: McGraw-Hill.

Holmes, P. (2004). Negotiating difference in learning and intercultural communication: Ethic Chinese students in a New Zealand University. *Business Communication Quarterly, 67*, 294–307.

Hu, G. W. (2002). English language teaching in the People's Republic of China. In R. E. Silver, G. W. Hu, & M. Iino (Eds.), *English language education in China, Japan, and Singapore* (pp. 1–77). Singapore: National Institute of Education.

Jackson, J. (2002). Reticence in second language case discussions: Anxiety and aspirations. *System, 30*, 65–84.

Jarrah, F. (1998). New courses will target transition to university. *China Morning Post, 23*, 28.

Jin, L. X., & Cortazzi, M. (1998). The culture the learner brings: A bridge or a barrier? In M. Byram & M. Fleming (Eds.), *Language learning in intercultural perspective: Approaches through drama and ethnography* (pp. 98–118). Cambridge: Cambridge University Press.

Kumaravadivelu, B. (2003). Problematizing cultural stereotypes in TESOL. *TESOL Quarterly, 37*(4), 709–719.

Ladd, P. D., & Ruby Jr., R. (1999). Learning style and adjustment issues of international students. *Journal of Education in Business, 74*(6), 363–367.

Li, M., & Campbell, J. (2008). Asian students' perceptions of group work and group assignments in a New Zealand tertiary institution. *Intercultural Education, 19*(3), 203–216.

Lin, Y. (1977). *My country and my people*. Hong Kong: Heinemann.

Littlewood, W. (2009). Participation-based pedagogy: How congruent is it with Chinese cultures of learning? In P. Cheng & J. X. Yan (Eds.), *Cultural identity and language anxiety* (pp. 179–202). Guilin: Guangxi Normal University Press.

Liu, J. (1998). Guanyu xushuti de pianhang jiaoxue – zenyang jiao xusheng ba juzi liancheng duanlo [Narrative text in Chinese discourse pedagogy: How to teach students to connect sentences into paragraphs]. Shijie Hanyu Jiaoxue [Chinese Teaching in the World], 1, 72–78.

Liu, N., & Littlewood, W. (1997). Why do many students appear reluctant to participate in classroom learning discourse? *System, 25*, 371–384.

Nakamura, H. (1964). *Ways of Thinking of Eastern People*. Honolulu: University of Hawaii Press.

Nield, K. (2004). Questioning the myth of the Chinese learner. *International Journal of Contemporary Hospitality Management, 16*(3), 189–196.

Northrop, F. S. C. (1946). *The meeting of East and West*. New York: Macmillan.

Phuong-Mai, N., Terlouw, C., & Pilot, A. (2006). Culturally appropriate pedagogy: The case of group learning in a Confucian Heritage Culture context. *Intercultural Education, 17*(1), 1–19.

Rajaram, K. (2010). *Culture Clash: Teaching western-based business education to mainland Chinese students in Singapore*. Unpublished doctoral dissertation, University of South Australia, Adelaide, Australia.

Rajaram, K., & Bordia, S. (2011). Culture clash: Teaching Western-based management education to mainland Chinese students in Singapore. *Journal of International Education in Business, 4*(1), 63–83.

Rajaram, K., & Bordia, S. (2013). East versus West: Effectiveness of knowledge acquisition and impact of cultural dislocation issues for mainland Chinese students across ten commonly used instructional techniques. *International Journal for the Scholarship of Teaching and Learning, 7*(1), 1–21.

Rodrigues, C. A. (2004). The importance level of ten teaching/learning techniques as rated by university business students and instructors. *Journal of Management Development, 23*(2), 169–182. https://doi.org/10.1108/02621710410517256

Ryan, J., & Louie, K. (2007). False Dichotomy? 'Western' and 'Confucian' concepts of scholarship and learning. *Educational Philosophy and Theory, 39*(4), 404–417.

Ryan, J., & Slethaug, G. (2010). *International education and the Chinese learner* (Vol. 1). Hong Kong: Hong Kong University Press.

Samuelowicz, & Bain. (2001). Revisiting academics' belief about teaching and learning. *Higher Education, 41*, 299–325.

Shi, L. (2006). The successors to Confucianism or a new generation? A questionnaire study on Chinese students' culture of learning English, language. *Culture and Curriculum, 19*(1), 122–147. https://doi.org/10.1080/07908310608668758

Tan, J. (2011). *Revisiting the Chinese learner: Changing contexts, changing education.* Taylor & Francis.

Tan, D., & Akhtar, S. (1998). Organizational commitment and experienced burnout: An exploratory study from a Chinese cultural perspective. *International Journal of Organizational Analysis, 6*(4), 310–333.

Tiong, K. M., & Yong, S. T. (2004). *Confucian heritage culture learners' and instructors' expectations and preferences in collaborative learning: Convergence or divergence?* In Proceedings of HERDSA annual conference, 4–7 July, Curtin University of Technology, Sarawak Campus, Miri, Sarawak, Malaysia. ISSN:1441-001x http://herdsa.org.au/conference2004/Contributions/NRPapers/A055-jt.pdf. Accessed 12 Feb 2011.

Tu, C. H. (2001). How Chinese perceive social presence: An examination of interaction in online learning environment. *Educational Media International, 38*(1), 45–60.

Tuener, Y., & Acker, A. (2002). *Education in the new China: Shaping ideas at work.* London: Routledge.

Tweed, R. G., & Lehman, D. R. (2002). Learning considered within a cultural context: Confucian and Socratic approaches. *American Psychologist, 57*(2), 89–99.

Valiente, C. (2008). Are students using the 'wrong' style of learning? *Active Learning in Higher Education, 9*(1), 73–91.

Wang, Y. (2012). Mainland Chinese students' group work adaption in a UK business school. *Teaching in Higher Education, 17*(5), 523–535.

Wang, M., Zhang, Y., Sanyk, W., & Velasco, M. (2016). Identifying cultural learning preferences: Develop effective training for Chinese learners. In Intelligent Environments 2016, IOS Press, 21: 139–148. DOI :10.3233/978-1-61499-690-3-139

Chapter 7
Concluding Thoughts

The chapter presents the concluding thoughts of the book, namely, overarching two key areas, (a) focusing on the contributions to the literature, theory and practice and (b) concluding the chapter by advocating educators to have a thorough and reflective understanding of the mainland Chinese learners so that a much better-suited curriculum with cultural sensitivity could be adopted to well-equip and educate these students effectively.

7.1 Contributions to Literature, Theory and Practice

With globalization and internationalization of higher education, students from a diverse cultural background from varying geographical locations explore internationally to pursue their undergraduate and postgraduate studies overseas. For the past two decades especially, a culturally diverse student population has been a common phenomenon in universities located in English-speaking countries such as the United Kingdom, the United States, Australia and New Zealand. The offering of academic courses in conjunction with overseas universities is relatively a rising phenomenon in some Asian countries, most evident in the city state of Singapore. The higher educational sector in Singapore comprises of several competitive local universities, supplemented with numerous overseas universities from Australia, the United Kingdom, the United States, New Zealand, France and other countries that have set up educational programs in collaboration with educational providers.

Singapore being a knowledge-based and forward-looking country aspires to be a global education hub; hence, it further strengthens its strategic position through the collaborations with overseas Western universities. This enables Singapore to progressively grow into an increasingly large potential export market in offering educational opportunities with high quality and reputation to other Asian countries. The research presented in this book aspires to address the gaps that would potentially assist in enhancing the rigor, quality of the educational standard. This eventually

© Springer Nature Singapore Pte Ltd. 2020
K. Rajaram, *Educating Mainland Chinese Learners in Business Education*,
https://doi.org/10.1007/978-981-15-3395-2_7

enables its compatibility with the Asian client base to be progressively reviewed and enhanced in terms of content intensity and educational services that are provided to students.

The primary intention of Singapore's government is for the country to be nurtured into a globally well-reputed, recognized, effervescent country and internationally embraced educational centre. The opening and fast evolving of China's economy have made Singapore a natural choice for many mainland Chinese. One of the key contributing elements could be largely attributed to the various similarities in the cultures of both countries. Tsang (2001, pp. 347–8) adds:

> During the past decade, there have been an increasing number of mainland Chinese academics and students coming to Singapore. These mainland Chinese have probably become the largest group of full-time and part-time international students.

Consequently, students learning effectively in their pursuit of study with the correct set of teaching and learning techniques have serious personal and policy implications.

The book's contribution includes the approach adopted in enhancing the learning process and experience by adopting the correct mix of instructional techniques for mainland Chinese learners. The interpretation derived from the findings enables us to evaluate from the perspective of curriculum design and development of an effective business educational framework to sustain profitability by offering tailor-made, superior quality course programs. Although the key focus is on the effectiveness in the students' learning process and delivery of instructional techniques for mainland Chinese students, the contribution can be appreciated from a much wider perspective. Students' learning quality and effectiveness in how they are taught to learn have an impact on their roles as managers, which is intertwined with their future performance in organizations that influences its growth. The progress of an organization could be viewed as part of an indirect contributing factor to the country's economy. The means in which knowledge is transferred and acquired by students through their learning processes and outcomes would allow them to competently perform and deliver quality outcomes in their future organizations.

Besides, the book makes an assenting contribution through deep insights on Chinese mainland learners, not only to Singapore's higher education sector but also to all who are involved in the internationalization of higher education. Universities and higher education institutions offer customized, cultural dislocation fit and quality courses that attract diverse students globally to Singapore for their pursuit of higher education. Consequently, the potential inflow of students increases the revenues generated from these international students who come to study, reside and, at a later phase, probably even work in Singapore. From the past trends and observational evidence, we could interpret and report that the total revenue generated from international students coming to Singapore has a positive trajectory on the economic growth and cultural diversity. This emphasizes the strong extrinsic contributions of the book, although the key research focus is on cultural dislocation, the learning process and its effectiveness aspects with the correct mix of instructional techniques adopted. To sustain the reputation of an institution and Singapore as an international educational hub for higher learning, offering a quality education and service experience is imperative. Students who have a positive and valuable learning experience from these institutions will potentially recommend them to prospective students in the future. To put it in context, for example, Singapore Institute of Management—SIM Global serves as an exemplary icon as a higher education institution partnering with overseas universities, which have been offering quality, well-established and reputable programmes with flexible learning curriculum for students. This largely contributes to its excellent reputation as an institution and serves as a strong influencing factor for its future students. It also strengthens its market position as one of the most well-established institutions dealing with affiliated overseas university partners in Singapore.

Fundamentally, variations exist in the preferred instructional techniques adopted in Asian and Western countries due to different reasons. Perhaps, the varying phases of the country's economic progress and expansion could be one of the reasons. Singapore has a consistently well-established economy, significantly, a high-quality, rigorous and strong academic standard. Hence, the varying instructional approaches adopted have a substantial influence on the way these mainland Chinese students learn and acquire knowledge, who come from varying provinces where they noticeably differ in terms of resources availability and its infrastructure of modern facilities. The studies included in this book are performed in Singapore to comprehend the specific yet complex issues from the perspective of cultural dislocation context. The findings of these studies in the book provide insights and rationale behind the selection of the correct mix of appropriate instructional techniques, which contributes to the learning framework of teaching mainland Chinese students. The instructional approaches adopted and practiced in Singapore's business education vary from those of other countries. Educators within Singapore, which is a multiracial country, may prefer differing styles of instructional approaches, which potentially influence the effectiveness on the delivery of lessons. Thus, advocating an evidence-based tested instructional framework will assist to enhance the quality and effectiveness of the lessons facilitated, which would potentially enhance the quality deliverables that contribute to the growth of these higher education institutions and universities. Moreover, the manner in which this higher education institutions and universities are regulated and conducted in Singapore has an impact on the quality standard in terms of curriculum design, basic facilities and infrastructure put in place, the faculty hired to teach and the reputation they offer in comparison to other countries. Differences prevail within Singapore in the governance and running of fully fledged government and private institutions; hence, it is vital to have a tailor-made instructional framework in addressing the different clusters and types of students in these institutions.

These insights and findings are significant for investment-related activities in the educational field as Singapore endeavours to sustain its strategic position as a global education hub. In today's evolving and rapid climate, sourcing for good investment opportunities is a crucial aspect leading a multinational educational business today. Evaluating the risk profile and reducing the dangers of business deals in foreign environments are unequivocally essential. A deep understanding of cultural values and norms will assist in business ventures in the Asian region. Wide-ranging knowledge on the social cultural environment would be a plus, providing higher efficiency which, in due course, potentially would result in achieving a higher profitability for the institution. The findings in the book reiterate the relative cultural influence on perceived learning effectiveness, which alleviates the business risks caused by cultural issues. The research insights constitute a practical contribution in enhancing the quality and academic standard of the international business education. The cultural and educational congruence among the institutions and students largely contributes to the academic success of the students. The shaping of curricula of these institutions requires a good comprehension of the social cultural impact on the learning styles and perceived learning effectiveness on instructional techniques of mainland Chinese students. To maintain a globally well-established reputation, these institutions and universities should continuously strive to achieve close cultural 'fit' in all their educational operations and endeavours.

The findings and discussions covered in the book will assist to identify the more effective instructional approaches by ranking its importance and preference when measured across mainland Chinese students. Besides, it also enables systematic contemplation by considering various aspects in shaping the course curriculum and adopting the instructional styles in line with mainland Chinese students in their pursuit of a Western-based education. Moreover, it facilitates effective decision-making in adopting the correct mix and appropriate instructional techniques in educating these students. These broad research agendas exclusively address the specific objectives of the studies in the book. Firstly, based on the academic literature, the studies in the book develop an empirically tested conceptual framework to comprehend the correct mix of appropriate instructional approaches preferred by the mainland Chinese students in terms of their perceived effectiveness in learning and acquiring knowledge. Secondly, the distinctively identified attributes were empirically tested with this conceptual framework.

The theoretical contribution will further add to the evolving and unique but significant sector of international business education. The study has practical implications in terms of enhancing the perceived learning effectiveness and learning effectiveness of these mainland Chinese students, thus contributing to the standard of quality of education providers. To be precise, our research in the book will further enhance the quality of academic curricula, instructional approaches adopted and market position with other Asian clients in terms of effective delivery of contents and services provided to students. Institution and universities collaborating with overseas Western universities will benefit from the conceptual framework, enabling them to further enhance the curricula to be focused on effective learning through the adopting of the correct mix of instructional approaches. By incorporating the findings of how students learn effectively in order to improvise and implement 'tailor-made' courses, this will eventually contribute to sound educational management strategies in the higher education institutions offering Western-based education.

The implication of our studies in the book includes its influence on the design and development of course curricula, principally regarding the instructional approaches adopted for business programs which are offered in conjunction with Western universities A thorough understanding of the cultural norms, values and aspects will assist in effectively delivering the contents using appropriate instructional approaches for mainland Chinese students. This will enable the course programs to be tailor-made to better orientate the contents to different students' needs, hence, leading to a much higher standard in learning effectiveness of the course contents, addressing the quality aspects of nurturing mainland Chinese students. The nurturing and moulding of these quality students will eventually lead to developing successful business managers in the future. Moreover, career coaches from the students' career centres of the higher education institutions could creatively use the findings of the study to assist and mentor students in identifying the possible career pathways most appropriate for them. A good understanding on how mainland Chinese students learn effectively enables one to examine the fit and appropriateness on the possible types of job characteristics as well as in the preparation towards their choice of career.

Apart from these higher education institutions, the results can be used in the development of business educational programs for mainland Chinese students at different types of higher education institutions with international students both in Singapore and other countries, especially in the Asia Pacific region. The value proposition could be largely attributed to an increased trend in Singapore and elsewhere as evidenced by the number of institutions in higher education sector that are being formed, with a large majority of them targeting international students as one of their key stakeholders. Tailor-made courses can be designed to deliver result-oriented outcomes by comprehending the influencing factors that affect students' effective learning when different instructional approaches are adopted. Organizations like the Ministry of Education (MOE), Consumers Association of Singapore (Case Trust), EduTrust [is a quality assurance certification scheme administered by the CPE for Private Education Institutions (PEIs) in Singapore] and Singapore Quality Class (SQC) (which sets the quality criteria for business excellence standards in organizations) will be very interested in the research findings and analysis as they could be used to design, develop and implement new project initiatives for nurturing mainland Chinese students pursuing Western-based business education. For example, the findings can help these institutions to align and have new inputs into the design of the learning objectives of their in-house certifications, diploma courses and university in-house designed or partner university-affiliated programs. Moreover, the results will also serve as an instrument to fine-tune the specific aspects pertaining to learning effectiveness of the various global business educational initiatives and nation-wide projects in relation to mainland Chinese learners.

The implications of the studies in the book will be associated with the educational activities and policies to be reviewed and new ones to emerge and be implemented for the development of the business educational curriculum and delivery methodologies for international students, where the large majority will be the mainland Chinese students, specifically in the undergraduate business education cluster.

The instructional strategies shared in this book for mainland Chinese students pursuing Western education serve as an evidence-based practice-oriented guide for educators teaching mainland Chinese students in universities and higher education institutions. The deep scope of discussion in this book is intended to shed light on how best to optimize the learning experience of mainland Chinese students in a culturally dislocated learning climate and environment away from their home, in our case in Singapore. A deep comprehension of the culturally dislocated aspects (to understand the variations in culture) and how effectively knowledge can be best transferred has to be deeply understood to offer quality education to students from a foreign country. The instructor requires some basic competency in understanding the fit of the varying instructional approaches that correlates to the cultural aspects to be able to identify the appropriate and correct mix of instructional techniques for the mainland Chinese students.

This book aims to further the understanding of the unknown aspects of learning approaches of the mainland Chinese students through the correct mix of instructional approaches and the cross-cultural influences in business education for them. It serves as a bridging platform for educators in a Western-based education to address elements of cultural dislocation and perceived learning effectiveness and learning effectiveness of mainland Chinese students. For example, the findings from the study show that the cultural dislocation variable of comfort does not affect the optimal perceived learning effectiveness of these Chinese mainland students.

'To optimize students' learning, essential characteristics like exposure, the right combinations of techniques, addressing comfort and familiarity aspects should converge to maximize module appeal and effectiveness' (Rajaram and Collins 2013, p. 195). The analysis of the study provides insights to educators in higher education on both theoretical developments and practical insights. The adoption of the correct mix of instructional approaches enhances the mainland Chinese students' learning process, perceived learning effectiveness and academic performance as part of their learning outputs. By understanding the subtle yet deep-rooted complex cultural characteristics of these mainland Chinese students, both local and Western educators facilitating Western-based education are able to design much better, more effective educational course programs.

The study findings in this book contribute to the higher education business by helping institutions to design a customized and quality curriculum to facilitate the mainland Chinese learners. With quality curriculum, we could expect higher-quality level of students being nurtured which will eventually show in their work performance and deliverables. This helps to progressively enhance the reputation and image of the institution where many others would want to pursue their higher education studies, which then apparently sustain the inflow of students' number which contributes to profitability at the output.

The quality of the learning process during their pursuit of higher education studies influences the learners their future performance as managers of organizations. The learning culture enables the nurturing and moulding of learners' cognitive thinking process as well as their behaviours at large. Their competencies, especially in the area of conceptual, problem-solving and thinking abilities, are fundamentally correlated deeply to how they were trained in their learning process. Organizations grow through the talents they attract and eventually help to boost the economy of a country. From another perspective, through offering of customized and quality courses, more Chinese students would be attracted to Singapore to pursue their higher education by reputation. This will in turn boost the education sector growth of Singapore's economy as well.

Having a holistic framework at large on the aspects of enhancing the quality of learning for international students will help to augment the quality and effectiveness of the education facilitated. It is imperative to offer quality educational experience in sustaining the reputation of an institution as well as Singapore as a global educational hub for higher learning. To sustain good reputation and promote quality education, higher education institutions need to achieve current and future cultural fit in their offshore operations (Bodycott and Lai 2012). The research discussed in the book provides useful insights and a holistic framework for instructors, corporate trainers and curriculum developer in understanding on how specific cultural group of learners learns effectively across various instructional approaches by comprehending the elements embedded within the cultural aspects. These insights can also explain the lack of motivation, ambiguity and frustration that emerge from these international students when inappropriate instructional approaches are used. Further to that, the quality of learning deteriorates due to the disconnectivity in terms of engagement that occurs between the instructors and students.

Although this book's main focus is on the learning effectiveness and preferences of the correct mixture of instructional approaches for mainland Chinese learners, its contributions address a much larger reach in terms of impact. This study findings in the book are beneficial not just to Singapore educators but also contribute to educators globally who have to teach the progressively increasing number of Chinese students. The book offers the following key value propositions:

(a) Enabling educators, who facilitate or teach international Chinese students, who are one of the larger clusters of international students, to have a deeper understanding of cultural dislocation issues which enables them to apply the knowledge within their own teaching and learning context.

(b) Providing insights to the numerous collaborating institutions and universities that provide such Western-based programs to a rising number of international Chinese students.

(c) Allowing course managers and staff either managing or directly dealing with these mainland Chinese learners to appreciate the issues that are interrelated with their learning process and effective learning,

(d) Creating awareness for educators so that they are able to reflect on their own styles of teaching, comprehend the mainland Chinese learners' cultural and social aspects and keep up with emerging key issues that could potentially affect the learning outcomes of these students.

Specifically, the research study provides evidence that with a prolonged exposure to varying instructional approaches in a different learning culture, the mainland Chinese students could shift their preference and become more adaptable to instructional approaches which may not be in their preference ranking priority list. These mainland Chinese students, after being exposed to prolonged western-based education instructional style, prefer a less guided instructional approaches. It shows that they can learn effectively using the active techniques as well, provided the instructional approaches were used in a structured and customized context. Hence, instructors could use the strategy of progressively exposing some approaches in a safe, nurturing and comfortable learning climate especially during their initial first year of study. Having to build these students' confidence through a well thought-through scaffolded process of learning that encompasses the integration of cultural and social aspects becomes a strategy to be adopted.

Additionally, the research study provides link to close the gap of understanding mainland Chinese students' learning behaviour through the proxies of cultural dislocation perspectives: comfort, familiarity and knowledge transfer. The actual processes embedded within the learning settings and the behavioural aspects arising from the cultural dislocation proxies were examined. The research also assists educators in comprehending the correct mix of instructional approaches to be adopted appropriately for effective learning of the mainland Chinese learners. This enables customization of the academic curriculum and instructional methodology to be adopted for this group of mainland Chinese students' optimal learning experience based on key learning effectiveness features, their cultural values, beliefs backgrounds and aspects associated with proxies of cultural dislocation.

7.2   Conclusion

Singapore, a knowledge-based economy, aspires to become a global educational hub where it provides a platform for others to excel in their pursuit of their investment, trade, economic growth, cultural exchange development and education interests and needs. International students view Singapore as an excellent academic platform where they could experience the 'best of both worlds', that is, to pursue a Western-based education within an Asian context. Investors are well aware that Singapore has stable governance that provides political stability and security and assures a growing national economy. Singapore's government supports and provides full autonomy to higher education private institutions to conduct their own international business programs, as long as they meet the stringent quality processes and procedures that are in place.

As such, this opportunity serves as an excellent platform where students are able to experience a Western education in an Eastern culture. Consequently, this creates a new era of Confucianism for the economic betterment of Singapore as a leading and evolving educational hub. Moreover, Singapore serves as an exemplary icon to neighbouring countries such as Indonesia, Vietnam, Thailand, India and Malaysia in offering Western-based education pursued in an Eastern cultural context. Being a developed country, well-reputed and highly advanced in the education industry, Singapore advocates other Asian countries to also adapt to the rapidly changing higher educational landscape, learn and progress with the trend. The evidence-based conceptual framework also serves as an excellent guide for developing countries in the Middle East and South Africa, which are now opening their doors to enhance their educational quality and to attain world-recognized educational standards.

Singapore extends its assistance to other developing countries for them to acknowledge the educational values and importance of developing into a global educational hub.

Business education today provides the global perspectives, skill sets and competencies required by future managers. Education—predominantly obtaining a global degree today—provides more than merely an academic qualification; it facilitates real-life experiences and expands the diversity of thoughts. It equips students with the relevant, current industrial exposure and facilitates a global networking platform for them to enhance their capabilities. These students are potentially the future managers who will be the primary workforce in the multinational corporations, statutory boards and government organizations. The learning culture and the process of learning in which these students are nurtured with will significantly influence the working styles and learning approaches to be adopted in the potential organizations that could employ them in the future. Hence, it is vital to facilitate a suitable platform for them to acquire information and learn optimally and notably, to adapt to the continuously and rapidly evolving learning environment, for example, by being able to appreciate the correct mix of instructional approaches with sensitivity to cultural values and norms that enable these students to learn effectively, nurtured and equipped with the needed competencies and skills.

The higher education institutions are nurturing the potential future workforce that will be the future backbone of skilled talents in Singapore. From this study, evidence shows that the instructional approaches have to be carefully and appropriately employed based on the diverse cultural backgrounds, values and instructional preferences of these international students. It is important for these international students to be adaptable to the Western-based educational approaches in order to assist them to transit, adapt and work well as future managers of global multinational corporations. It is essential to facilitate a versatile learning climate and conducive environment to enable these students to be ready and competent with the organizational learning aspects in their future workplace. Organizational performance is intertwined with and related to students' learning effectiveness. These students, who are potential future leaders, require to acquire knowledge in the most productive manner during their future organizational training and career development. Having a deep comprehension on the varying complex issues that are embedded in learning allows the organizations to customize their human capital framework to develop future leaders, perhaps from these international students' population, of those who decided to build their future in Singapore or even as part of their career stint here before they return back to their home.

Business education generally attracts a large pool of students to Singapore globally. A strong indication of its continuous and growing success is reflected through the yearly increasing number of enrolments of international students in business courses. The ability to put in place good cultural strategic policies that facilitate growth in the international business education sector is one of the primary challenges in today's rapidly evolving international business education field. For a country to have quality education targeted at a diverse group of international students coming from different foreign countries requires a well-grounded and thorough understanding of the cultural aspects and how knowledge is best delivered to these students. The key issues to be explored are (a) to understand the various types of instructional approaches and (b) to identify the correct mix of instructional approaches that best suit this cluster of international students. In this context, the study acts as a bridging platform to address the cultural dislocation elements and inferred learning effectiveness variables of mainland Chinese students when examined through the lenses of the different instructional approaches.

Teaching effectively with a high level of engagement in cultural dislocation contexts may be a challenge and daunting task. Majority of educators adopt instructional techniques that may not be aligned to the international students, in our case, the mainland Chinese students' preferences, learning styles, cultural values, norms and beliefs. This leads to large negative ripple effects causing the learning to be ineffective and inconsistent and knowledge transfer and acquisition not achieved optimally.

A quality education targeted at a culturally diverse population of students from different countries requires good understanding and sensitivity to social cultural influences in knowledge delivery. Some of the central issues are (a) understanding the correlation of various instructional approaches and distinctive learning cultural values and norms together with the learning styles embedded within that and (b) identifying the most appropriate mix of instructional approaches that fits these cluster of international mainland Chinese learners who represent a unique type of learners with their learning preferences, in our case, among these Chinese mainland students itself.

We could agree that there is a level of complexity in selecting the correct mix of instructional techniques. The identification of correct mix of instructional techniques requires a good understanding of students' learning culture, their preference style of learning and factors that engage and enable the level of their learning effectiveness and optimal acquisition of knowledge. This is imperative if the learning outcome is inclined towards facilitating an optimal, conducive learning environment and climate for these students. Having to understand the students' preference on instructional techniques helps to explicitly cater to their preference, comfort level and familiarity with the correct mix of instructional approaches through which their transfer of knowledge occurs. Hence, this enables educators to design a pedagogical framework customized to the learners' preference that correlates to their style of learning, learning engagement and interest, which enables a pathway for better acquiring of knowledge.

We trust the insights derived through the discussion on commonly used instructional approaches across cultural dislocation variables and the perceived effectiveness described in this book will benefit, especially allowing them to have a deeper understanding that builds their confidence and competency in teaching and facilitating these mainland Chinese learners. However, instructors should also be cautioned that the Chinese culture and the mainland Chinese population are not static and homogenous. With the rapid development and globalization, the mainland Chinese students are also evolving and adapting to the world. Therefore, this book aims to provide the foundation where the instructors can build their instructional repertoire from while still being aware of the particular characteristics and profile of the students they are teaching. We trust, with a much thorough and reflective understanding of these mainland Chinese learners, higher education institutions who enrol international students may be able to develop a much better-suited curriculum with cultural sensitivity with the distinctive, perhaps at times even subtle, differences embedded that will assist in the preparation of the students to be successful business managers and leaders in the future.

References

Bodycott, P., & Lai, A. (2012). The influence and implications of Chinese culture in the decision to undertake cross-border higher education. *Journal of Studies in International Education, 16*(3), 252–270.

Rajaram, K., & Collins, J. B. (2013). Qualitative identification of learning effectiveness indicators among mainland Chinese students in culturally dislocated study environments. *Journal of International Education in Business, 6*(2), 179–199.

Tsang, E. W. (2001). Adjustment of mainland Chinese academics and students to Singapore. *International Journal of Intercultural Relations, 25*(4), 347–372.

9 789811 533938